MILITARY AVIATION
OF THE
FIRST WORLD
WAR

MILITARY AVIATION
OF THE
FIRST WORLD WAR

THE ACES OF THE ALLIES
AND THE CENTRAL POWERS

ALAN C. WOOD
AND ALAN SUTTON

FONTHILL

Dedication by Alan C. Wood:

Dedicated to my Grandson James Francis BA (Hons)

Fonthill Media Limited
Fonthill Media LLC
www.fonthillmedia.com
office@fonthillmedia.com

First published in the United Kingdom and the United States of America 2016

British Library Cataloguing in Publication Data:
A catalogue record for this book is available from the British Library

ISBN 978-1-78155-422-7

Typeset in Minion Pro 10.5pt on 13.5pt
Printed and bound by CPI Group (UK) Ltd, Croydon, CR0 4YY

CONTENTS

PREFACE

T HE FIRST WORLD WAR—1914 to 1919—was a global conflict with 57 nations involved, but the main fighting powers were Britain (with its Dominions and Empire), France and Russia—known as The Allies or The Triple Entente and the Central Powers—Germany and Austria-Hungary.

As the war progressed other nations joined one or other of the main power blocks—Italy and Belgium joined the Allies and Turkey joined the Central Powers. In 1917 the United States of America aligned itself with the Allies.

With aviation being in its infancy only eight nations had a major air arm to their fighting services. All known lesser military air services are listed but not in great detail as they had but a minor part in First World War military aviation.

Alan C. Wood

INTRODUCTION

THIS BOOK IS NOT intended to be comprehensive, for to provide such a work would require many volumes totalling thousands of pages. Instead this should be viewed as an overview; a short general introduction to the topic of military aviation in the First World War. The aim has been to produce a well-illustrated book to maintain the interest of the reader with some short biographies of the leading aces and basic information on the aircraft types used, and their development during the First World War. Furthermore, this book focuses on the air arms initially developed by the respective armies, and therefore the air arms of the navies, although fleetingly touched upon, are not really dealt with in much detail. To provide reasonable coverage for the Royal Naval Air Service alone would require a separate and substantial additional volume. In a similar manner, although Zeppelins, other airships and balloons are briefly mentioned, little detail is given. Other Fonthill titles which do cover naval air services and airships are advertised at the back of the book.

In 1914 aviation was still in its infancy—to the extent that the no-one really knew how to use this new facility—this new weapon in the armoury of war. For the army generals the obvious starting point was for reconnaissance—to see where the enemy were and what they were doing. The navies of the world were also experimenting with floatplanes and seaplanes, and development went ahead in parallel in both services. Very soon, however, it became apparent that aircraft could be more versatile. They could be used to deliver blows and to bring attacks onto the enemy by strafing in ground attacks and in bombing. Such tactics, if used by the enemy, needed to be fended off and the reconnaissance aircraft of the opposition had to be stopped from snooping. This led to the development of the fighter, and the successful fighter pilots became the aces.

During the fours years of the First World War the development of aviation went through a dramatic revolution as airframes and engines went through revision after revision with each enhancement being played upon by thousands of engineers to improve the speed, the operational ceiling and the rate of climb. British and French captured aircraft were forensically investigated by German technicians and *vice versa*, and opposition innovations were copied, accelerating aviation technology. Coupled with this, combat tactics evolved and skills were developed. One of leading German aviators who introduced and developed

One of the more comical-looking aircraft of the War was the Rumpler Taube monoplane. Here a captured Taube is pictured on display in the courtyard of Les Invalides in Paris, during 1915. The Taube was a pre-First World War aircraft, only briefly used on the front lines, and replaced later by newer designs. (*Bibliothèque nationale de France*)

such tactics was Max Immelmann, who gave his name to one famous manoeuvre—the 'Immelmann Turn'. This is also known as a steep climb followed by a stall turn, or simply an 'Immelmann'; an aerobatic manoeuvre that results in level flight in the opposite direction at a higher altitude. After having made a high-speed diving attack on an enemy, the attacker then climbs back up past the enemy aircraft, and just short of the stall, applies full rudder to yaw his aircraft around. This puts his aircraft facing down at the enemy aircraft, making another high-speed diving pass possible. This is a difficult manoeuvre to perform properly as it involves precise control of the aircraft at low speed. With practice and proper use of all of the fighter's controls, the manoeuvre could be used to reposition the attacking aircraft to dive back down in any direction desired.

Apart from ever-developing technology and tactics, a third element was weight of numbers, and in this Germany failed. The western allies produced vastly more aircraft and Germany struggled to match production output. The Siemens company ended up building a copy of a captured French Nieport 11 which they named the Siemens-Schuckert. It is estimated that by the end of the war Germany had built 48,537 aircraft, and their ally the Austro-Hungarian Empire had built 5,431—a combined total of 53,968. France had built a staggering 67,987 and Great Britain had built 58,144. On the Allied side were added Italy at some 20,000; the USA at approximately 15,000 and Russia (up to the Revolution) some 4,700—mainly under licence from French designs. This resulted in an Allied total of 165,831 aircraft, an incredible number; more than three times that produced by the Central Powers.

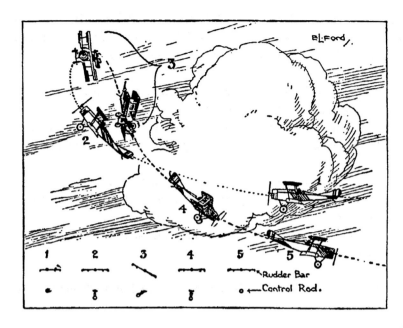

A manoeuvre illustrated from a First World War handbook.

Aerial aircraft-to-aircraft combat got off to a slow start. On 1 April 1915, French pilot Roland Garros shot down a German Albatros. Although this was not the first air-to-air kill, Garros's mount, a Morane Parasol, was the first aircraft to be modified specifically for the purpose of aerial combat. Working with designer Raymond Saulnier, Garros had developed reinforced propeller blades that deflected bullets from a forward-firing machine gun. This development made it easier to hit the target as the gun could be aimed at gunsight from the cockpit. Over the next few weeks, Garros and his Parasol scored three more victories until he was forced to land behind enemy lines and was taken prisoner before he could burn the aircraft—which fell into the hands of the Germans. The Parasol forward-firing mechanism was taken to Anton Fokker so that he could replicate the system for German fighters. In fact, Fokker and his engineering team had already been working on just such a system, and the available evidence points to a synchronisation device having been in development with Fokker's company for perhaps six months prior to the capture of Garros's machine. The end result—spurred on by obvious German interest—was that the Fokker team came up with a better solution—an interrupter mechanism. They developed a synchronized propeller system in which the the gun fired through the propeller arc thus avoiding damage to the propeller blade. The new mechanisn was fitted to the Fokker Eindecker and premiered on the battlefield with a victory for Max Immelmann on 1 August 1915.

Allied pilots soon found themselves helpless against the German Eindeckers. French bombing missions into German territory were halted. British pilot morale plummeted, as the pilots began to refer to themselves as 'Fokker fodder.' The German pilots steadily accumulated victories and medals. This one-sided battle came to be known in the West as 'the Fokker Scourge'. Max Immelmann and Oswald Boelke ruled the skies as they flew together, developing aerial combat tactics and techniques. The Germans carefully protected their advantage, never allowing the Eindecker to cross lines where it might be shot down, captured, and copied.

Oswald Boelcke became an early German ace while flying the Eindecker. He codified a set of rules for successful aerial combat; they were called the *Dicta Boelcke* and have been drilled into the heads of budding fighter pilots ever since. The rules are:

1. Try to secure the upper hand before attacking. If possible, keep the sun behind you.
2. Always continue with an attack you have begun.
3. Only fire at close range, and then only when the opponent is properly in your sights.
4. You should always try to keep your eye on your opponent, and never let yourself be deceived by ruses.
5. In any type of attack, it is essential to assail your opponent from behind.
6. If your opponent dives on you, do not try to get around his attack, but fly to meet it.
7. When over the enemy's lines, never forget your own line of retreat.
8. In principle, it is better to attack in groups of four or six. Avoid two aircraft attacking the same opponent.

Boelcke was killed after his 40th victory when he violated his own Rule 8. Trying to avoid von Richthofen, he collided with squadron mate Irwin Böhme while all three were jointly attacking a DH.2.

German superiority ended in 1916 and from then onwards the Allies were always in the ascendancy. An Eindecker pilot became lost in heavy fog and landed in France. Soon after, the British introduced the Sopwith Strutter and the French the Nieuport 17. Both aircraft used technology from the captured Eindecker, but combined the synchronized propeller system with more powerful engines gaining equality, and then superiority, in the skies.

Detail of an early Fokker Eindecker without the cowl showing Fokker's original *Stangensteuerung* gear connected directly to the oil pump drive at the rear of the engine. Fokker's gear was designed to *actively* fire the gun rather than *interrupt* it. Although frequently referred to as an interrupter, this is a misnomer. Operationally the end result was the same thing—the bullet fired through the propeller arc without hitting the propeller blades.

Basic Statistics

The difference between the number of aircraft available to each country in 1914 and 1918 is staggering:

	1914	1918
France	138	4,500
Great Britain	113	3,300
Germany	232	2,390
Italy	150	1,200
USA	55	740

The number shot down, crashed or damaged is equally staggering:

France   52,640
Great Britain 35,973
Germany   27,637

Taking the main three protagonusts, if this data is tabulated it produces the following picture:

	Built	Destroyed	Remaining	Difference	As % of built
France	67,987	52,640	4,500	10,847	15.95%
Great Britain	58,144	35,973	3,300	18,871	32.46%
Germany	48,537	27,637	2,390	18,510	38.14%

Source: Enzo Angelucci, *Illustrated Encyclopedia of Military Aircraft*, 2001.

Of course, the picture is skewed by the fact that the aircraft 'remaining' were probably front line aircraft only. There would have been many more with minor damage, or in reserve, or considered obsolete and perhaps already scrapped. Nevertheless, compared to the number of aircraft built, the front line totals at the end of the war appear modest.

The Main Aircraft Types Used by the Protagonists in Alphabetical Sequence

Careful study of the aircraft types and variations shows that literally hundreds of different 'models', 'types' and 'iterations' were designed or built during the four years of the war. Some of the iterations or variations may have been tiny, but the end result is that a comprehensive list of types used by each side would be beyond the scope of this book. The web site www. theaerodrome.com is a good place for the interested reader to get more information. In tabulating the main type used by each side, we have adopted those described by this web site. This produces a list of the most common aircraft used by each side. As the scope of this book is limited, this information has been given for the three main protagonists only. It starts with the France, the most advanced aeronautical nation at the start of the war and the largest manufacturer of aircraft.

France

1	Blériot XI	12	Morane-Saulnier A.1	23	Nieuport-Delage 29
2	Bréguet Br.14	13	Morane-Saulnier L	24	Paul Schmitt 7
3	Bréguet Br.M5	14	Morane-Saulnier N	25	Salmson 2
4	Caudron G.4	15	Morane-Saulnier P	26	SPAD A.2
5	Caudron R.11	16	Nieuport 11	27	SPAD S.VII
6	Dorand AR.1	17	Nieuport 12	28	SPAD S.XII
7	Dorand AR.2	18	Nieuport 16	29	SPAD S.XIII
8	F.B.A. Type C	19	Nieuport 17	30	Voisin 5
9	Hanriot HD.1	20	Nieuport 23	31	Voisin 8
10	Maurice Farman F.40	21	Nieuport 27		
11	Maurice Farman S.11	22	Nieuport 28		

Great Britain

1	Airco DH.1	15	Bristol Scout	29	Sopwith 1½ Strutter
2	Airco DH.2	16	Handley Page O/100	30	Sopwith Bulldog
3	Airco DH.4	17	Handley Page O/400	31	Sopwith Camel
4	Airco DH.5	18	Handley Page V/1500	32	Sopwith Cuckoo
5	Airco DH.6	19	Martinsyde F.4 Buzzard	33	Sopwith Dolphin
6	Airco DH.9	20	Martinsyde G.100 Elephant	34	Sopwith Pup
7	Airco DH.9a	21	RAF B.E.2c	35	Sopwith Salamander
8	Armstrong-Whitworth F.K.3	22	RAF B.E.12	36	Sopwith Snipe
9	Armstrong-Whitworth F.K.8	23	RAF F.E.2	37	Sopwith Tabloid
10	Armstrong-Whitworth F.K.10	24	RAF F.E.8	38	Sopwith Triplane
11	Avro 504	25	RAF R.E.7	39	Vickers F.B.5
12	Blackburn Kangaroo	26	RAF R.E.8	40	Vickers F.B.12
13	Bristol F.2b Fighter	27	RAF S.E.5 and S.E.5a	41	Vickers Vimy
14	Bristol M.1c	28	Short Bomber		

RAF in this sense refers to Royal Aircraft Factory.

Germany

1	A.E.G. C.IV	16	D.F.W. C.V	31	L.F.G. Roland D.II
2	A.E.G. G.IV	17	Fokker D.VII	32	L.F.G. Roland D.VIb
3	AGO C.II	18	Fokker D.VIII	33	Pfalz D.III
4	Albatros C.I	19	Fokker DR.I (Dreidecker)	34	Pfalz D.XII
5	Albatros C.III	20	Fokker E Series (Eindecker)	35	Pfalz DR.I
6	Albatros C.V	21	Friedrichshafen G.III	36	Rumpler 6B
7	Albatros C.VII	22	Gotha G.V	37	Rumpler C.I
8	Albatros C.X	23	Halberstadt C.V	38	Rumpler C.IV
9	Albatros C.XII	24	Halberstadt D.II	39	Siemens-Schuckert D.III
10	Albatros D.I	25	Hannover CL.II	40	Siemens-Schuckert D.IV
11	Albatros D.II	26	Hannover CL.IIIa	41	Siemens-Schuckert R.I
12	Albatros D.III	27	Junkers CL.I	42	Taube
13	Albatros D.V Series	28	Junkers D.I	43	Zeppelin Staaken R.VI
14	Aviatik B.I	29	Junkers J.I		
15	Aviatik C.I	30	L.V.G. C.II		

Further Aircraft Statistics for France, Great Britain and Germany

Type

Advanced Trainer	AT
Armed Reconnaissance	AR
Bomber/Night Bomber	B/NB
Carrier-borne Fighter	CBF
Carrier-borne Reconnaissance & Patrol	CBRP
Escort Fighter	EF
Fighter	F
Fighter/Reconnaissance/Light Bomber	F/R/B
Fighter/Scout	F/S
Floatplane Fighter	FPF
Floatplane Fighting Scout	FPFS
Flying Boat	FB
General Purpose	GP
Ground-Attack	GA
Ground Attack/Fighter	GA/F
Heavy Bomber	HB
Lightweight Bomber	LB
Lightweight Day Bomber	LDB
Observation	O
Reconnaissance	R
Reconnaissance/Fighter/Night Bomber	R/F/NB
Reconnaissance/Fighter/Trainer	R/F/T

Reconnaissance Flying Boat	RFB
Reconnaissance Scout/Trainer	RS/T
Reconnaissance/Bomber	R/B
Reconnaissance/Trainer	R/T
Reconnaissance/Light Bomber	R/LB
Reconnaissance/Torpedo Bomber	R/TB
Scout	S
Scout/Light Bomber	S/LB
Short-range Bomber	SRB
Tactical Medium Bomber	TMB
Trainer/Reconnaissance	T/R

Wings

Biplane	B
Monoplane	M
Triplane	T

Crew	Crew complement for each type
Ceiling	Recorded operation ceiling for each type in feet
Climb	Speed of climb in feet per minute
Range	Recorded range for each type where known in miles
Speed	Recorded speed (mph) for each type where known
Quantity	Recorded quantity built for each type where known

The models are shown alphabetically within year of first introduction. NK = 'not known'. France also used British aircraft and Britain used French aircraft, below only the indigenous models for each nation are given, and not any of the types that they 'bought in'.

France

Manufacturer and Model	Year	Type	Wings	Crew	Ceiling	Climb	Range	Speed	Quantity
Bleriot XI	1909	T/R	M	1	NK	NK	NK	47	850
Caudron G.3	1914	R/T	B	1	14,100	NK	NK	66	2,849
Farman MF.11 Shorthorn	1914	R/B	B	2	12,500	NK	217	66	300
Breguet Br.M5	1915	B	B	2	11,500	NK	NK	NK	NK
Caudron G.4	1915	B	B	2	14,100	NK	NK	82	1,421
Morane-Saulnier Type N	1915	F	M	1	13,100	820	140	103	49
Nieuport 11 (Bébé)	1915	F/S	B	1	15,100	660	205	97	7,200
Nieuport 12	1915	F/F/T	B	2	13,000	NK	264	90	1,000
SPAD A.2	1915	F	B	2	14,100	525	186	96	99
Voisin Type 5	1915	B	B	1	11,500	NK	NK	65	300
Hanriot HD.1	1916	F	B	1	21.000	894	342	114	1,200
Nieuport 17	1916	F/S	B	1	17,600	673	155	110	3,600

SPAD S.VII	1916	F	B	1	17,500	NK	224	119	6,000
Breguet Bre.14	1917	GP	B	2	14,000	NK	301	121	7,800
Caudron G.6	1917	GP	B	2	15,500	865	217	93	512
Dorand AR	1917	O	B	2	18,000	NK	171	92	142
Nieuport 27	1917	F	B	1	18,209	NK	155	115	1,000
SPAD S.XI	1917	F	B	2	22,966	788	249	112	1,000
SPAD S.XII	1917	F	B	1	22,474	1,090	217	126	300
SPAD S.XIII	1917	F	B	1	21,818	1,312	NK	138	8,472
Caudron R.11	1918	GP	B	3	19,521	NK	NK	114	370
Nieuport 28	1918	F	B	1	17,388	855	217	123	300
Salmson 2	1918	R	B	2	20,505	NK	311	117	3,200
SPAD S.XIV	1918	FPF	B	1	16,404	NK	155	127	40

This table accounts for 48,004 aircraft of the 67,987 that France is said to have built, 70.61 per cent. There were, of course, many minor marques and other variations. In addition France used British and Italian aircraft.

Figures are always misleading. For example the table above shows that 2,849 Caudron G.3 were built, whereas in France 2,450 were actually built and the remainder were built under licence; 233 were built in England and 166 in Italy.

Great Britain

Manufacturer and Model	Year	Type	Wings	Crew	Ceiling	Climb	Range	Speed	Quantity
Royal Aircraft Factory B.E.2	1912	RS/T	B	2	10,000	222	234	72	3,500
Avro 504	1913	R/T	B	2	13,000	NK	250	95	8,970
Bristol Scout	1914	F/S	B	1	14,000	540	NK	100	370
Sopwith Tabloid	1914	S	B	2	6,900	430	317	87	42
Airco DH.2	1915	S	B	1	14,000	549	249	93	453
Royal Aircraft Factory F.E.2	1915	R/F/NB	B	2	9,000	NK	NK	80	2,339
Short Type 184	1915	R/TB	B	2	9,000	NK	243	88	936
Sopwith Baby	1915	FPFS	B	1	9,800	285	224	101	286
Vickers FB.5 (Gunbus)	1915	S	B	2	9,000	310	249	70	224
Avro 523 Pike	1916	SRB	B	3	13,000	526	466	97	2
Royal Aircraft Factory F.E.8	1916	F	B	1	14,500	NK	NK	94	295
Royal Aircraft Factory R.E.8	1916	R/LB	B	2	13,500	300	217	103	4,077
Sopwith 1½ Strutter	1916	F/R/B	B	1/2	13,000	NK	351	102	5,939
Sopwith Pup	1916	F	B	1	17,500	460	NK	112	1,770
Airco DH.4	1917	LDB	B	2	22,00	1,000	478	143	6,295
Airco DH.5	1917	S/LB	B	1	16,000	815	273	102	552
Airco DH.9	1917	LB	B	1	15,500	503	503	113	4,091
Armstrong Whitworth FK8	1917	GP	B	2	12,100	NK	NK	95	1,650
Avro 529	1917	HB	B	3	13,500	715	360	95	2

Beardmore WB III / SB 3	1917	CBF	B	1	12,400	534	171	103	100
Bristol F.2b	1917	F/R/B	B	2	18,000	869	368	123	5,308
Fairey Campania	1917	CBRP	B	2	6,600	285	373	85	62
Felixstowe F.2	1917	FB	B	4	9,800	253	559	96	175
Royal Aircraft Factory S.E.5	1917	F	B	1	21,000	755	300	138	5,205
Sopwith Camel	1917	F	B	1	21,000	1,085	301	115	5,490
Sopwith Dolphin	1917	F	B	1	20,000	885	196	112	1,532
Blackburn R.T.1 Kangaroo	1918	R/TB	B	3	13,000	480	487	98	20
Fairey III	1918	R/LB	B	2/3	17,000	800	550	106	964
Felixstowe F.5	1918	RFB	B	4	6,800	216	590	88	280
Handley Page H.P. O/400	1918	HB	B	3	8,500	217	450	98	657
Martinsyde F.4 Buzzard	1918	F	B	1	25,000	NK	404	145	375
Sopwith Snipe	1918	F	B	1	19,500	1,500	40	121	2,097

This table accounts for 65,686 aircraft of the 58,144 that Great Britain is said to have built, 112.97 per cent. Clearly this is an obvious nonsense. There were, of course, many minor marques and other variations. In addition Great Britain used French and Italian aircraft. One reason for the big difference may be that the official total given of aircraft built was intended to specify those built for *British* use only, disregarding aircraft built for other nations. Whatever the cause, statistics rarely add up without a great deal of detailed explanation. One example of the confusion is the Airco DH.4. Of this model 6,295 were built, but 4,846 of this total were *not* built in Britain, instead they were built under licence in the United States for American war use when they entered the fray. This is another example where the the quoted numbers 'built' by a nation is shown to be deceiving.

Yet a further example of 'doubtful' figures relates to the Handley Page H.P. O/400. Some sources say 657 were built, but in Handley Page's history, written by the Company in 1949 (*Handley Page Forty Years On, 1909-1949*) the anonymous author from the Handley Page publicity department says: 'Some six hundred of these big Handley Page aircraft [O/400] were ordered and approximately four hundred built before the end of the war'. It is almost certain that the 657 is incorrect. This may have been the Government purchase order, but it would almost certainly have been countermanded at the cessation of hostilities with Handley Page receiving compensation. It may be assumed that a safer figure might be in the region of 400 to 450 having been built in Britain. The United States also built some O/400s under licence and approximately 107 were built in the USA by the Standard Aircraft Corporation. This adds further confusion to the numbers game.

Germany

Manufacturer and Model	Year	Type	Wings	Crew	Ceiling	Climb	Range	Speed	Quantity
Rumpler Taube	1910	GP	M	2	6,600	NK	87	62	100
Albatros B.II	1914	R	B	2	9,800	NK	NK	65	NK
Aviatik B.I	1914	R	B	2	15,000	NK	NK	62	NK
Rumpler B.I	1914	R	B	2	NK	NK	NK	90	224
AGO C.II	1915	R	B	2	14,800	NK	360	80	15
Albatros C.I	1915	R	B	2	9,800	NK	NK	87	500
Albatros C.III	1915	R	B	2	11,200	NK	NK	87	600
Aviatik C.I	1915	R	B	2	11,500	255	261	88	500
Fokker E (eindecker)	1915	F/S	M	1	11,800	633	123	87	420
LVG B	1915	RS/T	B	2	NK	NK	261	65	100
LVG C.II	1915	R/LB	B	2	13,100	NK		81	300
Rumpler C.I	1915	R	B	2	16,600	NK	360	94	1,000
Rumpler G.I	1915	B	B	3	16,400	NK	435	103	220
AEG C.IV	1916	F	B	2	16,400	NK	280	98	658
AEG G.IV	1916	TMB	B	3	14,800	NK	466	103	320
Albatros C.V	1916	R	B	2	16,400	NK	280	106	400
Albatros D.I	1916	F	B	1	17,000	547	180	109	50
Albatros D.II	1916	F	B	1	17,000	886	163	109	100
DFW C.V	1916	R	B	2	16,400	NK	NK	96	3,250
Gotha G.IV	1916	HB	B	3	16,400	NK	NK	84	230
LFG Roland C.II	1916	R	B	2	13,100	545	NK	103	400
Rumpler 6B	1916	FPFS	B	1	16,400	NK	224	95	88
Rumpler C.III	1916	AR	B	2	13,100	NK	298	85	75
Halberstadt D.II	1916	F	B	1	13,100	583	NK	93	65
Albatros D.III	1917	F	B	1	18,000	886	217	109	1,866
Albatros C.X	1917	R	B	2	16,400	NK	NK	109	NK
Albatros D.V	1917	F	B	1	18,700	820	217	116	900
Albatros D.Va	1917	F	B	1	18,700	908	232	116	1,662
Albatros J.I	1917	GA	B	1	14,800	400	217	87	240
Fokker Dr.I (dreidecker)	1917	F	T	1	20,000	1,090	186	103	320
Friedrichshafen G.III	1917	B/NB	B	3	14,800	NK	373	84	338
Gotha G.V	1917	HB	B	3	21,300	NK	522	87	205
Hannover CL.II	1917	EF	B	1	24,600	NK	NK	103	439
Hannover CL.III	1917	F	B	2	24,600	NK	NK	103	617
Hansa-Brandenburg W.12	1917	FPF	B	2	16,400	NK	323	99	181
Pfalz D.III	1917	F	B	1	17,000	820	NK	103	600
Rumpler C.IV	1917	R	B	2	21,000	NK	NK	106	650
Rumpler C.VII	1917	R	B	2	24,000	NK	364	109	NK
Rumpler C.VIII	1917	AT	B	1	13,100	771	336	87	125

Rumpler D.I	1917	F	B	1	23,000	NK	224	112	NK
Siemens-Schuckert D.I	1917	T	B	1	13,100	539	NK	97	95
Siemens-Schuckert D.III	1917	F	B	1	26,200	1,260	NK	112	80
Zeppelin-Staaken R-series	1917	HB	B	7	14,100	350	497	84	29
Fokker C.I	1918	R	B	2	13,100	NK	NK	109	250
Fokker D.VII	1918	F	B	1	18,000	772	NK	117	3,300
Fokker D.VIII	1918	F	M	1	20,700	NK	175	117	295
Halberstadt CL.IV	1918	GA/F	B	2	21,000	NK	300	116	700
Junkers CL.I	1918	F	M	2	19,700	NK	NK	100	47
LFG Roland D.VI	1918	F	B	1	19,000	860	249	124	350
LVG C.VI	1918	R	B	2	21,300	550	245	106	1,100
Pfalz D.XII	1918	F	B	1	18,500	NK	NK	106	800
Siemens-Schuckert D.IV	1918	F	B	1	26,200	400	NK	118	123

This table is the exact opposite of the British table in that the total for quantities built of all of these models comes to only 24,927; far short of the 48,537 aircraft said to have been built by Germany. Therefore, many minor marques, models and variations are missing making this a less than a comprehensive list. It is not helped by the fact that some types—notably the Albatros B.II were know to have been built in 'large numbers', and yet here all we can do is list it as 'not known'; this aircraft alone could easily account for 3,000 or more to go towards the missing number. As Curt Riess's 'Hauptmann Hermann' makes clear, (see the section below), the utter confusion in Germany at the end of the war makes it difficult to assess and compile accurate figures. Many aircraft were manufactured by sub-contract and accurate figures did not become available or the evidence was destroyed. Also, whatever brave attempts the interim German Government may have made to abide by the stringent Allied terms, those service personnel on the ground, profoundly in disagreement with the new authorities, did whatever they could to obfuscate, very often to the degree of downright disobedience.

The fact is that highly detailed information *was* kept; the German mind-set is such that *not* to keep detail is simply *unmöglich*, but it quietly got lost in the winter fog of 1918/1919. This makes an interesting contradistinction with April/May 1945 when the utter and absolute collapse of the Third Reich resulted in hundred of tons of vital papers falling into the hands of the Allies with very little being destroyed, (although it had been ordered to be destroyed). This did not happen in 1918 and 1919. The German collapse through internal revolution rather than outright defeat on the battleground resulted in the Army remaining in some form of underlying control, enabling them, or at least a large proportion of them, to operate a form of quiet disobedience.

Extreme caution is advised in interpreting facts and figures. In fact when compared to the figures for France and Great Britain, the statistics simply do not add up. Whichever web sites or reference books one goes to there are quite wide variations. In short, one should look at these figures with a metaphorical 'health warning' in mind, and understand that they should be viewed as indicative rather than gospel.

The End of the War on the German Side

Curt Riess's Hauptmann Hermann in *The Rise and Fall of the Luftwaffe* gives some interesting information about the last few days of the War and what happened after:

It was the night of 23 September 1918. Our air group was based on two airfields near the French-Belgian frontier. There were two squadrons on our field, the third along with the staff on the other field. I still remember the half-circle of tents silhouetted against the sky, rapidly disappearing in the dusk. I still hear the noise of the motors making a test run and drowning out every other sound. Then we could see a long stream of sparks from the exhaust until the throttle was eased and the engine, after releasing a long blue flame from the exhaust, was idling again smoothly. When all engines had been tested the ignition was cut.

The sudden silence gave us an unreal feeling of peace and of suspense. We were tense when we emerged from the tent of the squadron-leader who had given us the meteorological report and the itinerary for our separate take-offs, the route going out and the return, the latest intelligence reports about the anti-aircraft guns, the searchlight defences, and the information about the hundred and fifty night fighter airplanes that were supposed to defend Paris against us.

For Paris was the target. Our 'planes were loaded with hundreds of incendiary bombs. Each of them weighed two pounds. Other German bombers were to visit London that night. The idea was to start so many fires with this first incendiary attack that the fire brigades would not be able to put all of them out.

Then we took our seats and I was about to start my motors. But we never took off. Suddenly through the darkness a car came racing, a staff officer jumped out and rushed toward us. Orders from General Headquarters. We were not to take off. That day it had been decided to send a request to President Wilson to start negotiations for an armistice. Incidentally, the request did not leave Imperial Headquarters at Spa till late on 3 October—ten days later.

That sudden change in orders came as a severe shock to us. Only a week before we had attacked Paris heavily with high-explosive bombs totalling 22 tons, a terrific amount for that time. We had seen the heavy explosions and the fires that we had caused in Paris, and a few days later we were able to read reprints from Swiss papers with exciting reports of the terror we had created. It is true, we had lost a number of our 'planes, but not as many as in our first night attack on Paris in the spring of 1918, when I had returned alone—eight 'planes from our squadron had started out and had seen three of our 'planes shot down in flames. This time our squadron had lost only two 'planes—which wasn't too bad.

Then came something that should have tipped us off. We were requested to drop leaflets over the enemy lines. I still have one of those leaflets and on reading it over I understand why we didn't like the idea of dropping them.

Up to that point none of us flyers had doubted for a moment that Germany was going to win the war. That, indeed, was our reason for fighting the war. The leaflets which we had to drop were titled 'Pourquoi?' and under this title there were two pages of printed text in French, in which we, the Germans, asked the French why this war should be continued. We said that we should be only too happy to make peace, but that France was prevented from doing so by England and also by America, which had decided to continue the war until the utter destruction of Europe was achieved. There was some mention of the sufferings of women and children and the enormous sacrifices—and would it do anybody any good? Certainly not the French. So let's make peace. . . .

Well, that hadn't sounded too well. But somehow we never thought that the reason for such leaflets was that our war was already lost. In the beginning of August the Allies had broken the German lines north of the old Roman road from St Quentin to Amiens, and we had had to move our aerodromes steadily backward. Of course, we had no idea at that time that Ludendorff and Hindenburg had already declared that they could not win the war. It was only now, at the end of September, when our so-called 'fire circus' was suddenly cancelled, that we really became suspicious.

Still, our spirits were unbroken. Even when the backward movement started in earnest. From that night in September until the day of the Armistice we changed airdromes four times and were bombed more and more often by the Allies. Our own night bombing was continually reduced. 'The front lines are too uncertain,' we were told. They were uncertain, and naturally night bombing was out when you did not know whom you were going to hit. That was the end of the strategic air war as far as we were concerned. We had to assist the infantry on the battlefield. We were sent on reconnaissance. We had to strafe the ground and do some low-level bombing flights in order to support the 'planned retreat' of our troops—yes, already then it was called that.

The orders for this type of co-operational work were not as precise as our orders had been all these years. It was all very confusing. Commanders who asked for our co-operation didn't know themselves where their troops were stationed, and we had never been trained in this kind of observation work. Furthermore, these armed reconnaissance flights became costly. Not that we were not willing to take risks. But we began to feel that our actions no longer had any definite purpose, not even to mention a defined purpose, and that we were just being sent up to create some illusion of action. That made us mad, and we began to resent the useless murdering of our comrades and the damage to our 'planes. The emergency airports we now used were not well enough equipped to handle our heavily loaded bombers. The strain increased.

The worst, of course, was the fact that the Allied air forces were by now vastly superior in numbers, and their pilots were confident of the approaching breakdown of the German war machine. The Allied aircraft were superior also in quality, and the other side knew it only too well. Inspection of our 'planes shot down on the other side had indicated to them that we had no more copper nor rubber, that the welding work on our steel spars was faulty, that our fuel—a benzol-alcohol mixture—often contained so much water that the engines began to cough.

We were getting nervous. One night a German anti-aircraft battery near our aerodrome fired at my 'plane and with the first salvo shot half my tail off. This was the first time I had been hit by flak during the whole war. It seemed highly symbolic to me. What was the use of precisely calculated and daringly executed forays when everything around us was crumbling? What was the use anyhow?

We began to feel frustrated. We had just changed our aerodromes again, and I had to fly my twin-engined bomber eastward to the new airport early in the morning. It was bitter cold in the half-burnt-out house near our landing field where we spent the night, keeping warm by feeding some Louis XIV chairs to the fire in the enormous fireplace.

Shortly after I had fallen asleep, I heard light artillery and machine-gun fire on the ground. We soon learned that the machine-gun fire came from our troops aiming at reconnaissance parties. I went on sleeping, at least I tried to. Then my chief mechanic rushed in and told me to take off immediately if I didn't want to be captured. I rushed to the aerodrome where the mechanics had already warmed up the engines and climbed into the rear gunner's seat. Just before opening up the engines, I heard machine-gun fire from across the field and as I had to take off in the direction it came from, I didn't feel too good.

When I was up about a hundred feet, I saw that the troops who were firing were wearing British battle bowlers. The British were taking our airfield, and I managed to get away only on my few seconds' head start.

I flew in the direction of Liège. I still wasn't out of danger. My port engine didn't work properly and it overheated rapidly. I could not gain much altitude, what with my crew of three mechanics in the back, and the baggage and the supply of spare parts and tools which we had loaded into the 'plane. After we had flown about fifty miles, the ailing engine stopped altogether. It was clear to me that a piston had seized.

I found a field near a little village and landed there. We found that a bullet had pierced the cylinder and caused the failure. Immediately upon our landing, a disorderly crowd of young German soldiers swarmed all over the field, shouting at us that the war would be over shortly, that a revolution had broken out in Germany, and that Soviets were being formed by soldiers and workers in order to lead the German army back home.

I didn't believe a word of it. My observer fired a few rounds over the heads of the crowd when some of the soldiers tried to loot our 'plane for 'souvenirs.' That didn't look too good to us. Finally, an officer appeared and we requisitioned his car for my observer and the chief mechanic to drive to our headquarters for a new engine so we could fly back. That was at about eight-thirty in the morning.

At three o'clock in the afternoon they came back without an engine. My observer's face was deadly white. 'There is no use exchanging the engine,' he murmured. 'We have to give up the 'plane and return to the squadron by car.' And then, as an afterthought: 'The Armistice has broken out.' The Armistice conditions saw to it that there would be no German air force, even before the peace itself was negotiated.

Article IV demanded the surrender of 2,000 fighters and night bombers. The surrender of half the material had to take place before 21 November, the rest of it before 2 December. The number of 2,000 was later reduced to 1,700.

Then came a new order from the Armistice Commission, according to which 600 more airplanes had to be surrendered before the first of January, or, if that was impossible, twenty horses should be substituted for each missing 'plane. . . . By 12 December, the Armistice Commission stated that 2,000 'planes had already been surrendered or abandoned, but that only 750 fighters and 25 night bombers had been accounted for. The rest of the lot was made up mostly of obsolete 'planes and training machines. Many of the first-line squadrons had simply not obeyed orders.

Anyhow, that seemed to be the end of the German air force—at least, that's what it seemed in those days. It had not had a long life, so far. It had been created on 1 October 1912, and when the war broke out only 34 units were in service. But on this 10 November, when everything was over, 306 squadrons were in existence.

Between 1914 and 1918 the German air force had trained 17,000 men as pilots and crew. Of these 17,000 men, 4,600 had been killed in action, 2,000 had been killed behind the front lines, 4,300 had been wounded, and 3,100 were missing or were prisoners. So there were really only a few of us around when the curtain went down.

But we German pilots would never have given up. In spite of the depressing last weeks the morale of our men did not decline. . . . Yet, the fact that our morale was excellent while the mass of the German army was in a state of demoralization did not have so much to do with material things as with our mentality—the very special mentality of flyers everywhere in the world. I said we felt like an elite. Flying somewhere in the immense ether, often alone, made us feel superior to the little beings down below, to the small business being enacted miles beneath us. We felt somewhat as follows: Here I am all by myself, there are thousands of anti-aircraft guns, there are thousands of searchlights, there are hundreds of fighters after me. And in spite of them all I'll come back. . .

We had a special sort of pride.

And now that the war was coming to an end, our superiority, though perhaps imagined, seemed to come to an end. What were we going to do? Most of us were very young, in fact most of us had left school in order to become flyers. Now we had no place to go, we had nothing to do. Even before the war ended we felt nostalgia. We looked for an object for our dreams, an object for our idealism. . . .

The next weeks—my next weeks—were full of burning 'planes, of 'planes reduced to scrap. I don't remember very well all the phases of my return to Germany. I only remember that our ground crews revolted one night and left for Germany with all our supplies and cars and trucks. Finally we managed to repair a broken-down truck on which we transported our most valuable instruments, a few supplies, and those of our men who were not fit to march. But long before we reached the German frontier the car broke down. Then we just got out and marched home.

During my retreat I saw 'planes abandoned in France and in Belgium because they were no longer fit to be flown or had been damaged deliberately by the hostile population or by the revolutionary ground personnel or just because there was no fuel. Also abandoned were immense amounts of spare engines, spare parts, tools, ammunition, instruments—every kind of equipment farther behind in the reserve depots and in the repair centres, nearly all of which were located in the occupied countries. Nobody thought of salvaging all this material; nobody seemed interested.

A great many 'planes and engines were lost in the Rhineland and, indeed, everywhere in Germany. Training 'planes and also fighters and bombers which were about to be sent to the front. They were abandoned and pillaged and looted by souvenir hunters and by scrap thieves. Many of the 'planes which had already been put on freight trains were simply broken to bits for scrap, for fire wood, by the starving population. You couldn't blame those people. They needed the wood. They needed the few pennies they got for the scrap. And, anyhow, 'planes to them were the very symbol of war—which they hated above all.

The greatest number of 'planes was, of course, still concentrated in the factories and in the reserve depots and in training centres. The destruction of most of them started only after Versailles. But during the last weeks of 1918 some of them were already being torn to pieces and smashed with heavy hammers; propellers were broken, precision instruments were shattered, and some of the wrecks were thrown into yards where they rusted for years. It seemed the end. This return to Germany was a nightmare for those of us who loved flying. It was worse, much worse, than all the dangers of war I had been through.

This long extract has been given as Riess's fictional Hauptmann Hermann describes in vivid prose the post-war chaos of destruction and abandonment. This accounts in large for the discrepancies in numbers, for apart from outmoded aircraft, keeping front line services functioning inevitably left vast remants of damaged craft, parts, and the general detritus of war. For the Allies it would have been bad enough and some degree of chaos ensued on the Western Front as everyone simply wanted to go home, but on the German side the total collapse in morale, the retreat, and the ransacking must have been a heart-breaking sight for all those who had given so much. The handing over to the Allies of materiel and aircraft alone would almost have been impossible for the German Government to comply with. It was not through lack of willingness, it was simply because chaos ensued.

Quite who Hauptmann Hermann was has never been discovered. Riess writing in 1942 says that because this (then) senior serving Luftwaffe officer had family in Germany he did not wish for his name to be quoted. He may be real, he may be fictional, or he may be an alamalgam of several people who Riess interviewed, but the general tone of what Hauptmann Hermann says strikes as a vivid picture of the time.

The Scope of Coverage and the Methods used in this Book

As has been said above, the scope of this book is, by necessity limited. Therefore some subjectivity has been applied in deciding which of the aces to feature for each nation, and what to show by way of illustrations. We have tried to apply a balanced approach and hope we have been relatively successful. The method of giving titles to officers has generally been given in their own languages, but when it comes to the Cyrillic titles we have reverted to the Anglicised versions. When it comes to spelling this is also fraught with difficulty, and we have tried to adopt the most commonly used version of the name or word.

We are conscious that the illustration section for France does not do that nation justice, but many French aircraft, such as the Nieuport 11 *Bébé* are illustrated in other nations' sections as they were often manufactured under licence. Besides this, we believe that English language readers will probably wish for the weight of illustration to be given to the British, Commonwealth and German participants.

THE UNITED KINGDOM OF GREAT BRITAIN AND IRELAND, THE DOMINIONS AND EMPIRE

B RITISH MILITARY AVIATION STEMS from the first usage of observation balloons by the Royal Engineers—who had five such balloons at Woolwich Arsenal in 1879. Army interest in balloons had commenced in 1863 when a Mr Henry Coxwell was commissioned by the Army to make a series of ascents at Aldershot. One ascent was made by two officers from the Royal Engineers who made a favourable report.

In 1884 the Bechuanaland Expedition included a detachment of three balloons with a complement of sixteen personnel under the command of a Major Elsdale RE. Other campaigns saw the use of balloons. Meeting with success, the Balloon Section was enlarged and moved to the open spaces of Aldershot during 1881. During 1890 a Balloon Section was officially established as a Unit of the Royal Engineers. During the winter of 1905–06 the Balloon Section removed to Farnborough, Hampshire, where the RE Balloon Factory was firmly established.

On 1 April 1911 the aviation element of the Royal Engineers was expanded to battalion strength with Headquarters at South Farnborough, No. 1 (Airship) Company also at Farnborough, and No. 2 (Aeroplane) Company at Larkhill, near Stonehenge, Salisbury Plain, Wiltshire. This was the first British military unit equipped with heavier than air craft. Commander of the Royal Engineers Air Battalion was Major Sir Alexander Bannerman. Captain E. M. Maitland commanded the Airship Company and Captain J. D. B. Fulton the Aeroplane Company.

On 13 April 1912 the Royal Flying Corps (RFC) was constituted by Royal Warrant—the Government intention being that such a corps could serve both Army and Navy requirements—an obvious cost cutting plan. Accordingly, the original Royal Flying Corps consisted of a Military Wing, Naval Wing and a Central Flying School for training all pilots. This unwieldy state of affairs continued until 23 June 1914 when the Admiralty insisted that the Naval Wing become a service in its own right. The Royal Naval Air Service came into being on 1 July 1914 leaving the Royal Flying Corps comprising of the Military Wing and Central Flying School at Upavon, Wiltshire.

When the Royal Flying Corps came into being in April 1912 the Aeroplane Company of the Air Battalion, Royal Engineers, became No. 3 Squadron RFC and No. 2 Squadron RFC was formed from pilots from the Air Battalion Depot at Farnborough. No. 1 Squadron RFC was formed from No. 1 Airship Company, Air Battalion, Royal Engineers, and remained as the RFC Airship Detachment until 1 May 1914. On the same day a cadre No.

1 Squadron was formed at Brooklands with heavier than air craft. It is open to question whether No. 1 Squadron was the first RFC Squadron—it depends on what constitutes a squadron—heavier or lighter than air craft.

All Airships became the responsibility of the Royal Navy on 1 January 1914 and the RFC transferred its airships to the Navy by the end of that date.

One of the leading supporters of an air force in the early 1900s was a Royal Field Artillery officer—Captain Bertram Dickson. In a memorandum submitted to a sub-committee of the Imperial Defence Committee, Dickson emphasised Britain's need for an air force as: 'The fight for supremacy of the air in future wars will be of the first and greatest importance'. Dickson was no stranger to upsetting the status quo—he had learned to fly at his own expense at Châlons-sur-Marne in 1909—and had been reprimanded the following year for flying over British Army annual manoeuvres in a Bristol aircraft and 'unnecessarily frightening the cavalry's horses'.

The Imperial Defence Committee had been tasked with creating efficient Army and Naval air services, and evaluating the need for aerial navigation for their usage.

In Germany—the apparent war opponent—development of lighter than air rigid airships was progressing rapidly, with nearly all such aircraft capable of carrying out reconnaissance and bombing flights over the North Sea and English Channel. The German aircraft could carry a small bomb load—whilst the British aircraft had virtually nothing in comparison.

The Imperial Defence Sub Committee—far sighted—decided that a mere Air Battalion was insufficient for military needs, and decreed it be replaced with a 'Flying Corps'—separate from the Army. The army descriptive term 'Corps' had to be used—no one then—knew what else to call the new service. Accordingly, the Royal Flying Corps came into official existence on 13 May 1912.

Initially, the Royal Flying Corps had fewer than twenty aeroplane, many of which were monoplanes, but in September 1912, following a series of accidents, these were grounded until their safety could be confirmed, a serious setback to the fledgling service.

In time, with the further formation of squadrons, the fledgling Corps slowly built up its aircraft strength. B.E. (Bleriot Experimental) 2s, Maurice Farmans, Bréguets and Avros were obtained and built up a pool of aircraft. This progress was reflected when 4 Squadron was able to detach two complete Flights—consisting of eight aircraft—to the new Royal Naval Air Service.

In June 1914 the entire might of the RFC Military Wing was assembled at a 'concentration camp' (A Boer War term which later had evil connotations in the Second World War) at Netheravon on Salisbury Plain. Nos 2, 3, 4, 5 and 6 Squadrons were present with 1 Squadron being converted from airships and 7 Squadron being formed at Farnborough. The assembled 700 officers and men of the RFC were put through a month's intensive programme—they finished in time for the obvious looming war with Germany.

On 4 August 1914 Britain declared war on Germany. The RNAS assumed a Home Defence role—with the RFC ordered to support the British Army in France. 'An aerial cavalry reconnaissance unit' as one senior officer described their role. However, by the time the war ended the RFC, and later the RAF, had fought in East Africa, Italy, Mesopotamia, Palestine and Russia—some cavalry unit!

At the outbreak of war the RFC had Nos. 2 and 4 Squadrons equipped with B.E.2 biplanes; No. 3 Squadron with Blériots and Henri Farmans; No. 5 Squadron with Henri Farmans, Avro 504s and B.E.8s. No. 6 Squadron's personnel and airplanes had been dispersed among the other squadrons to bring them up to strength—but later the squadron acquired R.E.5s then B.E.s and Blériots. On 11 August 1914 the first RFC ground staff embarked at Southampton for France. The RFC's strength in France was 63 aeroplanes, 95 vehicles, 105 officers and 755 other ranks; a mobilised uniformed strength of 860 officers and men, under the command of Brigadier General Sir David Henderson, Argyll and Sutherland Highlanders. Lt-Col. Hugh M. Trenchard—then the adjutant at CFS Upavon—was appointed to command all that was left of the RFC in Britain and on 19 August 1915 he took over the command of the RFC in France from Henderson. In later years he became known as the 'Father of the Royal Air Force'.

In November 1914 two Wings of two squadrons each were formed; 1st Wing to serve with the First Army, 2nd Wing with the Second Army. The Royal Flying Corps was at war in small numbers, but by the end of hostilities its successor, the Royal Air Force, had become the largest air force in the world.

Opposing the RFC in France was the Imperial German Air Service with approximately 1,000 aircraft—with the advantage of mainly fighting over their own front lines. The first RFC casualties of the war were Lt R. R. Skene and Air Mechanic Barlow—killed in their Blériot aircraft flying to Dover *en route* for France.

On 13 August 1914 the first RFC Squadrons began to fly to France; the first aircraft to land at Amiens at 08:20 hours was a B.E.2a No. 471 of 3 Squadron flown by Lt H. D. Harvey Kelley. On 19 August 1914 the RFC lost its first aircraft in action—when an Avro 504 of 5 Squadron flown by Lt V. Waterfall was shot down by ground fire in Belgium. By early March 1915 the RFC's Order of Battle showed seven squadrons in the field in France with a total complement of eighty-five aircraft of twelve different types. Six months later there were twelve squadrons totalling 161 aircraft with some fourteen different types.

11 Squadron RFC was completely equipped with Vickers F.B.5s—the first fighter squadron to be so equipped with a single purpose aircraft. The first RFC Victoria Cross (VC) was awarded posthumously to Lt W. B. Rhodes Moorhouse of 2 Squadron flying a B.E.2 on a low level bombing raid on Courtrai railway station on 26 April 1915. One year later, most RFC squadrons were single purpose squadrons with each equipped with but one type of aircraft. On the 1 July 1916 the Battle of the Somme began with the RFC strength some 421 aircraft in twenty seven squadrons.

Squadron aircraft types in France at the commencement of the Battle of the Somme

B.E.2 c/d – 2, 4, 5, 6, 7, 8, 9, 10, 12, 13, 15, 16
R.E.7 – 21
Martinsyde – 27
Morane – 1, 3, 60
Sopwith 1½ Strutter – 70
D.H.2 – 24, 29, 32
F.E.2b – 11, 18, 22, 23, 25
F.E.2d – 20

The ferocious land battle sucked in seven more RFC squadrons and seven RNAS squadrons in a struggle of attrition. By the end of November 1916 the RFC and RNAS had established air superiority over the opposing German Air Service.

SShortly to arrive were the Sopwith Pup and Triplane. Later came the S.E.5, Bristol Fighter and the superb Sopwith F.1 Camel whose pilots shot down more enemy aircraft than did any other single British type used in the First World War.

By April 1917 the strength of the RFC at the Battle of Arras had increased to over 900 aircraft, organised into five Brigades of 10 Squadrons. The R.E.8 biplane with a 150 hp engine was coming on service and replaced the outdated B.E.2 for reconnaissance work. April 1917 however proved to be the lowest point of the RFC's fortunes with a third of its aircrews falling to the German Air Service aircraft with their Albatros D.III which out-classed the RFC's aircraft. The Battle of Third Ypres (July–November) saw the RFC regain its spurs in air combat flying the S.E.5, the SPAD, the Sopwith Pup and Camel, Nieuport Scout and DH.5.

The Royal Flying Corps began life with nothing but a couple of flimsy aircraft and a couple of balloons. When war was declared, the fighter aircraft itself had been developed to a degree, but the art of fighting in the air was an unknown quantity. It was those who were able to grasp and understand the rudiments of this new form of warfare that stood the greatest chance of survival —these men were to become the Aces.

AIRCRAFT FLOWN BY THE RFC AND RAF DURING THE FIRST WORLD WAR

B OTH THE RFC AND the RNAS had grown in strength to such an extent that they became unwieldy to manage as a global fighting force. In 1917, recognising this situation, Lloyd George appointed a special committee—The Committee on Air Organization and Home Defence against Air Raids—chaired by the South African General Smuts, to enquire into, and make recommendations as to the future of the two air services. In mid-August 1917 the Smuts Committee made their report. It recommended that the RFC and the RNAS be amalgamated into a single air service and that an Air Ministry be established to control the new service.

On 29 November 1917 King George V gave Royal Assent to The Air Force Bill and on the 2 January 1918 the Air Ministry came into being. Major General Sir Hugh Trenchard KCB, DSO, was appointed Chief of the Air Staff. Later he rose to the rank of Marshal of the Royal Air Force, The Viscount Trenchard.

On 1 April 1918 the Royal Air Force—and the Women's Royal Air Force—were formed by the amalgamation of the RFC and the RNAS; (women had been employed in the RFC from early in 1917). The new Royal Air Force was the first independent air force in the world—and 22 years later—the most famous air force in the world when it defeated the *Luftwaffe* in the Battle of Britain.

RFC AND RAF FIRST WORLD WAR ACES AND AIRMEN

T HE FIRST RECORDED INCIDENT involving British and German aircraft was on the 25 August 1914. Lieutenant Harvey-Kelly, RFC, and two other members of No. 2 Squadron, intercepted an unarmed German Rumpler observation aircraft whilst on a reconnaissance flight. The three British aircraft, also unarmed, dived repeatedly at the Rumpler and flew circles around it until the pilot was forced to land in a field. Upon doing so, the German pilot and his observer ran away, whilst Lieutenant Harvey-Kelly landed his aircraft alongside and set fire to the German aircraft. This was the first German aircraft to be brought down in the war—albeit without firing a shot.

As war progressed and the number of losses increased daily, taking its toll on the general morale of those back in England, a new word came into being—Ace. French journalists created the word for the pilot Roland Garros, after he had shot down his third enemy aircraft. It was picked up by an unknown American war correspondent, who stated that a pilot who shot down five enemy aircraft was an Ace. The British did not like the word and would not use it, but the Germans revelled in the term and saw the use of it in propaganda, but set out the requirement that 10 victories were needed for a pilot to become a Kanone (Ace).

One of the first Allied 'aces' was a shy young man, Captain Albert Ball, VC, DSO, MC. He flew a variety of aircraft in his short but illustrious career, among these were the Nieuport Scout, R.E.8 and S.E.5. He received his wings in January 1916 and died on 7 May 1917, during which time he had risen to the rank of captain and had shot down 44 German aircraft. He was just 20 years old.

There were over 1,000 'Aces' in the RFC, RNAS and RAF during the First World War, if one were to use the 'five kills' requirement as a measure, only a relatively small number of these pilots scored over 20. Among them were those who became household names like Major Lanoe George Hawker, VC, DSO, who although only scoring seven 'kills' was regarded as Britain's first 'Ace'. He was to die shot down by Manfred von Richthofen—the Red Baron. Then there was William Avery Bishop, VC, DSO, MC, a Canadian, who joined the RFC in July 1915 as an observer, but soon progressed to become a pilot, his score at the end of the war was the highest in the RFC—72; Major William George Barker, VC, DSO, MC, 50 victories, flying Sopwith Camels and Snipes; Captain Anthony Frederick Weatherby Beauchamp-Proctor, VC, DSO, MC, with a total of 54 victories flying S.E.5s. Major James Thomas Byford McCudden, VC, DSO, MC, who scored 57 kills. Then one of the most famous of all the RFC's pilots Major Edward 'Micky' Mannock, VC, DSO, MC, who in just 18 months destroyed 61 enemy aircraft, before he himself was brought down and killed by ground fire.

Then there were the others who never became household names, but contributed just as much and in some case even more. Men like Captain Alfred Clayburn Atkey, MC, who claimed 38 victories, flying DH.4s and Bristol F.2Bs; Lieutenant Leonard Monteagle Barlow, MC, 20 victories flying an S.E.5; Captain Douglas John Bell, MC, a South African who joined the RFC in June 1916 and was shot down less than a year later, but accounted for 20 enemy aircraft in that short period of time. Major Geoffrey Hilton Bowman, DSO, DFC, who shot down 32 enemy aircraft. Captain William Gordon Claxton, DSO, DFC, a Canadian, who shot down 37 enemy aircraft. Captain Philip Fletcher Fullard, DSO, MC, flying the Nieuport and whose score reached 40 in just six months. Major Tom Falcon Hazell, DSO, DFC, from southern Ireland, who flew Nieuports and S.E.5s and accounted for 43 enemy aircraft and Major Donald Roderick MacLaren, DSO, DFC, MC, a Canadian who in one year accounted for 54 enemy aircraft and balloons.

One member of the Empire who joined the RFC at the outbreak of war, was 2Lt Indra Lal Roy from Calcutta, India. He was at school in England when the war broke out and immediately joined up. On graduating as a pilot, he joined 40 Squadron and in the month of July 1918 accounted for ten German aircraft, before he himself was shot down and killed. He was the first Indian 'Ace' and probably still the only one.

The Sopwith Camel was one of the most respected, but also the most unforgiving aircraft, in the RFC. Tough, fast and reliable, it was a pilot's aircraft and could be devastating in the right hands. The F.E.2b on the other hand, although looking fragile, was one of the most durable of aircraft and more than capable of holding its own in battle. The S.E.5a was the aircraft most feared by the Germans, with its agility, speed and fire power. Between them—the S.E.5a, the F.E.2b, the French built Nieuport and the Sopwith Camel, they accounted for the majority of German losses.

Number of aces in the British, Dominion and Empire forces 1914 to 1918:

5 victories	246
6 victories	128
7 victories	133
8 victories	109
9 victories	80
10 victories	47
11-14 victories	157
15-19 victories	62
20 + victories	83
Total	**1,045**

This is an astonishing number, but when multiplied by the number of enemy 'downed' it rises to over 9,500 aircraft accounted for by the Aces. Of course, thousands more enemy aircraft were shot down by ground fire or as 1, 2, 3 or 4 'kills', not making the designation of an 'Ace', so the total of enemy downed must be in the of 20,000 or possibly more. Of course, the picture is mirrored on the other side, so in all the human tragedy was immense. Many thousands of aircraft were built. To cite just three British examples, of the Bristol F.2B, IYOS (Initial year of service) 1917, 5,308 were built, of the Royal Aircraft Factory S.E.5 IYOS 1917, 5,205 were built and for the Sopwith Camel, IYOS 1917, 5,490. Similar numbers are on the German side. All in all it was a race for mastery of the skies, and as is usual in warfare, the major race was with technology of airframes, engines and fuel to achieve superiority of speed, manouvreability and fire-power.

The following list of British and Dominion Aces and airman is representative and not exhaustive. It covers the majority of the key 'Aces' of the First World War fighting for King and Country.

Major Lanoe George Hawker, (1890-1916)
7 victories

Acknowledged to be the first British 'ace' and one of the RFC's first fighting pilots that was recognised by the award of the Victoria Cross.

Major Hawker was born on 30 December 1890 into a military family at Longparish, Hampshire. In June 1910 he joined The Royal Aero Club and on 4 March 1913 gained Flying Certificate No. 435. He was commissioned into the Royal Engineers, requested attachment to the Royal Flying Corps and moved to Upavon, Wiltshire, Central Flying School, (CFS) on 1 August 1914. Passing out from Upavon on 3 October 1914, Hawker was sent to 6 Squadron at Farnborough, and then on 6 October 1914 flew to France in Henry Farman No. 653. Two days later he was in action—flying as Observer in B.E.2a No. 492 observing the advancing German invaders. On 31 October 1914 he fired his first airborne shots at the enemy—six rounds from his Webley service issue revolver. His other airborne armament was a .303 inch issue service rifle.

On 18 April 1915 Hawker took off alone to bomb German Zeppelin airship LZ 35 in its hangar at Gontrode. His bomb load was only three 20 lb Hales bombs plus several hand grenades. He scored two hits on the hangar and threw his hand grenades at the crew of a captive balloon that were firing machine guns at him. The hangar proved to be empty, as LZ 35 had crashed five days before Hawker's bomb run. For this raid and previous good work he was admitted to The Distinguished Service Order and promoted to Captain.

On 3 June 1915 Captain Hawker was allocated a new aircraft—a single-seat Bristol Scout C, No.1609—which he promptly modified to his ideas of air fighting. A Lewis machine gun was fixed to the left side of the cockpit, pointing forward and outwards to clear the propeller arc.

On 7 June he fired his Lewis gun in anger at a German two-seat recce aircraft, causing it to spin earthwards. A week on 21 June 1915, later he attacked a DFW C which also spiralled earthwards. The next day Hawker made a bad landing when he ran out of petrol and 'broke' his Bristol Scout No. 1609. Eager to get back into action he acquired another Bristol Scout C, No. 1611, and fitted it with his 'local mod' (Airfield modification) Lewis gun.

On 25 July 1915 he took off in Bristol Scout 1611 on a combat patrol and spotted an Albatros C Type over Passchendaele. Closing, Hawker fired an entire pan of ammunition at the German causing it to force land. He then turned his attention to a second enemy aircraft and opened fire—again the enemy aircraft was forced to land. Continuing his fighting patrol Hawker saw another Albatros C two-seater. Closing to within 100 yards he riddled the Albatros with Lewis gunfire which caused it to burst into flames and crash. The Albatros was later found to be from Flieger Abeiltung 3, piloted by Oberleutnant Alfred Übelacker with Hauptmann Hans Roser as Observer; both German officers were killed.

Captain Hawker was recommended for the Victoria Cross for this and previous air combat. The recommendation was approved and gazetted on 24 August 1915. This was the first air VC awarded for air combat and gallantry over the months Hawker had been in France.

On 2 August 1915 flying a two-seater F.E.2b No. 4227 he forced down a C Type at Wulverghem—his official total now stood at four. His unconfirmed total many more. On 11 August—flying the same aircraft—with Lieutenant Noel Clifton as observer/gunner, he scored two more victories; an Aviatik C and a Fokker E. His last victory was on 7 September 1915 when he shot down a German Scout over Bixschoote whilst flying Bristol Scout No. 1611. On 20 September 1915 Captain Hawker was posted back to England, recommended for promotion to Major and command of a new Squadron—No. 24.

On 5 October 1915 Hawker was decorated by King George V with the Victoria Cross and Distinguished Service Order. On 3 February he was promoted to Major. On 7 February 1916 24 Squadron moved to St Omer, to work up into a fighting unit flying DH.2 fighters, (the first such squadron to reach the Western Front). On 12 February the squadron moved to Bertangles, near Amiens. As Commanding Officer, Major Hawker was forbidden to fly but continued to do so. At 1300 hours on 23 November 1916, Major Hawker took off in a four aircraft patrol. One DH.2 was forced to return to base with engine trouble but the three others carried on. At about 1400 hours German two-seater recce aircraft were spotted—it was a trap laid by the Richthofen Geschwader. Albatros D.IIs from Jagdstaffel 2 swooped on the DH.2s—led by Manfred von Richthofen, 'The Red Baron'.

Major Hawker was outclassed in his DH.2 against the superior Albatros D.II of von Richthofen but circling, gave combat to the Red Baron over the German lines; waving at one time to acknowledge his adversary. Major Hawker's aircraft ran out of petrol and he tried to reach British Lines—the Red Baron seized his chance and poured machine gun fire into the DH.2. (It is recorded that von Richthofen fired over 900 rounds). Major Hawker was killed by a single bullet that went through his head—his only injury. His aircraft went down two miles south of Bapaume and German Grenadiers buried his body next to his aircraft. Major Hawker was the Red Baron—Freiherr Manfred von Richthofen's 11th victim.

Major Edward Corringham 'Mick' Mannock, (1887-1918)
73 victories

Edward Mannock was born at Preston Cavalry Barracks, Brighton on 24 May 1887 into a military family of Irish parentage. As a youngster he developed astigmatism in his left eye that left him poorly sighted in that eye. He was working in Turkey when the war broke out and—as the Turks were aligned and allied with Germany—was interned until 1 April 1915.

Returning to Britain he was commissioned 2Lt into the Royal Engineers on 1 April 1916. In August 1916 he transferred to the Royal Flying Corps and was taught to fly at Hendon and Upavon—qualifying on 28 November 1916 with Aero Club Flying Certificate No. 3895. Training completed, he was sent to France on 1 April 1917 and posted to 40 Squadron at Aire five days later.

On 7 April 1917, Mannock flew one of 40 Squadron's Nieuport Scouts for his first sortie—but it was not until 7 May 1917 that he opened his score by downing a kite balloon. On 25 May and on the 1 June he downed a two-seater enemy observation aircraft but did not claim them as victories. Exactly one month later, on 7 June, he officially downed his first enemy aircraft—an Albatros D.III Scout—with a mere 30 rounds from his machine gun. Two more enemy aircraft followed on 9 June over Douai.

On 12 July Mannock—flying his Nieuport B1682—shot down a DFW CV of Schusta 12. This was followed next day by another DFW CV falling to his guns over Montigny.

He was awarded the Military Cross on 22 July 1917 and promoted Captain and Flight Commander. Between 28 July and 15 August Mannock shot down five enemy single-seaters—including the German ace Leutnant Joachim von Bertrab of Jagstaffel 30 on 12 August. During the next week he began to score victories steadily, five victories in seven days—exhibiting the hallmark of the finest fighter pilot—the desire to be at the throat of the enemy and shoot them out of the sky.

On 4 September 1917 Edward Mannock—in spite of being practically blind in one eye—downed three DFWs in the one day. During the rest of September another seven two-seat recce aircraft were added to his victory score. A Bar to his Military Cross followed on 18 October 1917.

On 1 January 1918 Mannock downed another recce two-seater a Hannover CL.III of Flieger Abteilung A 28, then—next day he left 40 Squadron—and was sent on a month's leave to England with a victory score of 23 victories.

Mannock returned to France on 31 March 1918, as a Flight Commander with 74 Squadron—which was a new squadron equipped with S.E.5a Scouts. On 12 April 1918 Mannock scored 74 Squadron's first victory, downing an Albatros Scout over Carvin and sharing another victory.

Most of the time he flew with his squadron formation into battle, but on occasion went on a lone hunt for the hated enemy and amazingly he downed another six German aircraft by the end of April 1918. His hunting skill was now coming to its zenith. During May 1918 he took his score upwards by another 24 victories. On 19 May he was awarded admission into the Distinguished Service Order (DSO). On 1 June 1918 he scored an incredible triple victory, shooting down three Pfalz D.III Scouts over Estaires. By 18 June Mannock had downed another eight German aircraft and on 21 June 1918 was promoted to Major. He was then placed in command of 85 Squadron which was equipped with S.E.5a aircraft.

By 3 July 1918 Mannock was airborne again with his new squadron—flying with his pilots as a formation—not as individuals. This method had brought great success to Mannock with 40 Squadron and he brought it to 85 Squadron. On 7 July 1918 Mannock was out in formation with his squadron and clashed with Fokker D. VIIs causing mayhem. Mannock shot one Fokker down and drove another down in a spin—two more Fokkers collided with one another with fatal results. Mannock scored another victory on 8 July 1918: another on the 10th, two more on 19th July, two more on the 20th and a Fokker Dr.I triplane on the 22 July 1918.

On 26 July 1918 a two-plane dawn sortie took off at 05:00 hours from St Omer and flew low to the Front. Mannock had as wingman—or rather tailman—2Lt Donald Inglis. Mannock and Inglis at 50 feet attacked a DFW CV and sent it down in flames over the German trenches. As Mannock and Inglis flew over the enemy trenches they met a hail of ground machine gun fire. Mannock's aircraft was hit and set on fire and he met his end in a ball of flames near Pacaut. The Germans buried the top ace's remains at La Pierre au Beure.

On 18 July 1919 Edward Mannock was awarded the Victoria Cross for Valour.

Lieutenant-Colonel William Avery Bishop, (1894-1956)
72 victories

Lt- Col. William Avery Bishop was born at Owen Sound, Ontario, Canada, on 8 February 1894. In August 1911 he entered the Royal Military College (Canada) and three years later was commissioned in the Canadian Army. At the end of June 1915 Bishop arrived in England. He did not like the idea of trench warfare and in July 1915 he applied for transfer to the RFC as an Observer. Bishop was posted to 21 (Training) Squadron at Netheravon, Wiltshire, for Observer training. Passing out as an Observer, he was posted to 21 Squadron which was due to be moved to France.

On 1 January 1916 Bishop's squadron—No. 21—was stationed at Boisdinghem, St Omer, flying two-seater R.E.7 observation and recce aircraft. Bishop remained on reconnaissance duties—coming under enemy fire on occasion—until 2 May 1916 when he, due to an injured knee—was taken off flying.

Bishop trained as a pilot at Upavon Central Flying School (CFS) on Salisbury Plain and applied for transfer to front line duties in France. On 9 March 1917 he was posted as a pilot to 60 Squadron, RFC, at Filescamp. Flying the small Nieuport Scout biplane aircraft, armed with a single Lewis machine gun mounted to fire over the top wing, Bishop had difficulty in landing the machine and after several heavy landings crashed on 24 March 1917. Authority ordered him back to England for further flying training but fate intervened. On 25 March 1917 Bishop was in formation with three other Nieuports of 60 squadron when they clashed with three German Albatros D.III Scouts over St Leger. Bishop closed with one Albatros and poured bullets into the pilot's cockpit—causing it to spiral out of control into the ground. This was his first victory and it caused his posting to England to be cancelled.

Bishop's marksmanship and his new found flying skills earned him five more victories; four Albatros's and one balloon by 8 April 1917. On 25 April 1917 Bishop was promoted to Captain and had his Nieuport's engine cowling and wing V struts painted bright blue. By the 30 April 1917 he had 14 victories to his credit—including another balloon at Artois and was awarded the Military Cross. By the 31 May 1917 he had downed 22 German aircraft—mostly Albatros D.IIIs. On 2 June 1917 he made a lone dawn attack—flying his Nieuport B1566—on the German airfield at Estmourmel destroying three Albatros D.IIIs in a half hour action. On the 11 June 1917 he was gazetted to be decorated with the Victoria Cross for this action.

By 16 August 1917 Bishop's victory score had reached an incredible 47, flying his S.E.5a Scout No. A8936 of 60 Squadron. During September 1917 he was decorated with; the Victoria Cross, DSO, to add to his Military Cross; then a Bar to his DSO. He was promoted to Major on 13 March 1918 and command of the new 85 Squadron which moved to Petite-Synthe, near Dunkirk, on 22 May 1918.

Bishop was back in the air at once seeking the enemy—he scored his 48th victory on 27 May, shooting down an Albatros C two-seater over Passchendale. A day later he shot down two Albatros D.Vs over Cortemarck. His victory total now stood at 50. By the end of May it was 55 and by 19 June 1918, was 72 enemy aircraft. Bishop survived the war and died in Florida on 11 September 1956.

Lieutenant-Colonel Raymond Collishaw, (1893-1976)
60 victories

A Canadian, Raymond Collishaw was born in British Columbia, Canada, on 22 November 1893. He served in the Canadian Merchant Marine and went on Scott's 1911 Antarctic Expedition.

In January 1916 Collishaw joined the Royal Naval Air Service, No. 3 Wing flying Sopwith 1½ Strutter aircraft on long range bombing missions to the Saarland. On 25 October 1916 he opened his victory score by shooting down two Fokker D.IIs over Luneville.

On 1 February 1917 he transferred to No. 3 Naval Squadron. On 15 February and again on 4 March 1917 he shot down a Halberstadt D.II bringing his score to four victories. In April he joined No. 10 Naval Squadron at Furnes as B Flight Commander flying Sopwith Triplanes. On 28 April flying his Triplane No. N5490 he shot down an Albatros D.II over Ostend. Two days later he repeated the feat over Courtemarck, bringing his total to six.

Collishaw chose four other pilots to form his Flight, all Canadians: Flight Sub Lieutenants Reid, Sharman, Nash and Alexander. These five pilots formed the 'Black Flight' ... their Triplanes were painted black on the engine cowling, wheel discs and forward fuselage with white lettering names thereon—Black Maria (Collishaw's 5492), Black Death (Sharman), Black Sheep (Nash), Black Roger (Reid) and Black Prince (Alexander).

From 9 May 1917—when his score stood at seven—until the 27 July 1917—he continued to score at an amazing rate. On 6 June he shot down three Albatros D.IIIs; on 15 June he destroyed four more enemy aircraft. Incredibly on 6 July 1917 he accounted for six Albatros D.Vs on the same day—this brought his score to 31. The 'Black Flight' was decimating the German Air Service and *Jasta* 11 was tasked with bringing their prowess to an end—they failed. By 27 July 1917 Collishaw's score stood at 38 enemy downed. By 10 December it was 39 when he shot down an Albatros C type over Dunkirk; on 19 December he reached his 40 score when he downed an Albatros D.V over Ostend. On 29 December 1917 Collishaw was placed in command of No.13 Naval Squadron equipped with new Sopwith Camels.

1 April 1918 saw the creation of the Royal Air Force and Collishaw was promoted to Major and placed in command of 203 Squadron RAF—which had been formed that day from No. 3 Squadron RNAS. From 11 June 1918 to 26 September Collishaw downed another 19 enemy aircraft bringing his score to 59. On 1 October 1918 he was promoted to Lieutenant-Colonel at the age of 25.

After the Armistice in November 1918 Collishaw was sent to southern Russia and by July 1919 he was in command of 47 Squadron, in aid of the White Russians. He scored his last victory on 9 October 1919 bringing down an Albatros D.V over Czaritsyn—this brought his total victories to 60. However, it is thought he scored at least another 15 unconfirmed victories. Lt-Col. Collishaw remained in the RAF post war and retired with the rank of Air Vice Marshal. He passed away in 1976.

Major James Thomas Byford McCudden, (1895-1918)
57 victories

Born at Gillingham, Kent, 28 March 1895, of an Army family, McCudden enlisted in the Royal Engineers as a boy on 26 April 1910. He transferred to the RFC as service number No. 892, Air Mechanic, Second Class on 28 April 1913. On 16 June 1913 he moved to 3 Squadron RFC, Netheravon, Salisbury Plain—then to France on 13 August 1914—still with 3 Squadron. By April 1915 he was a Sergeant Air Mechanic.

In June 1915 McCudden began to fly as an unofficial observer in Morane Saulnier two-seater monoplanes and on 19 December 1915 saw his first dog fight. On 1 January 1916 be became an official observer and continued to see action. He was awarded the Croix de Guerre on 21 January 1916, and on the 25 January was accepted for pilot training with promotion to Flight Sergeant. After flying training at Farnborough and Gosport he was sent to Upavon Central Flying School. He was awarded his RFC pilot's brevet on 30 May 1916.

Posted back to France on 7 July 1916, he joined 20 Squadron at Clairmarais equipped with F.E.2d two-seat bombers. On 7 August he joined 29 Squadron, C Flight, at Abeele flying De Havilland DH.2 fighters. On 6 September flying DH.2 5985, he had his first victory—an all white painted Albatros C two-seater which he sent down on the Menin Road. He was awarded The Military Medal on 1 October 1916.

On 1 January 1917 McCudden was commissioned as a Second-Lieutenant and remained on post with 29 Squadron. On 26 January he brought down another C type over Ficheaux and by 15 February 1917 his victories totalled five. On 16 February he gained his third gallantry decoration—the Military Cross—and was sent back to RFC Maidstone on a rest tour.

On 1 June 1917 he was promoted Captain and the following month joined 66 Squadron downing an Albatros D.V over Gheluwe and when on a brief spell with 56 Squadron—another Albatros D.V over 'Polygon' Wood. On 14 August 1917 he returned to the new S.E.5a fighter-equipped 56 Squadron as B Flight Commander. During August he shot down four German Albatros D.Vs whilst flying his S.E.5a No. B519—his score now stood at 11 victories. On 14 September 1917 he forced down an Albatros D.V flown by Leutnant Weigand of the famous *Jasta* 10 of Richthofen's 'Flying Circus'.

By the 23 September he had three more enemy to his credit but during the evening of that day his Flight became involved in a famous dog fight. The German ace—Werner Voss with 48 victories—flying a new Fokker Triplane and accompanied by two other scouts—was shot down and killed by 56 Squadron. On 3 October McCudden was awarded a Bar to his Military Cross.

At the beginning of December 1917 McCudden's official score was 23 victories and by the end of the month it was an incredible 37 victories. On 15 December 1917 he was admitted to the Distinguished Service Order and a Bar to the Order on 3 January 1918. That same month saw his score mount steadily with 56 Squadron to 46 victories.

His 50th victory came on 16 February 1918; At 10:35 hours he downed a Rumpler C type, at 10:45 hours he shot down a DFW C.V, at 11:10 hours another Rumpler C Type then, finally, at 12:30 hours yet another Rumpler C Type. His score now stood at 50 victories and by 26 February 1918 57 victories. 52 of which were scored with 56 Squadron. McCudden flew his final combat mission on 1 March 1918 and then returned to England on leave.

On 29 March 1918 he was gazetted the award of the Victoria Cross with which he was invested on 6 April 1918, together with the DSO and Bar and a Bar to his Military Cross. He succeeded in winning his battle to get back into the war and was given command of 60 Squadron at Boffles, Pas-de-Calais, with effect from 9 July 1918, in the rank of Major. Leaving Hounslow on 9 July 1918 in a new S.E.5a No. C1126 to take up his new command he crossed the Channel and landed in France at 17:30 hours at Auxi-le-Château. He found he was five miles short of his destination at Boffles. Major McCudden took off *en route* for his new command, but as his S.E.5a climbed the engine cut out, the aircraft side-slipped downwards and crashed into trees. Major McCudden died of his injuries and was buried next day at Wavans, where he still rests, a gallant fighter pilot.

Captain Anthony Weatherby Beauchamp-Proctor, (1894-1921)
54 victories

Beauchamp-Proctor was born on 4 September 1894 at Mossel Bay, Cape Province, South Africa. After university he enlisted in the Army and saw service in German South West Africa. On 12 March 1917 he enlisted in the RFC and sailed for England.

After ground and flying training at Farnborough, Oxford, Castle Bromwich, Netheravon and Upavon CFS he was awarded his RFC pilot's wings on 29 July 1917. Of small stature—5 feet 2 inches tall—2Lt Proctor had some difficulty in adapting to the controls of his aircraft, but overcame this and proved a brilliant pilot. His first squadron was No. 84 at Beaulieu, Hampshire, then commanded by Major Sholto Douglas. On 21 September 1917 the S.E.5a-equipped 84 Squadron moved to Flez, France, and began working up to battle state.

On 22 November 1917 Proctor shared in the demise of a German balloon, then another balloon, followed by forcing down two German observation planes. None of these were confirmed and it was on 3 January 1918 that Proctor—flying his S.E.5a B539—shot down a C type two-seater aircraft over St Quentin. By 28 February 1918 he had five enemy to his score. On 17 March 1918 he downed two Albatros D.Vs and one Pfalz D.III in one day—bringing his tally to nine. May 1918 proved a prolific month for Proctor. By 31 May his official record showed 21 enemy aircraft downed, his actual total was more but unconfirmed.

At the birth of the Royal Air Force on 1 April 1918 Proctor was promoted to Lieutenant (the RAF still used army ranks). Seven days later he was promoted Captain and placed in command of C Flight 84 Squadron. He was awarded The Military Cross on 28 May 1918. During the first fortnight of June Proctor downed seven more enemy aircraft, including four balloons. August resulted in fifteen more enemy going down, including five balloons. During September he concentrated on balloons, downing four, and was awarded the DSO. October 1918 saw his final tally and by 8 October he had 54 confirmed victories, but on that day he was wounded in action when he battled with eight of the enemy and was sent to hospital in England.

On 30 November 1918 he was awarded the Victoria Cross for valour in his aerial battles with the enemy. He remained in the RAF with a permanent commission but was killed flying Sopwith Snipe No. E8220 on 21 June 1921 while practising for an air display at Upavon. His body was returned to his native South Africa on 8 August 1921 and given a state funeral before being laid to rest at Mafeking.

Major Donald Roderick MacLaren, (1893-1988)
54 victories

Donald MacLaren was born at Ottawa, Canada, 28 May 1893. On 8 May 1917 he enlisted in the Royal Flying Corps as a trainee pilot, qualifying six months later when he received his pilot's brevet, and then sailed to Britain. On 23 November 1917 he was posted to 46 Squadron flying Sopwith Camels on the French Western Front. He began his victory score on 6 March 1918 when he shot down a Hannover C over East Douai. Four days later whilst flying his Camel No. B9153 he downed an Albatros D.V.

On 21 March 1918, flying alongside seven others from 46 Squadron, he bombed and crippled a German long range gun six miles behind enemy lines. *En route* to his base he encountered two German LVG.Cs and shot both down. Minutes later he closed with an observation balloon and brought that down too. For this action he was later awarded The Military Cross.

The German great offensive was in full flow and daily until 25 March 1918 he increased his victory total to 12. He made it 13 on the 27 March 1918 when he downed a Junkers J1. During April 1918 he scored three more victories, a balloon, a C Type and an Albatros D.V and was promoted to Captain. By the end of May 1918 he destroyed another 16 enemy aircraft, bringing his total to 32. June was somewhat quieter—two more victories. Nine more aircraft went down to his machine guns during July 1918—he was a deadly marksman—as were most of the Canadian pilots. Four more victories were gained during August 1918, making his total 45.

From the 15 September to 2 October 1918 he shot down no less than eight Fokker D.VIIs—a remarkable tribute to his shooting prowess.

At 14:30 hours on 9 October 1918 MacLaren scored his final victory—a Type C over Ricqueval Wood bringing his total to 54, including six balloons. He was awarded the DSO, MC and Bar, Legion of Honour and Croix de Guerre and was promoted to Major before the 11 November 1918 Armistice. He died in July 1988.

Major William George 'Billy' Barker, (1894-1930)
53 victories

Major Barker was born in Canada, 3 November 1894. He enlisted in the Canadian Army during December 1914 and was sent to France in September 1915, serving with a machine gun unit. In March 1916 he transferred to the RFC as an Observer with 9 Squadron flying B.Es then 4 and 15 Squadrons which also flew B.Es. He claimed two enemy aircraft, one on 21 July 1916 and another on 15 August. He was commissioned in April 1916 and decorated with The Military Cross (gazetted 10 January 1917) for excellent duty as an Observer.

He was sent for pilot training on 16 November 1916 then after completion, posted to 15 Squadron on 24 February 1917. On 25 March he forced down an enemy Scout and on 18 July he was awarded a Bar to his Military Cross. In April he began flying R.E.8 aircraft and was wounded by ground fire on 7 August 1917.

He was posted to England as an Instructor but chafed at the lack of action and was posted to 28 Squadron flying Camels as 'A' Flight commander. The squadron was posted to France, arriving on 8 October 1917. The same day Barker was airborne in Camel B6313 and shot down an Albatros D.V which he did not claim as a victory. Most of his following victories were in Camel B6313, which became the most successful individual fighter in the RFC/RAF, accounting for no less than 46 of the enemy in Barker's hands.

His first confirmed victory was on 20 October 1917 when he shot down an Albatros D.III over Roulers, followed by downing two Albatros D.Vs in flames on 26 October 1917.

On 7 November 1917 28 Squadron, commanded by Major H. Glanville, was sent to the Italian Front to aid the Italian fight against Austro-Hungarian and German forces. Barker scored the first three RFC victories over the enemy and by 29 December his score was at seven, including two balloons. He was admitted to the Distinguished Service Order at the end of December with his score cited at seven victories.

On 12 February he shot down (with others) five balloons over Fossomerlo, making his total 19. By 19 March he had downed another three bringing him up to 22. In spite of his outstanding record Barker, was passed over for command of 28 Squadron when Major Glanville was posted off squadron. Aggrieved, Barker applied for an exchange posting and was sent to 66 Squadron flying Camels on the Italian front. With 66 Squadron he scored another 16 victories making his total 43 by the end of July 1918. He was promoted to Major and given command of the newly formed 139 Squadron at Villaverla in northern Italy. Unusually, Major Barker took his Camel No. B6313 with him to 139 Squadron, which was otherwise equipped with Bristol F.2b Fighters. He was also awarded a Bar to his DSO.

On 12 September 1918 he was awarded the Italian *Medaglio d' Argento Valore Militare* (Silver Medal for Military Valour) for a clandestine exploit, when he flew an Italian Savoia-Pomilio SP.4 behind enemy lines, landed, dropped a spy, then took off back to Italy. His last combat flight and victory in Camel B6313 was on 18 September 1918 when he downed a D Type over Queroe. Major Barker was sent to England in command of an aerial fighting training unit but managed to return to a ten day combat mission in France, nominally attached to 201 Squadron, but free to fly where he thought he could find his aerial enemies in a Sopwith Snipe No. E8102 based on La Targette airfield. On 27 October he found his enemies—15 Fokker D.VIIs—and single-handedly took them on. Some contemporary ground based reports state 60 enemy fighters were ranged against him. Major Barker shot down a two-seat Rumpler then had to fight for his life. A Fokker machine gun bullet wounded him in the left thigh causing him to faint momentarily. Recovering, he gave battle with his Snipe's two .303 Vickers machine guns. He was wounded in his other thigh and then a bullet went through his left elbow. In spite of his wounds he shot down three Fokker D.VIIs and drove off the others—an incredible feat. Major Barker managed to crash land his badly shot up Snipe on British lines and was taken to No. 8 General Hospital, Rouen, where he remained unconscious for three days.

Major William George Barker was awarded the Victoria Cross for his epic fight and received the supreme honour from King George V on 1 March 1919. Major Barker left the RAF and returned to Canada and went into business with Fairchild Aviation Corporation of Canada. He was killed on 12 March 1930 whilst testing a Fairchild two-seat aircraft. He was buried at Mount Pleasant cemetery, Toronto.

Captain Robert Alexander Little, (1895-1918)
47 victories

Robert Little was born at Melbourne, Victoria, Australia, on 19 July 1895. He was one of the many Colonials who flocked to the British Colours during the First World War and enlisted in the Royal Naval Air Service during 1915. He qualified as a Naval pilot on 27 October 1915 and commissioned as a Flight Sub Lieutenant early in 1916 at RN Air Station, Eastchurch. Late in June 1916 he was posted to No. 1 Naval Wing, RN Air Station Dunkirk, flying Bristol Scouts and Sopwith 1½ Strutters. On 26 October 1916 he was posted to No. 8 (N) Squadron flying Sopwith Pups.

Little gained his first victory on 11 November 1916 when he shot down an Aviatiak C.I on the Western Front while flying Sopwith Pup No. N5182. By March 1917 his score stood at four and he was awarded the Distinguished Service Cross. 8(N) Squadron converted to Sopwith Triplanes and flying No. N5469 Little gained his fifth victory on 7 April 1917, south east of Lens, downing an Albatros D.III during a dogfight.

Little continued to score victories, a total of eight during the remainder of April 1917. On 30 April he and three others attacked 12 Albatros D.IIIs. Little shot down two of them and the other pilots accounted for three more downed. Another eight of the enemy went down during May 1917 and on the 25 May 1917 his score was 20, all while flying Sopwith Triplane N5393.

From 16 to 29 June 1917 he shot down two C Types and two Albatros D.Vs bringing his total to 24. By 10 July 1917 he had added another four victories in Triplane N5493, and he then switched to Sopwith Camel N6378 in which he shot down an Albatros D.V over Vitry on 12 July 1917. By 27 July 1917 his score had risen to 38, nine enemy went down during the remainder of July 1917, 24 of them downed while flying Triplanes.

In August 1917 Little was admitted to the Distinguished Service Order and awarded a Bar to his DSC, a bar to his DSO followed on 14 September 1917. Little was posted to 3(N) Squadron, which on the formation of the RAF on 1 April 1918, became No. 203 Squadron Royal Air force.

On 1 April 1918 Little brought down a German Fokker Dr.I triplane over Oppy while flying Camel No. B7198 bringing his score up to 39. Five more enemy aircraft went down in April 1918 then three more in May 1918, bring his victory tally to 47 enemy aircraft downed.

On 27 May 1918 he scrambled his aircraft at night to try and intercept an intruding enemy Gotha bomber over Noeux. Little found the Gotha and made an attack on its rear. Ground searchlights caught the Gotha in their beams and ground forces opened fire. Captain Little was hit by either the Gotha's rear gunner or ground fire, by a bullet which passed through his thighs. Bleeding heavily, he crash-landed his aircraft but succumbed to his wounds. He was the highest scoring Australian ace of the First World War.

Captain George Edward Henry McElroy, (1893-1918)
46 victories

Born at Donnybrook, Dublin, on 14 May 1893, McElroy enlisted in the Royal Irish Regiment in August 1914 and was sent to France in October 1914 where he saw action. He transferred to the RFC during February 1917 and after pilot training joined 40 Squadron in France flying Nieuport Scouts.

In October 1917 40 Squadron re-equipped with S.E.5a s and on 28 December 1917—flying S.E.5a B598—'McIrish' as he was nicknamed, shot down a LVG.C over Vitry. His second victory—a Rumpler C type—was on 13 January 1918 over Vendin Bridge. Two more victories followed during January making his total four then between the 2 February and 26 February 1918 his score stood at 13. Eight more were confirmed during March 1918 then another six during April 1918 taking 'McIrish' up to 27 victories. On 7 April he shot down three enemy aircraft between 1040 hours and 1115 hours!

Three more victories followed in June 1918—a DFW C Type and two balloons bring his score up to 30 confirmed. July 1918 proved incredible for 'McIrish'—he accounted for no less than 16 enemy up to the 25 July 1918—46 confirmed.

On 31 July 1918 'McIrish' took off from Bryas airfield at 0815 hours on what proved to be his last flight in S.E.5a No.E1310. He shot down a Hannover C Type over Laventie (which was unconfirmed by the RFC but confirmed by the German Air Service) but was hit by ground fire and fatally crashed. He was buried by the German Air Service at Laventie. Captain McElroy was awarded The Military Cross in February 1918 then a Bar to the Cross in March then a second Bar in April. The Distinguished Flying Cross was awarded in July followed by a Bar to the DFC in July.

Captain Albert Ball, (1896-1917)
44 victories

Albert Ball was born in Nottingham on 14 August 1896. He enlisted in the army as a Private on 21 September 1914—by 29 October 1914 he was a Second Lieutenant.

In June 1915 he paid for private tuition and trained as a pilot at Hendon with the Baumann Flying School. On 15 October 1915 he obtained Royal Aero Club Certificate No.1898 and requested transfer to the RFC. The transfer granted he further trained at Norwich and Upavon—being awarded his pilot's brevet on 22 January 1916.

On 18 February 1916 he was posted to 13 Squadron, RFC, at Marieux, France, flying two-seat B.E.2cs. Ball saw much action in the slow recce B.E.2cs but wanted to fly the fast fighters. His wish was granted on 7 May 1916 when he was posted to 11 Squadron flying Nieuport Scouts. Now in his chosen element Albert Ball began to display the hall mark of the finest troops—the urge to be at the enemy. He built a small wooden hut next to his aircraft hangar, in which he lived, ate and slept 'over the shop' so that he could be airborne almost immediately and into combat. On 16 May 1916—flying Bristol Scout 5512—he opened his score, shooting down an Albatros C Type over Beaumont at 0845 hours. On the 29 May 1916 he shot down two LVG.C types when flying his Nieuport 5173.

An example of Albert Ball's desire to be at the enemy's throat was when he took off in Nieuport 5173 on 1 June 1916, and deliberately circled over the German airfield at Douai—challenging and inviting combat. Two German pilots took up the challenge but were driven down by Ball who claimed one—A Fokker E type—as a victory making his total four.

On 26 June he attacked and destroyed an Observation balloon with phosphor bombs—next day he was gazetted to receive The Military Cross and cited for his continuous determination to be at the enemy.

Victories six and seven were; a Roland C11 and an Aviatik C on 2 July 1916—both shot down within the space of half an hour. On 29 July 1916, Ball was posted to 8 Squadron RFC flying lumbering B.E.2cs—this recce and artillery spotting role did not suit his desire to be in combat—and on 14 August 1916 (his 20th birthday) he was posted back to 11 Squadron flying Nieuports.

Ball was allocated a brand new Nieuport No. A201 and during the last two weeks of August he gained 10 victories—all but one being Roland C11s. On 22 August he scored a hat trick when he downed three Roland C11s within three quarters of an hour. His total now stood at 17 enemy downed. The next day—23 August—Ball was moved to A Flight of 60 Squadron with a 'roving seek and destroy the enemy' role. This pleased him as he preferred to fight alone.

On 1 September 1916 Ball went on leave for two weeks—and honours began to be heaped on him. Admission to The Distinguished Service Order, promotion to Flight Commander and the Russian award of The Order of St George 4th Class.

Returning from leave Ball was immediately in combat. From the 15 September to 30 September he scored 14 victories ... including three hat tricks! The first hat trick was on 21 September when three Rolands went down in the space of two hours. The next trio—three Albatros C Types—went down, again within the space of an hour and three quarters on 28 September. The final three—an Albatros C Type and two Rolands—went down at 1055 hours, 1830 hours and 1845 hours on 30 September 1916. Ball's victory total was now 31.

Ball was sent back to Britain for Rest and Recuperation and was fêted as a national hero. On 18 November 1916 Albert Ball went to Buckingham Palace to be invested with the DSO and Bar and MC. A week later he was gazetted with another Bar to his DSO—making him the first to be awarded three DSOs. Ball chafed at his lack of combat and managed to get a posting to 56 Squadron and on 7 April 1917 was back in France at Vert Galand.

On 23 April he was back in aerial combat flying his Nieuport B1522 as Flight Commander and shot down an Albatros C Type at 0645 hours. Four more victories followed during April when Ball was flying S.E.5 A4850 then he had three 'pairs' on 1 May, 2 May and 5 May 1917, making his total 43. Albert Ball had his final combat victory on 6 May 1917 when—flying Nieuport B1522 over Sancourt—he destroyed an Albatros D.III at 1930 hours taking his total to 44 victories.

Captain Albert Ball made his final flight on 7 May 1917 when he flew S.E.5 No. A4850 in an eleven strong hunting patrol into action against JG 11—led by Lothar von Richthofen (brother of Manfred von Richthofen). A large scale dog fight erupted over a large area and Albert Ball was last seen attacking Lothar von Richthofen's red Albatros, causing it to crash land. Albert Ball was seen to crash by several German ground based officers near

Seclin and died soon after of his crash injuries. He was given a full Military Funeral by the German Air Service at Annoeullin Cemetery, France, on 9 May 1917.

Captain Ball was awarded The Victoria Cross on 8 June 1917 and France admitted him as a Chevalier de Legion d'Honneur. His father and mother received his Victoria Cross from King George V on 22 July 1917.

Major Thomas Falcon Hazell, (1892-1946)
43 victories

Born Galway, Ireland, joined the Army when the War broke out and commissioned as a Second Lieutenant in the 7th Battalion, Royal Inniskilling Fusiliers ('The Skins'), on 10 October 1914, serving with 'The Skins' until June 1916 when he transferred to the RFC.

After flying instruction—and a bad crash—he was posted to 1 Squadron, RFC, in France which was equipped with Nieuport 17s in January 1917, Nieuport 27s in August 1917 and S.E.5a s in January 1918. On 4 March 1917 Lieutenant Hazel scored his first victory. Flying a Nieuport A6604 he sent a German Aircraft type down out of control over Westhoek at 1610 hours. It was not until the 24 April 1917 that he had his next victory—an Albatros C destroyed over Grenier Wood at 1200 hours while flying Nieuport A6738. Another Albatros C Type was sent spinning out of control on 9 May 1917 making his confirmed total three victories.

His fourth and fifth victories were two Albatros D.IIIs destroyed over Hollebeke at 0700 and 0702 hours on 4 June 1917. Two more victories followed the next day—an Albatros D.III and a C Type. This made his total seven.

On 8 and 9 June 1917, he sent two Albatros D.IIIs out of control earthwards and on 12 July another Albatros D.II met a similar fate. On 22 July 1917 he scored a hat trick when he destroyed three of the enemy: A DFW C. Type, and two Albatros D.Vs whilst flying Nieuport B3455. His victory total was now 14. He was made a Flight Commander in No. 1 Squadron.

On 13 August he destroyed an Albatros D.V at 0710 hours and an Albatros C at 0920 hours—he shared the later kill with Lieutenant H. G. Reeves. The next day Hazell repeated his feat of the previous day, downing two Albatros D.Vs within five minutes. Another Albatros D.V was sent out of control on 16 August 1917 making Hazell's total 20 victories and the award of The Military Cross (which had been gazetted on 26 July 1917).

Hazell was sent back to England as a Flying Instructor at Upavon CFS and returned to France in command of 'A' Flight, 24 Squadron, on 28 June 1918. Now flying S.E.5a s, Hazel commenced to score a further 23 victories with 24 Squadron. Six victories in July 1918, of which four were balloons. Eleven in August 1918, of which three were balloons then three in September of which two were balloons and lastly—three in October of which one was a balloon.

Hazell was promoted to Major and left 24 Squadron on 18 October 1918 then moved to the Camel-equipped 203 Squadron as Commanding Officer. He served with No. 203 Squadron until 2 April 1919—then was granted a Permanent Commission in the Royal Air Force. Major Hazell died in 1946. He was admitted to the Distinguished Service Order, awarded the Military Cross and Distinguished Flying Cross and Bar.

Captain Philip Fletcher Fullard, (1897-1984)
40 (46) victories

Captain Fullard was born at Wimbledon on 27 May 1897 and educated at Norwich. He loved football and played centre half for Norwich in 1914. Fullard learned to fly at his own expense and after a spell in the Army, transferred to the RFC in 1916. He proved to be an exceptional pilot and marksman—maintaining his aircraft guns himself. This proved invaluable in combat as—unlike so many other airmen—his guns never had a stoppage.

In April 1917 he was posted to 1 Squadron—who were flying Nieuport Scouts and S.E.5a s—and scored his first victory, an Albatros D.III, on 26 May 1917 when flying Nieuport B1559. Another victory over an Albatros D.III followed on the 28 May 1917. On 4 June 1917, on an early patrol, he shot down an Albatros D.V at 0800 hours then another Albatros D.V at 0815 hours. His aircraft then came under fire from an all red Albatros D.V—the trade mark of *Jasta* 18 (and others)—Fullard rolled his Nieuport away and the Albatros was shot down by an S.E.5 flown by F/Cdr. T. F. N. Gerrard of 1 Squadron—with whom he shared the kill.

During July 1917 Fullard continued to score victories at an amazing rate—eight downed, all but one—a Type C—the other seven Albatros D.Vs. August 1917 was even more productive for Fullard—twelve enemy went down, eight of them Albatros D.Vs. In September, Fullard was awarded The Military Cross and Bar followed a month later by the award of The Distinguished Service Order.

October 1917 saw Fullard continue his rate of victories with eleven more enemy downed—his last two confirmed victories came on 15 November 1917 when he shot down an Albatros D.V at 1155 hours then another at 1156 hours! As usual there are differences of opinion as to how many Captain Fullard downed—40 or 46 seems to be the approximate total. He is sometime credited with two balloons but these are unconfirmed.

Captain Fullard broke his leg playing football and was returned to England. He did not score any more victories before the war ended in November, but remained in the RAF on a permanent commission, gaining Air Rank and the CBE and AFC. He passed away on 24 April 1984.

Major John Inglis Gilmour, (1896-1928)
39 (44) victories

John Gilmour joined the Argyll & Sutherland Highlanders (The Thin Red Line) then transferred to the RFC and was posted to 27 Squadron (with which the author served) and flew Martinsyde G.100 'Elephants'—which were designed as Scouts but lacked agility and were used instead for recce and bombing runs.

Gilmour scored three victories in September 1916 flying G.100s—unusual for this type of aircraft. He was awarded The Military Cross in 1917.

In November 1917, he was posted to 65 Squadron as a Flight Commander flying Sopwith Camels and scored two victories on 18 December 1917, flying Camel 9166 followed by three more victories on 4 January 1918. By 29 June 1918 his victory tally had reached 31 confirmed—which included one balloon.

On 1 July 1918 he downed three Fokker D.VIIs, one Pfalz and an Albatros D.V—all within 45 minutes. Next day he downed a Pfalz D.III, then on the 3 July 1918 another final two Pfalz D.IIIs making his confirmed total 39.

He was admitted to The Distinguished Service Order and received Two Bars to his Military Cross and promoted to the rank of Major. In October 1918 he was posted to Italy in command of 28 Squadron flying Camels from Treviso. He did not add to his victory score.

Captain Alfred Clayburn Atkey, (1894-1971)
38 Victories

The son of Alfred Atkey, and Annie Evelyn, née Shaw, Alfred Clayburn Atkey's family left Toronto to pioneer western Canada in 1906. From Minebow, Saskatchewan, Atkey returned to Toronto as a journalist for the *Toronto Evening Telegram*. On 19 October 1916, he enlisted in the Royal Flying Corps as a probationary Second Lieutenant. By September 1917, he was a bomber pilot assigned to 18 Squadron, flying the D.H.4, and on his way to becoming the highest scoring two-seater pilot of the First World War. In his fitness reports, he was described as an 'expert in gunnery, bombing, photography, reconnaissance.' In May 1918, Atkey assumed command of 'A' flight in 22 Squadron. Abandoning the D.H.4, he began flying the Bristol F.2b. For his gunner and observer, he chose Lieutenant Charles Gass. Together, they were deadly, shooting down 29 enemy aircraft in less than one month. They were lucky too. On one occasion, their Bristol Fighter was so badly shot up that Gass had to crawl out onto the lower wing to counterbalance the aircraft so that Atkey could fly it back to base.

In an historic dogfight known as 'Two Against Twenty,' Atkey and Gass, together with John Gurdon and his observer, Anthony Thornton, encountered 20 German scouts during the evening of 7 May 1918. In the epic battle that followed, Atkey and Gass shot down five enemy aircraft while Gurdon and Thornton knocked down three. Two days later, Atkey and Gass again shot down five enemy aircraft in one day.

When Atkey received the Military Cross the following was written in the *The London Gazette*: 'For conspicuous gallantry and devotion to duty. When engaged on reconnaissance and bombing work, he attacked four scouts, one of which he shot down in flames. Shortly afterwards he attacked four two-seater planes, one of which he brought down out of control. On two previous occasions his formation was attacked by superior numbers of the enemy, three of whom in all were shot down out of control. He has shown exceptional ability and initiative on all occasions.' The following was written in the *Gazette* when he received the a bar to his MC: 'For conspicuous gallantry and devotion to duty. During recent operations he destroyed seven enemy machines. When engaged with enemy aircraft, often far superior in numbers, he proved himself a brilliant fighting pilot, and displayed dash and gallantry of a high order.'

Atkey emigrated to the United States in 1923. On 23 January 1924, at age 29 and employed as a writer in Los Angeles, California, he filed a Declaration of Intention to become an American citizen.

Captain William Gordon Claxton, (1899–1967)
37 victories

Yet another great Colonial fighter pilot—born in Gladstone, Manitoba, Canada, on 1 June 1899—Claxton was a natural marksman (as were many of the Colonial fighter pilots) and superb pilot—in three months he shot down 37 enemy aircraft and two balloons. He enlisted in the RFC in Canada, on his eighteenth birthday in June 1917, and trained for his pilot's brevet at Camp Borden. Qualifying as a pilot, Claxton was posted to 41 Squadron flying S.E.5a s and began an incredible period of victories.

On 27 May 1918 he opened his score by shooting down a Fokker Dr1 over East Estaires while flying S.E.5a B38—next day he shot down two Pfalz D.IIIs making his score three in two days. From 12 June 1918 to 30 June 1918 he shot down no less than seventeen aircraft and one balloon... on 30 June 1918 he downed six enemy aircraft on that one day—an amazing feat. Six more enemy went down during July—making his total on 31 July 1918—27 victories.

On 3 August he was awarded The Distinguished Flying Cross: between 1 August and 13 August 1918 he shot down a further nine enemy aircraft and one balloon. On 17 August 1918, Claxton took off with another Canadian Frederick Robert McCall of 41 Squadron and clashed with a 40 strong enemy *Jasta* (believed No. 20). Outnumbered twenty to one—the two Canadians fought hard—each shooting down three Germans. Claxton was wounded in the head by a machine gun bullet fired by Leutnant Hans Gildmeister of *Jasta* 20. Claxton managed to crash land his S.E.5a within German lines and suffered no further injuries on crash landing. Skull surgery by a German surgeon saved his life and Claxton recovered from his near death wound.

He was awarded a Distinguished Service Order on 2 November 1918, and had been awarded a Bar to his DFC on 21 September 1918. Captain Claxton died on 28 September 1967 in Canada.

Captain James Ira Thomas 'Taffy' Jones, (1896-1960)
37 victories

Welsh born Jones enlisted in the RFC at the outbreak of the War. He had been serving in the Territorial Army since 1913, but decided to join the new Service. After training he was posted to 10 Squadron as an Air Mechanic (Wireless).

His squadron went to France in July 1915 and during January 1916 Jones took to the air as an Observer. He was awarded The Military Medal, and Russian Order of St George, in May 1916 when on ground duties—when he saved two wounded artillerymen whilst under enemy fire. Jones began his flying career in earnest when he gained his Observer's flying brevet in October 1916 flying in B.E.2cs, Ds and 2es. He was detached to England for pilot training on 27 May 1917 and commissioned.

He was returned to 74 Squadron on 30 March 1918 flying S.E.5a s alongside his Flight Commander Captain Edward Mannock. He scored his first victory on 8 May 1918, while flying S.E.5a No. C6406 over Bailleul, when he shot down a German C Type in flames.

On 12 May he put an Albatros D.V down out of control—on 17 May he shot a Hannover C out of the sky in flames at 0930—followed within a minute by putting an Albatros C down to earth out of control.

On 18 May he shot down another Albatros C Type followed by a Kite balloon on the 19 May making his total six victories—with none shared. By 31 May his total was 15 and he was awarded The Military Cross. He scored a double victory on 27 May, another double on 30 May followed by yet another on 31 May 1918.

During June 1918 he took another seven enemy aircraft out of the sky—all destroyed with three going down in flames. The aggressive fighter pilot Jones was elevated to Flight Commander and went at the enemy with vigour. On 24 July he scored three victories over three DFW C.s in the one day—one at 0720 hours the other two at 1730 hours.

On 30 July 1918, when he had 28 kills, he scored another triple victory during an afternoon's flying. On 3 August he was gazetted as being awarded The Distinguished Flying Cross for destroying six enemy aircraft in only eleven days.

On 3 and 4 August he increased his score by two more victories then on 6 August he shot down in flames two Fokker D.VIIs. The next day—7 August 1918 he scored his final victories—another double—at 1225 and 1715 hours. His confirmed total was now 37 but probably several more. On 25 August he was admitted to The Distinguished Service Order and awarded a Bar to his DFC for scoring 21 victories in but three months.

After the November Armistice he remained in the RAF becoming Officer Commanding of 74 Squadron—the squadron he had first served with as an NCO—a splendid achievement. He served in the RAF until 1936 leaving as time expired (time ex). He was recalled to the Colours in August 1939 in the rank of Group Captain—and put in charge of Fighter Operational Training Units (OTUs). He flew Spitfires—probably without permission—over enemy occupied France on operational sorties. His indomitable, aggressive spirit was still to the fore—as was shown when he was flying an unarmed Hawker Henley target tug—when he attacked a German Ju 88 bomber with the only weapon he had—a Very flare pistol.

Group Captain Jones survived the Second World War but died on 30 August 1960 at 65 years of age.

Flight Lieutenant Samuel Marcus Kinkead, (1897-1928)
35 victories

Samuel Kinkead was born in Johannesburg, South Africa, to an Irish father and Scottish mother who had recently emigrated to South Africa. He joined the Royal Naval Air Service in September, 1915. He earned his wings by the end of 1915. Kinkead served in 2 Wing RNAS during the Battle of Gallipoli. While flying a Bristol Scout, he shot down a Fokker on 11 August 1916. He also scored on 28 August 1916 while flying a Nieuport, and was credited with a third victory while flying a Nieuport. He fell ill with a serious case of malaria and was shipped home to convalesce. Upon recovery, he was sent to England, where his older brother Thompson was training as a pilot in the Royal Flying Corps. While on his second solo flight on 3 September 1917, Thompson died in a crash at Shoreham. Samuel signed for his deceased brother's personal effects.

Samuel Kinkead was assigned to 1 Naval Squadron to fly Nieuports on the Western Front. Exactly two weeks after his brother's death, on 17 September 1917, he drove down a DFW two-seater out of control. A month later, he repeated the feat to become an ace. He went on to claim three more triumphs in October.

In November and December 1917, he downed three planes each. In mid-November, he switched to fly a Sopwith Camel, with which type of plane he continued to fly until the end of the War. On 22 February 1918, he was awarded the Distinguished Service Cross.

In March, 1918, he started accumulating victories by ones and twos, finishing up May with his total at 26. Most of the time, he drove enemy craft out of the fight; he reported few destroyed. However, he received a Bar to his DSC on 26 April 1918. Then, on 30 May, he broke his string of victories for two months. He scored on each of the last three days of July, and four times in August, bringing his total to 33. He had become the leading ace out of the 18 in his squadron, now renumbered 201 Squadron when it was merged into the newly formed Royal Air Force. On 3 August, he received the Distinguished Flying Cross. On 2 November 1918, he was awarded a bar to his DFC.

Out of the victories whose details are recorded, Kinkead claimed 23 enemy planes 'out of control' including 3 shared. He destroyed 5, and shared in the destruction of 2 others. 1 aircraft was claimed captured.

Kinkead volunteered to serve with 47 Squadron after war's end, when they were sent into Russia to intercede in the Russian Civil War. He served as B Flight Commander under Raymond Collishaw. The squadron operated from an equipped train. It was while supporting General Denikin's Royalists that, on 12 October 1919, he won the Distinguished Service Order for a crucial ground attack against a Bolshevik cavalry division near Kotluban, thus saving the city of Tsaritsyn from capture. He also shot down three Russian fighters during this campaign: on 30 September 1919, at Chernyi Yar; on 7 October, at Dubovka; and on 18 October at Peskovatka.

He was a member of the British 1927 Schneider Trophy team, retiring in the Gloster IV after five laps. His third lap speed of 277.18 mph was the fastest biplane seaplane flight ever recorded. In 1928, while in command of the RAF High Speed Flight, Kinkead was killed in a plane crash as he tried to become the first man to travel at more than five miles a minute in a Supermarine S.5 near Calshot England. The circumstances of his death have never been satisfactorily explained although a verdict of death by misadventure was passed at the inquest. The witnesses to the crash thought Kinkead was flying very low and very fast when his S.5 dived into moderately deep water near the Calshot Lightship. Sam Kinkead had died instantly.

Captain Frederick Robert Gordon McCall, (1896-1949)
35 (37) victories

Captain McCall was born on 4 December 1896 at Vernon, British Columbia, Canada. He enlisted in the Alberta Regiment in February 1916, and in December 1916, arrived with his regiment in England. He was commissioned and transferred to the RFC in March 1917. He completed his flying training and was posted to 13 Squadron, RFC, on 4 December 1917. No.

13 Squadron was flying R.E.8 (nicknamed Harry Tate) two-seater reconnaissance aircraft.

McCall crewed up with 2nd Lieutenant F. C. Farrington as Observer/Gunner and between them they scored several victories in their 'Harry Tate' No. B6523. An amazing feat for a recce aircraft and a fatal shock for attacking German airmen. Other victories were scored in R.E.8 No. B5090. On 4 March 1918 McCall was awarded a Military Cross—two weeks later after another two victories—he was awarded a Bar to his MC. After a short leave he was posted to 41 Squadron flying S.E.5a s and by 1 June he had scored three more kills which brought him a well deserved DFC.

June 1918 was an excellent month for McCall but not for the opposing Germans whom he met in aerial combat—four went down on 28 June and five went down on 30 June, bring his total to 20 victories confirmed—all gained when flying S.E.5a D3927. His five victories in one day (30 June 1918) brought him admission to the Distinguished Service Order when his score stood at 24 victories.

On the 17 August 1918 his tally was 35 confirmed. On that date he and William Gordon Claxton were on patrol with other airmen from 41 Squadron when they clashed with a large force—some say 40 to 60—German aircraft. McCall and Claxton are believed to have shot down three enemy aircraft each but this was unconfirmed (but probably correct). Claxton was shot down behind German lines but McCall returned to base.

Captain McCall was taken ill and returned first to England then home to Canada where he was when The Great War ended in France in November. Captain McCall died on 2 January 1949. A gallant, aggressive fighter pilot—a credit to his country, one of the illustrious band of Colonial airmen who came to Britain's aid in The Great War.

Captain Henry Winslow Woollett, (1895-1969)
35 victories

Suffolk born Henry Woollett was commissioned into the Army when war broke out and transferred to the RFC in 1916. He passed out as a pilot after only a few hours dual instruction and was posted to 24 Squadron at Bertangles on 30 November 1916. 24 Squadron was flying DHs when Woollett joined them but it not until 5 April 1917 that he gained his first victory—an Albatros D.III over Honnecourt—which he claimed as destroyed. 24 Squadron then converted to the superior DH.5s and Woollett—flying DH.5 A9165—shot down an Albatros D.V and a Type C within a few minutes on 23 July 1917, bring his score to three confirmed. A Rumpler C was destroyed on 28 July and an Albatros D.V on 17 August 1917.

Lieutenant Woollett was promoted to Captain—with effect from (WEF) 13 July 1917 and made 'A' Flight Commander. He returned to England where he was awarded The Military Cross and became a Flying Instructor. He returned to France in March 1918 being posted to 'C' Flight, 43 Squadron, flying Sopwith Camels. On 8 March 1918 he reopened his victory total by sending an Albatros D.V down in flames over La Bassee—this brought him up to six confirmed.

Between the 11 and 27 March he destroyed six aircraft and two balloons—scoring a double on the 24 March and two balloons on the 27 March. On 2 April he shot down three balloons followed on the 12 April 1918 by an incredible feat of arms. Taking off on an early fighting patrol in Camel 6402, he met An Albatros D.V and a C Type over La Gorgue. Minutes later the two were downed—the Albatros in flames. Ten minutes later at 1040 hours he shot another Albatros out of the sky in flames. Landing to refuel and re-arm his guns he took off and met three Albatros D.Vs over La Gorgue at 1700 hours. Closing to the attack he sent all three down destroyed within minutes. All were confirmed making his total for the one day six enemy downed and became the second RFC pilot to claim six victories in a day (the first pilot was Captain J. L. Trollope also of 43 Squadron).

He was admitted to The Distinguished Service Order and received a Bar to his MC also the French Legion of Honour and Croix de Guerre. Captain Woollett resumed his offensive on 22 April with two balloons destroyed, then an Albatros D.V and a balloon on 9 May 1918. This brought his total to 28 confirmed but it is thought he scored several more unconfirmed. By the 9 August he had 35 confirmed victories—making his official total 20 destroyed, four driven down out of control and 11 balloons. An unofficial total was around 43 to 45

Captain Woollett survived the war and remained in the new RAF. He became commanding officer of his old squadron—No. 23—during 1930–31. He died on 31 October 1969.

Captain Francis Grainger Quigley, (1894-1918)
34 (33) victories

Captain Quigley—another gallant Canadian of that band who flocked to The Colours—was born 10 July 1894 in Toronto. He arrived in England in May 1915 with Canadian Army Engineers and was sent to France. He transferred to the RFC in the spring of 1917 and after flying training he was posted to 70 Squadron in France—the squadron being equipped with Sopwith 1½ Strutters until July 1917 then Camels for the rest of the war.

His first victory was an Albatros D.V, destroyed on 10 October 1917 while flying Camel B2356 at 0805 hours—twenty minutes later he sent another Albatros D.V down out of control. Both victories were confirmed. A German type C was destroyed on 20 October making his score three victories; then on 12 November he attacked an Albatros D.V and sent it spinning out of control—this was also confirmed. He was awarded The Military Cross and Mentioned in Despatches several times during the Autumn of 1917. By the year's end he had a victory total of nine German aircraft to his credit and entered into history as one of the Canadian Aces who displayed aggressive fighting spirit and a natural aptitude for combat in the air.

A brief spell of inactivity followed, but on 3 January 1918 he was back in action sending a C type out of control earthwards—this brought his total score to 10. Three days later he destroyed two Albatros D.Vs within 15 minutes over Stadenberg and Passchendaele while flying his Camel B2447. The first Albatros was shared with two other pilots of 23 and 70 Squadron—the German opponent was Leutnant Walter von Bulow Bothkamp, of *Jasta* 'Boelke') 92 with 28 victories to his credit. On 22 January 1918 he shared in downing three Albatros D.Vs upping his total to 15—by 17 February it was up to 18 victories.

Between 8 March and 23 March 1918 he had another 15 confirmed victories making his score 33. On 9 March, over Menin and Quesnoy, he destroyed—or sent down out of control—four Albatros D.Vs between 0930 hours and 1310 hours while flying Camel B7475. On 11 March he had another four victories: a balloon and three Pfalz D.IIIs over Menin/Passchendaele—next day he accounted for three Albatros D.Vs within five minutes over Dadizeele.

During March 1918 he was admitted to The Distinguished Service Order—in part due to his offensive action in attacking German ground troops during the last German offensive of the war. He fired more than 3,000 rounds from his guns at the ground enemy and dropped bomb after bomb—flying almost non-stop during the short daylight hours of March.

On the 22 March 1918 he destroyed two enemy aircraft in aerial combat—an Albatros D.V and a Fokker Dr1 Triplane. The next day he scored his final victory, a Pfalz D.III—sending it down to crash at Morchies. He was promoted to Captain.

On the 27 March 1918 he was wounded in the ankle and hospitalized and sent home to Canada. In September 1918 he managed to get himself back to England, with a view to resume combat—sadly he contracted the deadly influenza virus prevalent at the time—and died in hospital at Liverpool on 20 October 1918.

Major Roderic Stanley Dallas, (1891-1918)
32 (39) victories

Major Dallas was born on 30 July at Mount Stanley, Queensland, Australia, and served in the Australian Army in 1913. He applied for transfer to the RFC in 1914 but was turned down. Undaunted and eager to get into the air and combat, he applied and was accepted by the Royal Naval Air Service and began pilot training in June 1915. Qualifying and gaining his pilot's certificate on 5 August 1915, he joined No. 1 Wing, RNAS, at Dunkirk on 3 December 1915.

He made his first victory on 22 April 1916 when flying a Nieuport Scout near Dunkirk. He was awarded The Distinguished Service Cross on 6 September 1916 and the French Croix de Guerre. By February 1917 his score had risen to seven victories. Several of his victories were gained when flying a prototype Sopwith Triplane No. N500. On 14 June 1917 he took command of 1 Naval Squadron—renamed from No.1 Wing RNAS— equipped with Sopwith Triplanes. The same month he was awarded a Bar to his DSC.

In April 1917 No. 1(N) Squadron was put under RFC control and sent to the Somme Front where Dallas gained eight more victories. On 1 April 1918 the Royal Air Force was formed from the RFC and RNAS and Dallas was posted in command of 40 Squadron flying S.E.5a s. Flying with 40 Squadron Dallas notched up another nine victories flying his allocated S.E.5a B4879.

The exact number of enemy aircraft that Major Dallas brought down is uncertain—but it is *circa* 40. On 19 June 1918 he took on three Fokker Dr1s over Lievin but was shot down and killed. So died a gallant Australian ace who typified his country.

Lieutenant Colonel Andrew Edward McKeever, (1894-1919)
30 (31) victories

Yet another outstanding ace from Canada Andrew McKeever was born in Listowel, Ontario, on 21 August 1894, and came to Britain with the Canadian Army in 1914. In 1916 he transferred to the RFC and was sent to 11 Squadron on 28 May 1917 flying two-seat Bristol Fighters. He was to become the leading and outstanding ace of two-seater aircraft scoring a confirmed 31 victories—mostly with Sergeant L. F. Powell as his observer/gunner. Sergeant Powell is credited with shooting down eight German aircraft.

He scored his first victories on 26 June 1917 when he downed two Albatros D.Vs within minutes of each other. Lieutenant E. Oake being his observer/gunner. On 7 July 1917 he shot down three Albatros D.Vs with ten minutes while flying Bristol Fighter A7144 with Sergeant Powell. By 13 July he had taken out another three Albatros D.Vs making his (their) total eight victories. On 5 August 1917 he downed three Albatros D.Vs with Sergeant Powell—again—within minutes of each other.

By 28 September 1917 he had downed another seven Albatros D.Vs making his score 18 victories. Between 1 and 31 October 1917 he accounted for another eight aircraft—one C Type and seven Albatros D.Vs making his tally 26. During November he had five more victories—one C type and four Albatros D.Vs. Total confirmed—31 enemy aircraft, destroyed or downed out of control.

McKeever was awarded The Military Cross on 17 September 1917; a Bar to his MC on 27 October 1917 and admission to The Distinguished Service Order for his actions on 30 November 1917. Sergeant Powell was awarded a richly deserved Distinguished Conduct Medal.

Lieutenant Colonel McKeever survived the war but was injured in a road traffic accident and died from his injuries on 25 December 1919. He was the leading ace of the two-seat fighter aircraft with his redoubtable Sergeant Powell.

Flight Sergeant Ernest John Elton, (1893-1958)
16 victories

Ernest John Elton enlisted in the RFC in 1914 as an Air Mechanic and in 1915 was with 6 Squadron in France servicing Martinsyde S.1s, Bristol Scouts, B.E.2ds and B.E.2es. He assisted Major Lanoe Hawker VC in the fitting of an offset machine gun to Hawker's Bristol Scout.

Elton was accepted for pilot training late in 1917, promoted to Sergeant and posted to 22 Squadron flying Bristol Fighters. His first success came on 26 February 1918, when flying a Bristol with Sgt J. C. Hagen as observer/gunner, he accounted for two Albatros D.Vs at 1030 hours over Lens. Flying Bristol No. B1162 with 2Lt G. S. L. Hayward as observer/gunner, he scored another double on 6 March 1918 when two more Albatros D.Vs were destroyed.

Sergeant Elton was the most successful NCO pilot in the RFC as he and his observers/gunners—Sgt J. C. Hagen, 2Lt G. S. L. Hayward, Sgt S. Belding and Lt R. Critchley—shot 16 enemy aircraft out of the sky in 32 days action. Elton shot down ten with his front machine gun and his gunners six with the rear mounted machine gun.

2nd Lieutenant Indra Lal Roy, (1898-1918)
10 victories

Roy was born in Calcutta, India, and educated in England. He enlisted in the RFC in July 1917 and after training, was sent to 56 Squadron, RFC, on 30 October 1917. On 6 November he made a bad landing in an S.E.5a and was medically downgraded. Determined to get into the fight, Roy managed to get back to France and combat in June 1918.

Posted to 40 Squadron he joined the high scoring Captain George McElroy's Flight and began his brief but valiant combat as a fighter pilot—flying a S.E.5a No. B180. Between 6 July and 19 July 1918 he scored ten victories (two of them shared). On 8 July he downed three enemy aircraft in less than four hours. On 13 July he destroyed two enemy aircraft then on 15 July he destroyed a Fokker D.VII and sent another Fokker D.VII out of control in minutes.

His final victory was a Hannover C shot down on 19 July 1918, then on 22 July he was shot down and died in the cockpit of his S.E.5a B180 in flames—aged 19 years. He was awarded a DFC in September 1918. He was and probably still is—the only Indian—fighter pilot ace.

Lieutenant Croye Rothes Pithey, (1895-1920) and Lieutenant Hervey Rhodes, (1895-1987)
The top scoring R.E.8 pilot and observer/gunner aircrew
10 victories

Lieutenant Pithey was born in South Africa and Lieutenant 'Dusty' Rhodes enlisted in the Yorkshire Regiment before transferring to the RFC. Pithey was the pilot and Rhodes the observer/gunner in an R.E.8 Observation and recce aircraft —which was not exactly a fast fighter aircraft. However the R.E.8 had two Lewis machine guns in the rear cockpit for the observer/gunner and the pilot had a synchronised Vickers fixed on the port side of the fuselage. 120 lb of bombs could also be carried. By September 1917, 16 squadrons were flying the R.E.8 on the Western Front. Slow and cumbersome it was regarded as an easy kill by the Germans—but not always. On August 21 1917 Oberleutnant Dostler (26 victories) was killed by an R.E.8 gunner.

Pithey and Rhodes joined forces during March 1918—flying the slow R.E.8s of 12 Squadron, RFC. They opened their victory account on 7 May 1918 when they destroyed a balloon which was followed by another balloon on the 4 June 1918. Incredibly, on the 7 June 1917 at 0920 hours, they shot out of control three Pfalz D.IIIs making their total five victories. On 8 May 1918 Lieutenant Rhodes whilst flying with another officer, also shot down another enemy aircraft.

By 3 September 1918, the two officers in their R.E.8 No. F6097, had taken their total to 10 enemy aircraft (including two balloons) accounted for. But on 27 September 1918 their partnership came to an abrupt end when they were both shot up and wounded. Both airmen survived the war—Pithey died in 1919 and Rhodes in 1987. Two splendid airmen.

Captain Robert Henry Magnus Spencer Saundby, (1896-1971)
5 victories

Born on 26 April 1896 and educated at St Edwards School. Saundby served with the Royal Warwickshire Regiment during 1914 and was seconded to the RFC in January 1916. He went to France during 1916, flying DH.2s with 24 Squadron, and scored his first victory—a Fokker Eindecker—on 31 July 1916. Wounded during his dogfight he continued flying and scored two more victories in September and November.

Saundby was posted to 41 Squadron on Home Defence on 31 March 1917. On 17 June 1917—he and Lieutenant L. P. Watkins attacked the German Zeppelin L48 over Orfordness Theberton, Suffolk, at 0330 hours. Bringing the massive airship down Saundby and Watkins returned to base in their DH.2 No. A5058. Captain Saundby was awarded The Military Cross for destroying the L48. With the destruction of the L48 Saundby's score now stood at five.

After the War he remained in the RAF and was awarded the DFC. During Second World War he became Deputy Commander in Chief, Bomber Command, was knighted in 1944 and promoted to Air Marshal in 1945. He retired as Air Marshal Sir Robert Saundby, KCB, KBE, MC, DFC, AFC and DL in 1946 and died on 25 September 1971—a gallant officer.

Major Keith Rodney Park, (1892-1975)
20 victories

A New Zealander, Keith Park was born on 15 June 1892, and served with the New Zealand Artillery, gaining his commission in July 1915. He served in France with the Royal Artillery during 1916 being wounded in October. He transferred to the RFC in December 1916, underwent pilot training then became an instructor. He was posted to 48 Squadron flying Bristol Fighters on 7 July 1917 and by 11 September was a Flight Commander.

On 24 July 1917, he began to take the air war to the enemy when he sent an Albatros D.III down out of control off Ravensdyke. August 1917 proved a good month for Keith Park who scored nine victories—four in one day—17 August when he (and his observer) downed four Albatros D.IIIs in 30 minutes. Two Albatros D.Vs went down on 21 August followed by another Albatros D.V on the 25 August. His total score was now ten victories. He was awarded The Military Cross and French Croix de Guerre.

By the end of September 1917 he accounted for another six Albatros D.Vs taking his score to 16 confirmed. He was shot down once by anti-aircraft fire and once in aerial combat on the 3 January 1918 by Unteroffizer Ungewitter of Schlachtstaffel 5—but managed to crash-land his Bristol A7229 safely. On 10 April 1918 he assumed command of 48 Squadron with 17 confirmed victories to his credit and by 25 June 1918 he added three more victories—two downed on 25 June making his total 20. This was his final confirmed score.

Park remained in the RAF on a Permanent Commission and achieved high rank—during the Second World War he became Air Officer Commanding (AOC) of 11 Group Fighter Command during the Battle of Britain. He became AOC Fighter Command Malta and Burma and retired in the rank of Air Chief Marshal Sir Keith Park, GCB, KBE, MC, DFC and DCL. He returned to New Zealand and died on 6 February 1975 aged 83 years.

Major Arthur Travers Harris, AFC; (1892-1984)
5 victories

Bomber Harris—as he was later to be nicknamed—was born in Gloucestershire on 13 April 1892 and went to West Africa at an early age. He served in the Rhodesian Regiment as a boy bugler, then in 1915, enlisted in the RFC. Qualifying as a pilot, he served with 70 (Home Defence) Squadron which was formed at Farnborough on 22 April 1916 flying Sopwith 1½ Strutters. He was posted to 51 Squadron—which had been formed as a home defence squadron using bases in East Anglia—to combat the German Zeppelin menace, flying B.E.s as 'night' fighters. After a spell with 51 Squadron, he was posted as Flight Commander with 45 Squadron—again flying Sopwiths.

Taking off—on 5 July 1917, from Fienvillers in a Sopwith 1½ Strutter—he intercepted an Albatros D.V and sent it down out of control at 1720 hours. The later to be famous Harris had scored his first victory. Four more downed Albatros aircraft were confirmed victories for Harris—his last victory on 3 September 1917 while flying a Camel—was an Albatros D.V—sent down in flames over Ledeghem.

In 1918 Harris was posted to England in command of No. 44 (Home Defence) Squadron which was stationed in Essex to combat Zeppelin airship and German bomber attacks. 44 Squadron—under Harris—flew Camels on night patrols with success and Major Harris was awarded The Air Force Cross (AFC). After the War Harris remained in the RAF and commanded squadrons in India and Iraq. He joined the staff of Air Ministry in 1934 then commanded 4 Bomber Group 1937–38 and 5 Bomber Group 1939–40.

He came into his own in 1942 when he took command of RAF Bomber Command as AOC and began the great bombing offensive against Germany—which was supported by the great mass of the British (and other) people—as it meant that the Allies were fighting back against Nazi tyranny. Bomber Harris retired from the RAF as Marshal of the Royal Air Force Sir Arthur Harris, GGB, OBE, AFC, LL.D and numerous foreign decorations. A statue is his memory was placed in London and unveiled by H.M. Elizabeth, The Queen Mother, a fitting tribute to a great Commander.

Major Arthur 'Mary' Coningham, (1895-1948)
14 victories

An Australian, Arthur Coningham was born 19 January 1895 and served in the New Zealand Army in Egypt and Somaliland when the First World War broke out. He was discharged as medically unfit through typhoid in 1916—and somehow—managed to get back into combat be enlisting in the RFC in 1917. After flying training he was posted to 32 Squadron flying DH.2s and DH.5s and scored his first victory flying a DH.2 when he sent a C Type down in flames over Ervillers.

During July 1917, flying a DH.5, he scored nine victories—seven Albatros D.Vs and two C Types—between the 11th and 30th of that month. He was admitted to The Distinguished Service Order and awarded The Military Cross. He was elevated to Flight Commander. In early 1918 he was promoted to command 92 Squadron and scored another four victories—a

C Type and three Fokker D.VIIs. He always led his Flight or Squadron and was twice wounded in air combat—once with 32 Squadron and once with 92 Squadron. Being a Kiwi—Arthur Coningham was nicknamed 'Maori' which was corrupted to 'Mary'. A strange nickname for a brave gallant officer.

He was granted a Permanent Commission in the RAF after the Armistice and during the Second World War became AOC Desert Air Force 1941 to 1943. He then took command of 2 Tactical Air Force (2 TAF) until 1945. He was made Air Marshal and Knighted as Sir Arthur Coningham. He died on 30 January 1948 *en route* to Bermuda in an Avro Tudor of British South American Airways (BSAA).

Captain Leslie Norman Hollinghurst, (1895-1971)

'Holly' as he came to be known to servicemen (including the Author) was born on 2 January 1895 and enlisted in the Royal Engineers in 1914 but transferred to the RFC in 1916. Completing his pilot training with distinction he was 'creamed off' to instruct new entrants in flying.

He managed to get to battle in April 1918 with 87 Squadron, flying Dolphin aircraft, and opened his score on 6 July 1918 when he sent a Fokker D.VII out of control earthwards at Bapaume.

On the 9 August he downed a Pfalz D.III and an LVG C within minutes—sending the Pfalz down in flames. Next day he destroyed a Fokker D.VII which brought his score to five victories. By the 4 October 1918 his score had risen to 11—which included another five Fokker D.VIIs. The November Armistice brought an end to the air war with a DFC being awarded to the now Captain Hollinghurst. Hollinghurst remained in the RAF after the war and reached high rank within the service, being made an OBE in 1932. During the Second World War he became Commanding Officer of No. 38 Group (with which the author served) on 6 November 1943 in the rank of Air Vice Marshal.

Against orders (he was in possession of airborne battle plans) he flew on Operation Overlord (D Day Invasion) and Operation Market Garden (Arnhem).

He was knighted in 1948 and retired from the RAF in 1952 (as did the author!) with the rank of Air Chief Marshal Sir Leslie Norman Hollinghurst, GCB, KCB, OBE, DFC. Sir Leslie died suddenly on 8 June 1971 after attending a D Day reunion in Normandy, a well-liked officer, gentleman and Commander.

THE INVALUABLE SERVICES OF DOMINION FORCES

THERE WERE CLOSE TO 80 British Dominions that fought in the First World War. Many soldiers were from undivided India (which today comprises of India, Pakistan, Bangladesh and Sri Lanka), Australia, New Zealand, Canada, Nepal and various different parts of Africa with a sizeable army from the Caribbean recruited into the British West Indies Regiment taking part on the Western Front and in the Middle East.

For the purposes of this book the focus is on Canada, Australia, New Zealand and South Africa where most pilots and observers came from, but in fact pilots came from all across the Empire.

Of even greater importance than quantity was the quality. Two Canadians—Billy Bishop and Raymond Collishaw—are among the top 10 scorers overall. Three of the 10 are Germans, with Manfred von Richthofen, the fabled Red Baron, leading everyone with 80 victories. For Canada to have two in the top 10 compared to Germany's three is an astonishing ratio when considering the respective populations at the time. Another ace, William George Barker, who was Canada's most decorated war hero, was involved in one of the first war's most famous dogfights in October 1918 when he went up against 15 German fighters all by himself and was wounded three times. Despite passing out from his injuries twice, he shot down three of the enemy and drove the rest off before crashing.

Canada produced more than 190 aces, representing 18 per cent of the British and Dominions total.

Like Canada, Australia produced a wealth of aerial fighting talent with no less than 81 aces, of whom Robert Alexander Little came out top with 47.

New Zealand did more than its share. While New Zealand did not have its own military air service during the First World War, many New Zealanders joined Australian or British military aviation units to fight in the war. Some of New Zealand's first class of aces continued to serve post-war, whether in the Royal Air Force or the Royal New Zealand Air Force; some served in the Second World War. Indeed men like Keith Caldwell and Keith Park went on to have astonishingly important careers.

The following sections are a tribute to the Dominion support and in reality these few lines hardly do justice to the contribution they made.

CANADA

Royal Canadian Naval Air Service

C ANADIAN MILITARY FLYING BEGAN in the summer of 1914 when the Canadian Aviation Corps was formed with an establishment of just one aircraft! This solitary machine was sent to France on the outbreak of war and lasted only until February 1915, when it had to be scrapped.

The Royal Canadian Naval Air Service was founded in 1918, with eight ex-RNAS Sopwith Baby floatplanes. Two Canadian squadrons were formed that year—one flying DH.9a bombers, the other flying S.E.5a fighters.

Although Canada did not have a large number of squadrons, it had some of the most distinguished pilots of the First World War:

Lt Col. William Avery Bishop—*72 victories*
Lt Col. Raymond Collishaw—*60 victories*
Maj. Donald Roderick MacLaren—*54 victories*

Maj. William George Barker—*50 victories*
Capt. Alfred Clayburn Atkey—*38 victories*
Capt. William Gordon Claxton—*37 victories*
Flight Commander Joseph Stewart Temple Fall—*36 victories*
Capt. Frederick Robert Gordon McCall—*35 victories*

Compared to the following section on Australia, the Canadian contribution appears shorter. This is unfortunate and does not reflect Canada's true contribution which was out of proportion to its population. Unlike Australia which formed Australian Flying Corps in 1912, Canada had no air arm until the formation of the Canadian Air Force on 19 September 1918. Until that time, all flying activity was within the RFC or RNAS. Canadian airmen served in the British armed forces in surprisingly large numbers and in virtually every theatre of the war. Many of them entered service by volunteering for the Canadian Overseas Expeditionary Force. To do so, they were required to complete an Attestation Paper in which they declared an oath of allegiance to King George the Fifth and agreed to serve in any arm of the service for the duration of the war between Great Britain and Germany.

AUSTRALIA

The Australian Flying Corps

T HE FLEDGLING AUSTRALIAN FLYING Corps' first squadron was formed in September 1912 with two Deperdussins and two B.E.2a aircraft, two Farmans later being acquired to supplement the four original aircraft. In January 1914, the first flying school was founded at Point Cook, Victoria. The majority of the first pilots came from the Australian Light Horse, because it was felt that they had the delicate touch required to fly these early aeroplanes. On 31 March 1921, the Australian Air Corps (as it had become) took the name of the Royal Australian Air Force (RAAF).

The first two instructors—Capts H. A. Petre and E. Harrison—had been trained in England and began the first flying instruction course on 17 August 1914. It was attended by four officers—Capt. T. W. White and Lts G. P. Merz, R. Williams and D. T. W. Manwell—all of whom qualified.

When the First World War broke out, the Australian Flying Corps (AFC) used a Maurice Farman seaplane and a B.E.2a in support of a short campaign to invade and occupy part of Germany's Far East Empire—German New Guinea—on 15 September. The invading Australian Naval and Military Expeditionary Force met no resistance from the Germans.

On 8 February 1915, the Australian Government received the following cable message from the Viceroy of India:

Could you provide any trained aviators for service in Tigris Valley? All our trained officers are in Egypt and England. If officers available, can you also send machines complete with motor-transport, mechanism, personnel, spares, etc? We should prefer biplanes. If available, we should like particulars of machines. Should you be unable to send machines, we can obtain Maurice-Farman or Blériot types from England. Have you any aviators who have handled either type?

The reply was that they could supply everything except the aircraft. The pilots available were the four who had qualified the previous year, the two instructors and a lieutenant, W. H. Treloar, who had learned to fly in England. Lts White, Treloar and Merz were assigned to the Mesopotamian Half-Flight under the command of Capt. Petre. The selection of ground crews was deemed to be of the greatest importance, and only the best mechanics, carpenters and riggers were considered. Once the Half-Flight were on the move in the campaign, their effectiveness would depend solely on what they had taken with them and their ability to improvise. The AFC was about to come into its own.

The Australian officers were given equal commissions in the RFC and temporarily appointed to the Indian Army, but they insisted on retaining their own uniforms with 'Australia' shoulder-badges. Two Indian Army officer pilots—Majs Brooke-Smith and Reilly—who, together with four British and five Indian mechanics formed the nucleus of the Indian Flying Corps, were assigned to be in overall command.

Mesopotamia (now Iraq) was not the most hospitable of places at the best of times, but was even worse when fighting a war. The heat was intense, and Basra in the south-east of the country was surrounded by swamps. It was not long before mosquitoes got to work, and malaria and a number of other tropical diseases became rampant. Quinine was issued every other day, and cases of sunstroke were commonplace.

The first attack involving the AFC was in June 1915 during a campaign along the Tigris Valley towards Baghdad. The Army, intent on capturing the enemy stronghold at Kut, realised that the enemy garrison at Nasirayeh would have to be taken care of, and two Caudron aircraft were ordered up from Basra to carry out reconnaissance flights. However, in an atmosphere of intense heat and humidity, the two aircraft—flown by Reilly and Merz with NCO observer/mechanics—struggled to stay in the air. First, Reilly had engine trouble and was forced to land, but fortunately the Arabs nearby were friendly; then Merz had engine trouble and was forced to crash land in the desert. Later, an eyewitness who saw his aircraft go down said that the two crew members had a running battle with heavily armed Arabs and were killed. Their bodies were never found, but later the remains of the aircraft were discovered, smashed to matchwood.

Problems started to manifest themselves in the shape of spares and more importantly fuel. Lighters that brought the fuel and spares up the River Tigris from Ali Al-Gharbi were being delayed because of shipping problems, and aircraft that were becoming unserviceable were having to be cannibalised in order to keep the others flying.

The Tigris campaign was a desperate, deplorable muddle—a perfect example of arrogant British complacency—and combined with the underestimation of enemy forces, ended in the besieging of Kut. Gen. Charles Townshend surrendered Kut to the Turkish Army on 29 April 1916. This marked the end of the Australian Half-Flight, as by this time all their aircraft had been destroyed, and three of the four officers and most of the ground crew had been killed or captured during the campaign. Over 13,000 British and Indian soldiers were captured and marched more that 700 miles to Anatolia. Those who survived the horrendous march were put to work on building a railway through the Taurus Mountains. Only 2,000 survived captivity, and only six of the forty-four captured mechanics survived.

No. 1 Squadron AFC consisted of twenty-eight officers and 195 NCOs and airmen. The squadron was divided into three Flights—'A', 'B' and 'C'—with four aircraft to be allotted to each. The only problem was that they had no aircraft! Under the command of Lt Col. E. H. Reynolds, 1 Squadron AFC embarked from Port Melbourne on 16 March 1916 for Egypt. (It is interesting to note that the majority of the men in the squadron had never seen an aircraft at this stage, let alone an aircraft engine.)

On reaching Egypt on 14 April, the squadron was equipped with aircraft supplied by the RFC (under whose control it was placed) and put into service in the desert between the Suez Canal and El Arish. The Australian ground crews were trained by the RFC personnel there, whilst some of the officers were sent to England for flying training.

The aircraft used by the RFC and the AFC at that time consisted of old B.E.2c two-seaters with a 90-hp engine. The RFC had two squadrons in Egypt: 14 Squadron on the Suez Canal at Ismailia and Kantara, and 17 Squadron at Heliopolis. The Germans had one squadron equipped with single-seat Fokker scouts and two-seat Aviatiks, both of which could outclimb and outfly the British aircraft. Luckily, most of the flights consisted of either reconnaissance or bombing missions and the two rarely met in aerial combat.

Fortunately for the Australians, the build-up to any form of aerial combat was slow, giving them time to familiarise themselves with the aircraft and conditions. However, by the end of July 1916, the Germans had become more aggressive and were regularly bombing Port Said and Cairo. When the B.E.2cs were sent up to intercept, the German aircraft just climbed away using their superior speed. However, on the ground, British troops were gaining the upper hand and had forced the Turkish Army to withdraw from its stronghold at Bir el Mazar.

The Egyptian Expeditionary Force was making inroads toward Palestine, and in between was the strongly held garrison at El Arish. On 30 October 1916, 1 Squadron AFC began photo reconnaissance flights and photographed the whole route of the El Arish and Magdhaba line. They also started to carry out bombing raids behind the enemy lines. What was surprising to the Australians was that they were able to carry out these missions without aerial interference from the Germans, although there was the odd occasion when a German aircraft took a look and moved away. It was somewhat mystifying, bearing in mind the superiority in speed and firepower of the German aircraft and the fact that the British had no AA guns in the field.

Throughout this time the railway from Kantara was continuing to be built unmolested, while the AFC were carrying out bombing raids on the Turkish Hejaz railway almost unchallenged. The AFC were slowly but surely taking over control of the skies.

Back in Australia, three more AFC squadrons were created for the Western Front in France: 2 Squadron (formerly 68 Squadron RFC); 3 Squadron (formerly 2 and 69 Squadron RFC); and 4 Squadron (formerly 71 Squadron RFC). These arrived on station in September 1917.

The second squadron, 2 Squadron AFC, was formed under the command of Capt. W. O. Watt, who had been in command of 'B' Flight of 1 Squadron AFC. Watt was a very experienced pilot and no stranger to aerial warfare. He had learned to fly in England in 1911, qualifying for his certificate in a Bristol biplane. At the outbreak of war, Watt was in France and enlisted in the Foreign Legion as a third class air-mechanic, but when it was discovered that he was a qualified pilot he was transferred to Escadrille MF 44. During his time with the squadron he was awarded the Légion d'honneur and the Croix de Guerre for exploits in combat, but because he was not a French citizen was never given a position of command. He transferred to the AFC in 1916, with the rank of captain and flight commander.

Nos 2, 3 and 4 Squadrons AFC arrived in England at the end of 1916, untrained and ill-equipped but ready for a fight. Maj. Watt's squadron was sent to the 24th Training Wing at Harlaxton near Grantham in Lincolnshire; 3 Squadron, under the command of Maj. Blake, went to the 23rd Training Wing at South Carlton in Lincolnshire; and 4 Squadron, under the command of Maj. Sheldon, to the 25th Training Wing at Castle Bromwich near Birmingham.

The first of the three squadrons to finish their training and be posted to France was 3 Squadron. There it was given the role of support squadron to the British Corps squadrons who were on duty with two Army Corps in the line—5 Squadron (with the Canadian Corps) and 16 Squadron (with XIII Corps). To ease them into the war zone, the pilots were set to work artillery spotting and carrying out reconnaissance flights.

When 2 Squadron finished their training, they flew from Harlaxton to Saint-Omer in their DH.5s on 21 September 1917. The following day the squadron left to fly to Warloy near Baisieux, where they were attached to the 13th (Army) Wing RFC operating with the British Third Army. Within two days of arrival they were engaged in the first Australian aerial combat; whilst on a routine patrol, they attacked two German two-seater reconnaissance aircraft. However, both enemy aircraft escaped unscathed using their superior speed.

Nos 2 and 3 Squadrons' baptism of fire was on the Western Front at the Battle of Cambrai. The Germans put up a desperate major offensive, the like of which had not been seen throughout the war. Gen. Julian Byng, who was commanding the Third Army, decided to attack the Hindenburg Line—not with an artillery bombardment followed by ground troops, but by a massed attack of tanks. On the morning of 20 November 1917, a thick mist hung over the whole area, but the first patrol of DH.5s belonging to 2 Squadron AFC lifted off just after dawn. Their objective was to carry out low-level attacks on ground targets, with the intention of opening up a gap for the tanks to break through. Because of the thick mist, the aircraft were having to fly as low as 20-30 feet above the ground at enormous risk. As the first patrol returned, the second was already airborne and continuing the attack.

On one of the missions, Lt H. Taylor was shot down by ground fire as he strafed the enemy lines. Crawling from the wreckage, Taylor made for cover where he found a party of British soldiers who had lost their officer. Grabbing a rifle that belonged to a dead German, he led the infantry in an attack against the enemy. The skirmish was brief, but it lasted long enough to enable the party to make their escape, and Taylor proceeded to make his way back to his airfield. The incident was witnessed by his fellow pilot Lt Wilson, who circled overhead keeping a watching brief.

On 22 November, Maj.-Gen. Hugh Trenchard, Commander of the RFC, visited 2 Squadron AFC and later wrote to Gen. William Birdwood, commander of the Australian Corps:

> I have just been to see the Australian fighting Squadron No. 68 [2 Squadron AFC] for the second time in the last week, and I have talked to some of the pilots who carried out the great

work on November 20th, 21st and today. Their work was really magnificent. These pilots came down low and fairly strafed the Hun. They bombed him and attacked him with machine-gun fire from fifty feet, flying among treetops; they apparently revelled in this work, which was of great value. You might like to let some of your people know that I think them really great men, and I am certain that in the summer next year they will all give a very fine account of themselves. They are splendid.

The Battle of Cambrai, however, was not the success that Byng had hoped. His tanks did not penetrate the Hindenburg Line, due mainly to the fact that the Germans were able to bring reserves up to plug the holes when penetrated, whereas Byng had no such reserves to maintain the pressure. However, one section of the line—Bourlon Wood—was taken by ferocious attacks from both ground and air. For the next couple of days the German infantry, supported by aircraft, tried to retake the wood, but despite the ferocity of the attacks the defence held. Some of the fiercest aerial fighting the Australians had ever encountered took place over the wood during this period.

On the Messines Front in November 1917, 3 Squadron AFC looked on in horror at the muddy mess that unfolded before their eyes on the Ypres battlefield. The mud in places was waist deep, and the infantrymen stuck in it were almost literally unable to move forwards or backwards. When the order came for the Battle of Passchendaele to begin, it was like passing a death sentence on the battalion that had to begin the assault. The AFC in their R.E.8s took to the air at every opportunity in an attempt to relieve the nightmare being enacted below them, but the weather was dreadful and by December had got decidedly worse.

The squadron got to work artillery spotting and, surprisingly, suffered very few casualties, although one aircraft taking off on a mission was caught by a sudden squall, which carried the machine across the field and into the brick wall of Bailleul Cemetery. Both the pilot, Capt. H. H. Storrer, and his observer, Lt W. N. E. Scott, were killed.

Then, on 17 December, came a spell of unseasonably sunny weather. The squadron got all available aircraft into the air artillery spotting, and it was during one of these missions that a second crew were lost when Lt J. L. M. Sandy and his observer Sgt H. F. Hughes were attacked by six Albatros fighters. Lt Sandy turned his aircraft and met the enemy fighters head-on, shooting down one of them. Joined by another R.E.8 from 3 Squadron, the two of them attacked the five remaining enemy for ten minutes before the German fighters broke off on seeing another R.E.8 about to join in.

Lt E. H. Jones, one of the Australian pilots who had joined Lt Sandy in the fight, left the area to continue his patrol, but on returning to the airfield much later he discovered that Sandy and Hughes were missing. A search discovered the wreckage of their aircraft, with the bodies of the two crew members still inside. It transpired that during the encounter with the Albatros fighters, an armour-piercing bullet had hit the observer in the chest, passing through him and into the base of the pilot's skull. The aircraft had then continued to fly around in circles until its fuel ran out and it nose-dived into the ground.

At the beginning of 1918, it soon became obvious that the Allied advance was starting to gain momentum and that a major German offensive was on the cards. All the reconnaissance squadrons were set to work photographing different sectors for the Intelligence

Section and the map-makers. The aerodrome at Bailleul came under attack from Gotha bombers, and shelling, although inaccurate, was so heavy was that it was decided to move the squadron to Poulainville alongside the Australian Corps HQ at Bertangles.

Equipped with Sopwith Camels, 4 Squadron AFC had arrived in France at the end of December 1917. Ordered to Bruay, they came under the command of 10th (Army) Wing who were operating with the British First Army. The following month they were joined by 2 Squadron AFC in their new S.E.5s.

The squadron had a disastrous start to the war, losing a number of pilots through flying accidents whilst getting used to the idiosyncrasies of flying the Sopwith Camel in tight formation. The sector that was to be patrolled by both the Australian squadrons contained a number of German airfields, especially around Lille and Douai.

As the weather improved, there was no shortage of opponents on both sides. Although a number of famous German fighter aces—Boelcke, Immelmann, Wolff and Voss—had died in action, there was a cadre of battle-hardened pilots to replace them. The Red Baron, however, was still alive, and when his red Albatros appeared in the skies it struck fear into the hearts of the opposing novices. It was a war of survival—kill or be killed. Chivalry belonged in romantic stories and not on the battlefield, whether in the air, on the ground or on the sea. But the Germans, renowned for their ruthlessness, soon found that the newly arrived Australians could be equally ruthless.

On 21 March 1918, Gen. Ludendorff opened what was to be Germany's final offensive against the Allies. Both sides knew that this was to be the fight to the finish. The Americans had now entered the war, and their added weight of numbers and armament was to be a crucial turning point.

Almost immediately, 2 Squadron AFC was in the fight around the Cambrai and Saint-Quentin areas. As they returned to their airfield, they were replaced by squadrons from the RFC—making the aerial attack unrelenting—and 4 Squadron AFC started carrying out bombing and strafing raids on the advancing German troops as they crowded into the town of Bapaume. The roads became clogged with enemy, leaving them with nowhere to go as the Australian fighters swooped in to attack.

The occasional enemy fighter would appear and snap at the heels of the Australians, but in the main there was very little opposition in the air. One incident, on 24 March, showed how the 'novice' Australian pilots had turned into battle-hardened pilots within a matter of months. A squadron of S.E.5s encountered eight Albatros fighters and two Aviatiks, and in the short skirmish that followed, the Australians shot down two of the fighters and one of the two-seater Aviatiks with no loss to themselves.

The German Army was using up all its reserves in the offensive, but the British and French troops were holding the line. Germany's advance was beginning to falter. One Australian observer noted whilst on a reconnaissance flight:

> I saw fully 25,000 Germans advancing below under our very eyes, when from the direction of Chauny there flew seven French fighting squadrons, 105 machines glinting in the sun. They spread fanwise and dived upon the German troops, dropping 100-lb bombs and other smaller bombs. Hundreds and hundreds were killed. I saw 5,000 men flat on their faces trying to hide—it was awful.

All of the AFC squadrons were now fully committed to the battle, as indeed were all the RFC squadrons in the area.

The Allied offensive on the Somme opened on 8 August 1918, the Australian infantry carrying out some of the most daring raids on enemy-held positions. No. 3 Squadron AFC was assigned to the area to carry out reconnaissance and photographic missions, and throughout the offensive and right up to the Armistice, the AFC fought doggedly alongside the RFC. At the end of February 1919, the three Australian squadrons handed over their machines and stores to the British and departed for home.

The AFC lost over sixty aircraft in France. One-tenth (430,705) of Australia's population served in the armed forces, of whom 59,000 were killed fighting for the Empire. Australian forces won sixty-three VCs, and many Australians flew with the RFC and RNAS, gaining numerous victories. Outstanding among them was Capt. Robert Alexander Little, DSO and Bar, DSC and Bar, RNAS, RFC, with forty-seven victories. Other top Aces were:

Maj. Roderic Stanley Dallas—*39 victories*
Capt. Arthur Henry Cobby—*29 victories*
Capt. Elwyn Roy King—*26 victories*
Capt. Alexander Augustus Pentland—*23 victories*
Capt. Edgar McCloughry—*21 victories*
Capt. Richard Pearman Minifie—*21 victories*
Capt. Edgar Charles Johnston—*20 victories*

NEW ZEALAND

WHILE NEW ZEALAND DID not have its own military air service during the First World War, many New Zealanders did join Australian or British military aviation to fight in the war. Some of New Zealand's first class of aces continued to serve post-war, whether in the Royal Air Force or the Royal New Zealand Air Force; some served in the Second World War. Several earned advanced rank in the process. New Zealand produce fourteen Aces, the top three being:

Capt. Keith Caldwell—*25 victories*
Capt. Keith Park—*20 victories*
Capt. Ronald Bannerman—*17 victories*

SOUTH AFRICA

The South Africa Flying Unit

THE SOUTH AFRICAN MILITARY owe their existence to the Defence Act of June 1912, setting out the new basis for military forces in what was then the Union of South Africa, which had been created on 31 May 1910. In 1913, the South African Government selected several officers and sent them for flying training to form the cadre of the proposed South African Aviation Corps. Two years later, the South African Flying Unit was formed, equipped with a few B.E.2s and Henri Farman aircraft. In spite of difficulties with engines and the adverse climatic conditions, the South African Flying Unit flew recce missions to aid ground forces.

When Britain declared war on Germany in 1914, Gen. Louis Botha was Prime Minister. The German Empire in Africa at that time consisted of Togo, Cameroon, German South West Africa and German East Africa. On 26 August 1914, Togo surrendered after three weeks of fighting, whilst German forces held out in Cameroon until 18 February 1916.

Following a request from Britain for the South African Government to occupy the German colony of South West Africa, operations began in April 1915 and were concluded on 9 July. Three months later, on 8 October, 26 (South African) Squadron RFC was formed from personnel of the South African Flying Unit which had been operating against the Germans in South West Africa. The squadron—equipped with B.E.2c, B.E.2e and Henri Farman aircraft—carried out valuable bombing and recce flights for the military. Bases as such were hard to find, but the squadron operated out of Mombasa, Mybuyuni, Taveta, Kahe, Marago, Lokua, Dakawa, Morogoro, Tulo, Kilwa, Songea, Likuju, Mtua and Dar es Salaam.

The difficulty with operating early aircraft in German East Africa (as elsewhere in Africa) was that there were no detailed maps—the vast country was mostly unexplored and unsurveyed. The featureless bush was easy to get lost in, and water and aircraft fuel were in short supply.

Another squadron—8 (Naval) Squadron—arrived at Zanzibar under the command of F. W. Bowhill and took part in the last stages of the war against the forces of German East Africa under the command of Gen. von Lettow-Vorbeck. They proved to be worthy opponents, and it took four years before their final surrender came on 23 November 1918 (twelve days after the Armistice in France).

Among the outstanding pilots of the First World War were these South Africans:

Capt. Anthony Frederick Weatherby Beauchamp-Proctor—*54 victories*
Flight Lieutenant Samuel Marcus Kinkead—*35 victories*
Capt. Douglas John Bell—*20 victories*
Capt. Charles Gordon Ross—*20 victories*
Capt. Horace Dale Barton—*19 victories*

The first Central Flying School 1912 with Major Hugh Montague Trenchard, (1873-1956), 3rd from left, back row. The school was established at Upavon Aerodrome, near Upavon, Wiltshire on 12 May 1912. During the summer of 1912 Trenchard learned to fly and gained his aviator's certificate (No. 270) on 31 July flying a Henry Farman. He was subsequently appointed as second in command of the Central Flying School. He held several senior positions in the Royal Flying Corps during the War, serving as the commander of the Royal Flying Corps in France from 1915 to 1917.

Major Charles Dawson Booker, DSC, *Croix de guerre*, (1897-1918). On 13 August 1918, Booker was leading a rookie pilot on an orientation tour of their aerial battlefield. The two Camel pilots ran into a formation of at least six expert pilots from *Jagdgeschwader 2*. Booker tackled them single-handedly to cover the green pilot's retreat. It was the greenhorn who verified Booker's final three wins. However, *Jasta 12*'s ace Leutnant Ulrich Neckel finally shot Booker down. Booker was credited with 29 victories. He was promoted to high rank while relatively young as a result of his gallantry and unswerving dedication to the service.

Captain Robert Alexander Little, DSO & Bar, DSC & Bar, (1895-1918). Little is generally regarded as the most successful Australian flying ace, with an official tally of 47 victories. Born in Victoria, he travelled to England in 1915 and learned to fly at his own expense before joining the Royal Naval Air Service. Posted to the Western Front in June 1916, he flew Sopwith Pups, Triplanes and Camels with No. 8 Squadron RNAS, achieving thirty-eight victories within a year and earning the Distinguished Service Order and Bar, the Distinguished Service Cross and Bar, and the French Croix de Guerre.

Rested in July 1917, Little volunteered to return to the front in March 1918 and scored a further nine victories with No. 3 Squadron RNAS. On the night of 27 May 1918 On 27 May, Little received reports of German Gotha bombers in the vicinity, and took off on a moonlit evening to intercept them. As he closed with one of the bombers, his plane was caught in a searchlight beam and he was struck by a bullet that passed through both his thighs. He crash-landed in a field near Nœux, and bled to death before he was discovered the following morning by a passing gendarme.

Left: Major Edward Corringham 'Mick' Mannock, VC, DSO & Two Bars, MC & Bar, (1887-1918). At the outbreak of the war Mannock was working as a telephone engineer in Turkey and was interned at the onset of war. Through poor health he was repatriated and in 1915 he joined the Royal Army Medical Corps. By 1916, he had become an officer in the Royal Engineers and in August 1916 transferred to the Royal Flying Corps. In 1917 he transferred to No. 40 Squadron RAF where his working class manners did not fit in with the ex-public schoolboys who made up the majority of his comrades. On his first night, he inadvertently sat down in an empty chair—a chair which a newly fallen flier had occupied until that day. At first, Mick held back in the air to the extent that some pilots thought he was cowardly. He admitted that he was very frightened and like many top-scoring fliers Mannock initially had to to overcome his fears.

Right: After the troubled start in No. 40 Squadron Mannock began to accumulate victories, and his tally was 15 by the end of his first combat tour. He gained a reputation for ruthless hatred of his German adversaries, delighting in seeing them burn to death and in turn he also became phobic about burning to death in mid-air. He was sent home on leave in June 1918 and returned a few weeks later as Officer Commanding No. 85 Squadron. He scored nine more victories that July. By now, his phobias had spread to include excessive tidiness, and he also had presentiments of his coming end. Just a few days after warning fellow ace George McElroy about the deadly hazards of flying low into ground fire, Mannock did just that on 26 July 1918. His plane was set on fire, and he was killed in action.

Mannock was one of the first theorists of aviation tactics, and was renowned for his prudent but aggressive leadership in the air. He is regarded as one of the greatest fighter pilots of the War.

Captain Albert Ball, VC, DSO & Two Bars, MC, (1896-1917). Alert Ball photographed in front of a Caudron G.3, widely used as a trainer in 1915-16. Ball gained his pilot's wings on 26 January 1916. Joining No. 13 Squadron RFC in France, Ball flew reconnaissance missions before being posted in May 1916 to No. 11 Squadron, a fighter unit. From then until his return to England on leave in October, he accrued many aerial victories, earning two Distinguished Service Orders and the Military Cross. He was the first ace to become a British popular hero with 44 victories to his name.

No. 56 Squadron, France, 1917. Albert Ball is seated front row, second from the right. After a period on home establishment, Ball was posted to No. 56 Squadron, which deployed to the Western Front in April 1917.

Albert Ball in is S.E.5 cockpit. S.E.5 no. A4850, fresh from the factory, was extensively modified for Ball. In particular he had the synchronised Vickers machine gun removed, to be replaced with a second Lewis gun fitted to fire downwards through the floor of the cockpit. He also had a slightly larger fuel tank installed. On 9 April, A4850 was refitted, and the downward-firing Lewis gun removed and replaced by the normal Vickers gun mounting.

Albert Ball with some trophies. On the evening of 7 May 1917, near Douai, 11 British aircraft from No. 56 Squadron led by Ball in an S.E.5 encountered German fighters from *Jasta 11*. A running dogfight in deteriorating visibility resulted, and the aircraft became scattered. Ball was last seen by fellow pilots pursuing the red Albatros D.III of the Red Baron's younger brother, Lothar von Richthofen, who eventually landed near Annœullin with a punctured fuel tank. A German pilot officer on the ground, Lieutenant Hailer, then saw Ball's plane falling upside-down from the bottom of the cloud, at an altitude of 200 feet with a dead prop. Brothers Franz and Carl Hailer and two other men from a German reconnaissance unit hurried to the crash site, but Ball was already dead when they arrived. Ball's death sparked a wave of national mourning and posthumous recognition, which included the award of the Victoria Cross for his actions during his final tour of duty. His most renowned enemy, Manfred von Richthofen, remarked upon hearing of Ball's death that he was 'by far the best English flying man'.

The Germans buried Ball with full military honours. After the war the British discovered Ball's grave, which had been behind enemy lines, in the Annœullin Cemetery. In December 1918, personnel of No. 207 Squadron RAF erected a new cross in place of the one left by the Germans. 23 British bodies in graves in the location where Ball was buried were moved to the Cabaret Rouge British Cemetery, but at his father's request Ball's grave was allowed to remain. Ball's is the only British grave from the First World War in this cemetery extension, the remainder being German.

14 Squadron RFC B Flt, Commanding officer Lieutenant Jenkins (with his dog). No. 14 Squadron was formed on 3 February 1915 at Shoreham with Maurice Farman S.11 and B.E.2 aircraft. After a few months of training it departed for the Middle East in November of that same year for Army co-operation duties during the Sinai and Palestine Campaign. It remained in the Middle East until the end of the War.

Captain Andrew (Anthony) Frederick Weatherby Beauchamp-Proctor, VC, DSO, MC and bar, DFC (1894-1921). Beauchamp-Proctor, a South African officer, did not gain his first victory until 3 January 1918, but thereafter successes mounted rapidly. On 3 August, he was granted one of the first ever Distinguished Flying Crosses and by the end of that month he was up to 43 victories. Beauchamp-Proctor's victory total was 54; two (and one shared) captured enemy aircraft, 13 (and three shared) balloons destroyed, 15 (and one shared) aircraft destroyed, and 15 (and one shared) aircraft 'out of control'. His 16 balloons downed made him the leading British Empire balloon buster. On 2 November 1918, he was awarded the Distinguished Service Order, followed by the Victoria Cross on 30 November.

Lieutenant William Barnard Rhodes-Moorhouse, VC, (1887-1915). Rhodes-Moorhouse was the first airman to be awarded the VC. He enlisted in the RFC and obtained a posting to No. 2 Squadron on 20 March 1915 at Merville, flying the B.E.2. On 26 April 1915 at Kortrijk, Belgium, Rhodes-Moorhouse swept low over the railway junction that he had been ordered to attack. He released his 100 lb bomb and was immediately plunged into a heavy barrage of small arms fire from rifles and a machine-gun in the belfry of Kortrijk Church; he was severely wounded by a bullet in his thigh, and his plane was badly hit. Returning to the Allied lines, he again ran into heavy fire from the ground and was wounded twice more. He managed to get his aircraft back, and insisted on making his report before being taken to the Casualty Clearing Station. He died the next day, 27 April 1915. For this action he was awarded the Victoria Cross.

Major James Thomas Byford McCudden, VC, DSO & Bar, MC & Bar, MM, (1895-1918). McCudden joined the Royal Engineers in 1910. Having an interest in mechanics he transferred to the RFC in 1913 and at the outbreak of war in 1914 he flew as an observer before training as a fighter pilot in 1916. McCudden claimed his first victory in September 1916. He claimed his fifth victory—making him an ace—on 15 February 1917. For the next six months he served as an instructor and flew defensive patrols over London. He returned to the frontline in summer 1917. That same year he dispatched a further 31 enemy aircraft while claiming multiple victories in one day on 11 occasions. With his six British medals and one French, McCudden received more awards for gallantry than any other airman of British nationality serving in the First World War. He was also one of the longest serving. By 1918, in part due to a campaign by the *Daily Mail*, McCudden became one of the most famous airmen in the British Isles.

Left: James Macudden with his dog 'Bruiser'. At his death he had achieved 57 aerial victories, placing him seventh on the list of the war's most successful aces. Just under two-thirds of his victims can be identified by name. This is possible since, unlike other Allied aces, a substantial proportion of McCudden's claims were made over Allied-held territory. The majority of his successes were achieved with 56 Squadron RFC and all but five fell while flying the S.E.5a. On 9 July 1918 McCudden was killed in a flying accident when his aircraft crashed following an engine fault. His rank at the time of his death was major, a significant achievement for a man who had begun his career in the RFC as an air mechanic.

Right: Captain Keith Logan 'Grid' Caldwell, MC, DFC & Bar, (1895-1980). A New Zealander, Caldwell was commissioned by the RFC in April 1916. On 29 July 1916 he was posted to No. 8 Squadron RFC flying BE2Cs and Ds on observation duty. On 18 September 1916, flying a BE2D, he and his observer shot down a Roland CII. In November he transferred to 60 squadron flying Nieuport 17 fighters. In February 1917 he was promoted to Captain. In October 1917 he was posted back to England as an instructor. In March 1918 he was promoted to Major and given command of 74 'Tiger' squadron equipped with the SE5A, which he took to France on 30 March. Caldwell fought his last combat on 30 October 1918, claiming his 9th Fokker D.VII. Altogether he is credited with 11 aircraft destroyed, 2 shared destroyed, 1 shared captured, and 10 and 1 shared 'out of control'. Caldwell rose to become Air Commodore in the Royal New Zealand Air Force during the Second World War.

Lieutenant-Colonel William Avery 'Billy' Bishop, VC, CB, DSO & Bar, MC, DFC, ED, LL.D, (1894-1956). In November 1916 Bishop received his wings. On 17 March 1917, he arrived at 60 Squadron near Arras, where he flew the Nieuport 17 fighter. On 25 March he claimed his first victory against an Albatros D.III Scout near St Leger. On 30 March 1917, Bishop was named a flight commander and the next day he scored his second victory. Bishop, in addition to the usual patrols with his squadron comrades, soon flew many unofficial 'lone-wolf' missions deep into enemy territory. As a result, his total of enemy aircraft shot down increased rapidly. On 8 April he scored his fifth victory and became an ace. The successes of Bishop and his blue-nosed aircraft were noticed on the German side, and they began referring to him as 'Hell's Handmaiden'. Ernst Udet called him 'the greatest English scouting ace'. On 2 June 1917, Bishop flew a solo mission behind enemy lines to attack a German-held aerodrome, where he claimed that he shot down three aircraft that were taking off to attack him and destroyed several more on the ground. For this feat, he was awarded the Victoria Cross.

Bishop returned home on leave to Canada in fall 1917, where he was acclaimed a hero and helped boost the morale of the Canadian public, who were growing tired of the war. Upon his return to England in April 1918, he was promoted to Major and given command of No. 85 Squadron, the 'Flying Foxes'. This was a newly formed squadron and Bishop was given the freedom to choose many of the pilots. The squadron was equipped with SE5a scouts and left for Petit Synthe, France on 22 May 1918. On 27 May, after familiarising himself with the area and the opposition, Bishop took a solo flight to the Front. He downed a German observation plane in his first combat since August 1917, and followed with two more the next day. From 30 May to 1 June Bishop downed 6 more aircraft, including German ace Paul Billik, bringing his score to 59 and reclaiming his top scoring ace title from James McCudden. By the end of the war, he had claimed some 72 air victories, including two balloons, 52 and two shared 'destroyed' with 16 'out of control'.

Left: Lieutenant William George 'Billy' Barker, VC, DSO & Bar, MC & Two Bars, (1894-1930). After serving as an observer, Barker commenced pilot training in January 1917. On 24 February 1917 he returned to serve a second tour on Corps Co-operation machines as a pilot flying B.E.2s and R.E.8s with 15 Squadron. After service in France, on 7 November 1917, 28 Squadron was transferred to Italy with Barker temporarily in command. By September 1918 Barker's personal Sopwith Camel (serial no. B6313) had become the most successful fighter aircraft in the history of the RAF, Barker having used it to shoot down 46 aircraft and balloons from September 1917 to September 1918, for a total of 404 operational flying hours. Having flown more than 900 combat hours in two and one half years, Barker was transferred back to the UK in September 1918 to command the fighter training school at Hounslow Heath.

Right: On Sunday, 27 October 1918 while returning his Snipe to an aircraft depot, Barker crossed enemy lines at 21,000 feet above the Forêt de Mormal. He attacked an enemy Rumpler two-seater which broke up, its crew escaping by parachute and he was then bounced by a formation of Fokker D.VIIs of *Jagdgruppe 12*. In a descending battle against 15 or more enemy machines, Barker was wounded three times in the legs, then his left elbow was blown away, yet he managed to control his Snipe and shoot down or drive down three more enemy aircraft. The dogfight took place immediately above the lines of the Canadian Corps. Severely wounded and bleeding profusely, Barker force landed inside Allied lines, his life being saved by the men of an RAF Kite Balloon Section who transported him to a field dressing station. For this feat Barker was awarded the Victoria Cross. Barker is the most decorated serviceman in the history of Canada, and in the history of the British Empire and Commonwealth.

Lieutenant-Colonel Raymond Collishaw, CB, DSO & Bar, OBE, DSC, DFC, (1893-1976). A Canadian, Collishaw joined the RNAS, No. 3 Wing flying Sopwith 1½ Strutter aircraft on long range bombing missions to the Saarland. On 25 October 1916 he opened his victory score by shooting down two Fokker D.IIs over Luneville. On 1 February 1917 he transferred to No. 3 Naval Squadron. On 15 February and again on 4 March 1917 he shot down a Halberstadt D.II bringing his score to four victories. In April he joined No. 10 Naval Squadron at Furnes as B Flight Commander flying Sopwith Triplanes. On 28 April flying his Triplane no. N5490 he shot down an Albatros D.II over Ostend. Two days later he repeated the feat over Courtemarck, bringing his total to six. Collishaw chose four other pilots to form his Flight, forming the 'Black Flight' . . . their Triplanes were painted black on the engine cowling, wheel discs and forward fuselage with white lettering names thereon.

Ray Collishaw, of 13(N) Squadron, *c.* January 1918 with his F.1 Camel, Black Maria. From 9 May 1917—when his score stood at seven—until the 27 July 1917 when he had downed 38 enemy aircraft—he continued to score at an amazing rate. On 6 June he shot down three Albatros D.IIIs; on 15 June he destroyed four more enemy aircraft. Incredibly on 6 July 1917 he accounted for six Albatros D.Vs on the same day—this brought his score to 31. On 29 December 1917 Collishaw was placed in command of No.13 Naval Squadron equipped with new Sopwith Camels. With the creation of the RAF and Collishaw was promoted to Major and placed in command of 203 Squadron RAF—which had been formed that day from No. 3 Squadron RNAS. From 11 June 1918 to 26 September Collishaw downed another 19 enemy aircraft bringing his score to 59. On 1 October 1918 he was promoted to Lieutenant-Colonel at the age of 25. His total tally of victories was 60.

Major Roderic Stanley Dallas, DSO, DSC & Bar, (1891-1918). An Australian, Dallas's score of aerial victories is generally regarded as the second-highest by an Australian after Robert Little. Dallas sailed to England at the start of the War, seeking flight training and after being accepted into the RNAS, was commissioned as a Flight Sub Lieutenant, joining No. 1 Squadron in December 1915. During his service on the Western Front, in 1916 and 1917, he proved himself as an exceptional pilot and on 14 June 1917 he was made Commanding Officer of his Squadron. In 1918 after the amalgamation of the two air services to form the RAF, he was transferred to 40 Squadron RAF and held the rank of Major.

While on a reconnaissance operation, Dallas was struck by three bullets to his leg, after his safe return to base he was awarded the Distinguished Service Order, having already been awarded the Distinguished Service Cross and Bar and the French award, the Croix de Guerre and Palm.

Roderic Dallas was killed in action on 1 June 1918. It was later learned that he had been killed over Liévin during combat with three Fokker Triplanes from *Jagdstaffel 14.* There are several theories as to how he died. The common elements are that he was on patrol near the front line when he pounced on a German plane flying at a lower level, that there might have been another unknown British pilot in trouble, and that the Germans who shot Dallas down had dived from a still higher altitude. News of Dallas's death was greeted with shock and disbelief by his squadron, one pilot recording: *The world is upside down ... Dallas has been killed ... Too good for this world I suppose.* He is buried at Pérnes British Cemetery, Pas de Calais, France.

Captain Samuel Marcus Kinkead, DSO, DSC and bar, DFC and Bar, (1897-1928). A South African, Kinkead served in 2 Wing RNAS during the Battle of Gallipoli. While flying a Bristol Scout, he shot down a Fokker on 11 August 1916. He also scored on 28 August 1916 while flying a Nieuport, and was credited with a third victory while flying a Nieuport. Kinkead was later assigned to No. 1 Squadron RNAS to fly Nieuports on the Western Front. On 17 September 1917, he drove down a DFW two-seater out of control. A month later, he repeated the feat to become an ace. He went on to claim three more triumphs in October. In November and December 1917, he downed three planes each. In mid-November, he switched to a Sopwith Camel, the type of plane he would fly through war's end. Then, with his tally at 14, he went on hiatus for three months. During this time, on 22 February, he was awarded the Distinguished Service Cross.

In March, 1918, Kinkead started accumulating victories by ones and twos, finishing up May with his total at 26. Most of the time, he drove enemy craft out of the fight; he reported few destroyed. However, he received a Bar to his DSC on 26 April 1918. Then, on 30 May, he broke his string again, this time for two months.

He scored on each of the last three days of July, and four times in August, bringing his total to 33. He had become the leading ace out of the 18 in his squadron, now renumbered 201 Squadron when it was merged into the newly formed RAF. On 3 August, he received the Distinguished Flying Cross. On 2 November, he was awarded a bar to his DFC. In 1928, while in command of the RAF High Speed Flight, Schneider Trophy team, Kinkead was killed in a plane crash as he tried to become the first man to travel at more than five miles a minute in a Supermarine S.5 near Calshot.

Captain Frederick Robert McCall, DSO, MC & Bar, DFC, (1896- 1949). A Canadian, McCall was commissioned in March 1917 and joined No. 13 Squadron RAF in France flying the two-seat R.E.8 reconnaissance aircraft. After his first victory McCall was awarded the Military Cross with the citation: 'for conspicuous gallantry and devotion to duty', and two weeks later the accompanying Bar for downing an enemy scout while on photographic reconnaissance. After his third victory McCall was transferred to No. 41 Squadron flying the S.E.5. He was awarded the Distinguished Flying Cross after scoring four 'kills' in May 1918. On 28 June 1918 McCall downed five German aircraft in one day, and for this was awarded the Distinguished Service Order. On 17 August 1918, accompanying fellow Canadian ace William Gordon Claxton they ran into *Jagstaffel 20*, of at least 40 fighters. In the ensuing fight Claxton was shot down and McCall scored a victory. With his total at 35, McCall was ordered to England, and eventually to Canada, on convalescent leave. The Armistice was signed during his absence.

Left: Flight Sergeant Ernest John Elton, DCM, MM, (1893-1958). Elton enlisted in the RFC as an Air Mechanic. While serving in France he assisted Captain Lanoe Hawker in developing a machine gun mount for the Bristol Scout. In late 1916, he trained as a pilot, and was later assigned to No. 22 Squadron. On 26 February 1918, Elton piloted a Bristol F.2 Fighter to his first victory, when he destroyed two Albatros D.Vs near Lens. Following the engagement his engine failed, and he glided the six miles back to the Allied lines, crash-landing in no man's land. In the next month, Elton would be credited with destroying twelve more aircraft and driving two down out of control. He scored ten of his wins, and his gunner in the rear seat scored six times. His string culminated in a triple victory on 29 March 1918, when he destroyed three two-seater reconnaissance planes in ten minutes. They were the only two-seaters he ever destroyed; the remainder of his wins were over fighters, principally Albatros D.Vs. Elton was the highest scoring British non-commissioned flying ace during the War, credited with 17 victories.

Right: Captain Sir Ross Macpherson Smith, KBE, MC & Bar, DFC & Two Bars, AFC, (1892-1922). An Australian, Macpherson Smith enlisted in 1914 and served at Gallipoli. In 1917 he volunteered for the Australian Flying Corps and was later twice awarded the Military Cross and the Distinguished Flying Cross three times, becoming an air ace with 11 confirmed aerial victories. Smith was pilot for T. E. Lawrence and fought in aerial combat missions in the Middle East. He is mentioned several times in Lawrence's book, *Seven Pillars of Wisdom*. In 1919, he and his brother Keith, Sergeant James Bennett and Sergeant Wally Shiers flew from England, on 12 November 1919 in a Vickers Vimy, eventually landing in Darwin on 10 December, taking less than 28 days, with actual flying time of 135 hours. Smith was killed while testing a Vickers Viking amphibian aircraft which crashed soon after taking off from Brooklands on 13 April 1922.

Pilot Captain Ross Macpherson Smith and gunner Lieutenant E. A. Mustard, DFC, Australian No. 1, AFC, Middle East, 1918 in a Bristol F.2b.

The Australian No. 1, AFC suffered on of their number forced down, but they landed safely. Lieutenant Palmer, (skull cap) and Lieutenant Floyer. Victims of Oblt G. Felmy (*second from left, front row*). The Germans are smiling at their victory, the less-smiling British officers are probably simply glad to be alive.

Balance was restored to the RAF when Albatros D.III, 636/17 was brought down by Lieutenant R. C. Steele, of No. 111 Squadron, Palestine on 8 October 1917. The pilot was Oberleutnant Haegelstern. No. 111 Squadron was formed at Deir el-Balah, Palestine on 1 August 1917, with a mixed bag of single seat fighters as the first dedicated fighter squadron in the region. Its mission was to restrict enemy reconnaissance flights and challenge the German fighter presence over Suez. It was reinforced by Bristol F.2 Fighters in September. This capture of 8 October was the first aerial victory for No. 111. It handed over its Bristol Fighters to No. 1 Squadron, Australian Flying Corps in February 1918. In the background is an F.2b, soon to be handed over to the Australians.

The same Albatros DIII, 636/17, a different view of the German plane in Allied captivity with Australians of No. 1, AFC taking a good look.

Same again, the capture obviously was a matter of great pride and interest.

Sub-Lieutenant Reginald Alexander John Warneford, VC, Légion d'honneur, (1891-1915). Warneford's initial training took place at Hendon, passing then to Upavon where he completed his pilot training on 25 February 1915. During the course of training, the Commander of Naval Air Stations, R. M. Groves was quoted as saying: 'This youngster will either do big things or kill himself.' Warneford was initially posted to 2 Wing on the Isle of Sheppey in Kent but was quickly posted to an operational unit with 1 Wing at Veurne on the Belgian coast. Over the next few weeks, Warneford was involved in attacks on German troops and guns, as well as actions against enemy aircraft. His aggressiveness and effectiveness led to his being given his own aircraft and a roving commission.

On 7 June 1915 at Ghent, Warneford, flying a Morane-Saulnier Type L, attacked the Zeppelin LZ 37. He chased the airship from the coast near Ostend and, despite its defensive machine-gun fire, succeeded in dropping his bombs on it, the last of which set the airship on fire. LZ37 subsequently crashed in Sint-Amandsberg. The explosion overturned Warneford's aircraft and stopped its engine. Having no alternative, Warneford had to land behind enemy lines, but after 35 minutes spent on repairs, he managed to restart the engine and returned to base. On 17 June 1915, Warneford received the award of Légion d'honneur from General Joffre. Following a celebratory lunch, Warneford travelled to the aerodrome at Buc in order to ferry an aircraft for delivery to the RNAS at Veurne. Carrying with him an American journalist, he climbed to 200 feet when the right-hand wings suddenly collapsed leading to a catastrophic failure of the airframe. Accounts suggest that neither were harnessed and they fell, suffering fatal injuries. Warneford died of his injuries on the way to hospital. He was buried at Brompton Cemetery, London on 21 June 1915 in a ceremony attended by thousands of mourners.

Captain Henry Winslow Woollett DSO, MC & Bar, Légion d'Honneur, Croix de Guerre with Palm, (1895-1969). In 1916 Woollett qualified as a pilot and was assigned to No. 24 Squadron flying the Airco DH.2. On 5 April 1917 he claimed his first victory destroying an Albatros D.III. In the summer of 1917 No. 24 squadron switched to flying the Airco DH.5 and on 17 August 1917 Woollett became an ace, and was promoted to flight commander. Woollett returned to combat in March 1918 with No. 43 Squadron, operating Sopwith Camels. He achieved ten victories in March and was a triple ace by month's end. Beginning on 24 March, he began a series of 22 victories with Camel number D6402, making it one of the more successful airframes in the war. April saw him claim six more aircraft and five balloons. He shot down six planes on a single day—12 April. It was a record day unsurpassed by any pilot in the entire war. His total consisted of 20 aircraft destroyed, (including 4 shot down in flames), 4 more down 'out of control' and 11 balloons destroyed.

Captain James Ira Thomas 'Taffy' Jones DSO, MC, DFC, MM, (1896-1960). Jones was commissioned and undertook pilot training in August 1917. After completing his training, Jones was posted to No. 74 Squadron, where he formed a friendship with one of the flight commanders, Captain Edward 'Mick' Mannock, and it was with this Squadron that he earned his decorations for bravery. Jones recorded 37 victories in just three months whilst flying the S.E.5. Jones was once quoted as saying: 'It is wonderful how cheered a pilot becomes after he shoots down his first machine; his morale increases by at least 100 per cent. . . . My habit of attacking Huns dangling from their parachutes led to many arguments in the mess. Some officers, of the Eton and Sandhurst type, thought it was "unsportsmanlike" to do it. Never having been to a public school, I was unhampered by such considerations of form. I just pointed out that there was a bloody war on, and that I intended to avenge my pals.'

Major S. W. Addison (pilot) and Lieutenant Wilmot Hudson Fysh, (1895-1974) in Bristol F.2b Fighter, A7200. No. 1 Squadron AFC RAF. Addison had been promoted to major on 28 June 1918 and was the commander of No. 1 Squadron. Fysh, after being promoted to lieutenant, had been transferred to the Australian Flying Corps in July 1917. With No. 1 Squadron he scored five victories as an observer flying Bristol Fighters. All five victories were in Palestine where the squadron was based.

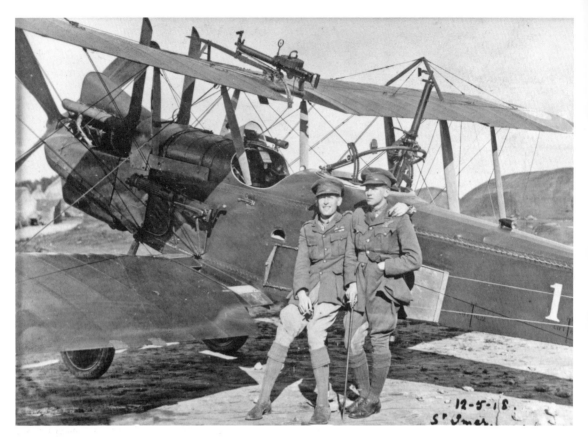

Captain D. F. Stevenson, DSO, MC; (*left*) in a somewhat familiar pose with his observer, Lieutenant J. W. Baker, MC, both with their 'gaspers' in hand, in front of their Royal Aircraft Factory R.E.8, E20, of No. 4 Squadron at St Omer, 12 May 1918. No. 4 Squadron concentrated on reconnaissance, standardising on the Royal Aircraft Factory B.E.2 in 1916. In the Battle of the Somme, 4 Squadron flew contact patrols keeping track of the position of advancing troops at low level, in addition to more regular reconnaissance and artillery spotting missions. The squadron re-equipped with the Royal Aircraft Factory R.E.8 in June 1917, in time to take part in the Battle of Messines and the Battle of Passchendaele. It remained equipped with the R.E.8 until the Armistice.

Captain George Edward Henry McElroy MC & Two Bars, DFC & Bar, (1893-1918). Looking older in this photograph than his 25 years, McElroy is standing by the nose of an S.E.5a , carrying four 25 lb Cooper bombs under its fuselage.

McElroy was appointed a flying officer on 28 June 1917. By the year's end McElroy was flying S.E.5s and claimed his first victory on 28 December. An aggressive dog-fighter, McElroy's score grew rapidly. He shot down two aircraft in January 1918, and by 18 February had run his string up to 11. He transferred to No. 24 Squadron and steadily accrued victories by ones and twos.

Captain George Edward Henry McElroy in an S.E.5 of 40 Squadron. McElroy transferred to No. 40 Squadron in June 1918, scoring three times, on the 26th, 28th, and 30th. The latter two triumphs were balloons, bringing his tally to 30. On 26 July, his friend, Edward 'Mick' Mannock, was killed by ground fire. Ironically, on that same day, 'McIrish' McElroy received the second Bar to his Military Cross. He was one of only ten airmen to receive the second Bar. On the 31 July he reported destroying a Hannover C for his 47th victory. He then set out again, but failed to return, having become the victim of ground fire.

Major Charles Philip Oldfield Bartlett DSC & Bar, (1889-1986). Bartlett was an RNAS officer of 5(N) Squadron with 8 victories. On 25 January 1918 he took his C.O. Colonel Dugdale up in his DH.4 N5974 for a 'joy ride' and to test weather conditions. Dugdale had never flown before, so he had the joy of experiencing heavy anti-aircraft fire! Here the pair pose for the camera.

Lieutenant Harry Rogers Jenkinson, (b. 1893). Jenkinson was born in New Jersey, but both of his parents had been born in England. Harry was part of the 'First 300', a group of US pilots trained under the aegis of the RFC. On 18 May 1918, he was posted to 73 Squadron, RAF, a Sopwith Camel Squadron then stationed at Beauvais. A few days later while on a ground strafing mission in the early evening, Harry's Camel took a direct hit from German anti-aircraft. His Camel was thrown upside down by the impact, but Harry managed to roll the airplane back over. When he finally got the machine under control he saw that the shell had torn away the rear spar of his lower left wing from the aileron all the way to the fuselage and there was a large hole in the bottom of the fuselage. He managed to get back across the lines and landed at Godevillers, but the plane was too close to the lines to salvage.

In January 1918 Captain Alan Pratt 'Lally' Maclean and Lieutenant Frederick H. Cantlon, MC, both Canadians of No. 11 Squadron, RFC, posed in Bristol F.2b C.4844, which they had named *Rickadamdoo*. They were flying this aircraft when they were shot down by fighters from *Jagdgeschwader I* on 18 March 1918. On 14 February 1918 in *Flight* magazine Maclean's engagement to Kathleen Fernihough had been announced.

Alan Maclean in his Bristol F.2b, C.4844, *Rickadamdoo*. The wedding was not to be. Maclean's obituary was announced in the unlikely publication of *Wisden's Almanack* for 1919. The crash on 18 March 1918 had been fatal for both men.

Sopwith Camel F.1 D8101, 'P', 66 Squadron, flown by Lieutenant Gerald Alfred Sigourney Birks, MC & Two Bars, (1894-1991). Birks was a Canadian pilot from Montreal. In October 1917 66 Squadron moved to join No. 14 Wing in Italy. Birks' third victory was on 2 May 1918, when he wounded Leutnant K. Kosiuski and drove him into a crash-landing his Albatros D.V. Two days later, Birks shot down and killed ace Karl Patzelt, as well as F. Frisch. In addition to killing both Austro-Hungarian pilots, he destroyed both their Albatros D.Vs. The new ace flamed another D.V a week later, on 11 May. He destroyed two Berg fighters in five minutes on a morning patrol on 19 May. The following day, he ruined another. On 24 May 1918, while flying wing with the redoubtable Barker, Birks was credited with shooting down Hungarian ace Leutnant József Kiss, CO of *Flik 55j*; Birks thus became a double ace. On 9 June 1918, Birks set another Albatros D.V afire in mid-air. On the 21st, he capped his list of triumphs by destroying another D.V over Motta. Birks' final tally at the end of the War was 12 victories.

Sopwith Camel D8239, 'R', 28 Squadron, with Clifford Mackay 'Black Mike' McEwen MC, DFC & Bar, (1896-1967). McEwen poses at Florence after the War; he was a Canadian Ace with 27 victories. McEwen had a long service career, he attained the rank of Air Vice-Marshal and retired in 1946.

Captain William Lancelot Jordan DSC & Bar, DFC, (1896-1931). Jordan was a South African who enlisted in the RNAS as a mechanic in September 1916, and subsequently volunteered to fly as a gunner. He received his pilot's training in 1917 and was posted to RNAS 8 Naval Squadron to fly Sopwith Triplanes. Shortly after his arrival, Naval 8 upgraded to Sopwith Camels. Jordan scored all 39 of his victories flying a Sopwith Camel. Jordan scored his first victory on 13 July 1917, driving a German Rumpler down out of control. His third through seventh victories were triumphs shared with other squadron members. One of these victories, his fourth, was achieved over German ace Adolf Ritter von Tutschek on 11 August 1917. RNAS 8 became No. 208 Squadron RAF when the amalgamation took place on 1 April 1918. Jordan thus scored 18 victories for the RNAS and 21 for the RAF without changing squadrons.

Camel B6344, 'G' aircraft of Captain James Hart Mitchell, MC, DFC, Italian Medal of Honour (1899-1921), 28 Squadron and his ground crew. After training, Mitchell was assigned to No. 28 Squadron. After his first three wins in France while flying a Sopwith Camel, the squadron transferred to the Italian Front. Mitchell scored eight more wins before being transferred out of combat duty in July 1918. By the end of the War No. 28 Squadron had claimed 136 victories. It numbered eleven flying aces among its ranks, including: future Air Vice-Marshal Clifford MacKay McEwen, William George Barker, Harold B. Hudson, James Hart Mitchell, Stanley Stanger, Arthur Cooper, Percy Wilson, Thomas Frederic Williams, and Joseph E. Hallonquist.

Lieutenant Arnold Shepherd and his Camel, No. 44 (Rhodesia) Squadron, 1918. No. 44 Squadron of the RFC was newly formed at Hainault Farm, Essex, on 24 July 1917. They were a Home Defence Squadron that pioneered the use of the Sopwith Camel fighter aircraft for night operations and achieved their first victory on 28/29 January 1918. One of their number was Clayton Knight, (1891-1969), born in Rochester, New York. He enlisted in the US Army Signal Corps hoping to join the aviation section. To speed up American training some 2,500 future pilots were sent to England and France for advanced pilot training. Clayton Knight was one of the original 150 American pilots sent to England in the summer of 1917. Clayton began his training with No. 44 Squadron. Knight was flying a DH9 on 5 October 1918 when he was shot down by Oberleutnant Harald Auffahrt the Commanding Officer of *Jasta 9*. The war ended while Knight was a prisoner of war in a German hospital. The knight's helmet may be no connection, but extra information would be welcome. At the end of the War No. 44 Squadron was commander by Arthur Harris, later to be known as 'Bomber Harris.'

Above: The life expectancy of a pilot was not high and many thousands died. Here German soldiers carry the body of a dead Allied airman.

Left: An aerial battle. This dramatic photo is one of Wesley D. Archer series of 'fake' shots, made using models, and included in *Death of an Airman*.

Early Aircraft used by the RFC and RNAS

The Avro Type E, Type 500, and Type 502 made up a family of early British military aircraft, regarded by Alliott Verdon Roe as his firm's first truly successful design. It was a forerunner of the Avro 504, one of the outstanding aircraft of the First World War. This early model was bought by a private individual, J. Laurence Hall, which was commandeered by the War Office at the outbreak of the War. Here Hall proudly stands in front of his Avro.

A Henri Farman of No. 30 Squadron takes off to drop food sacks over Kut, Mesopotamia, now Iraq.

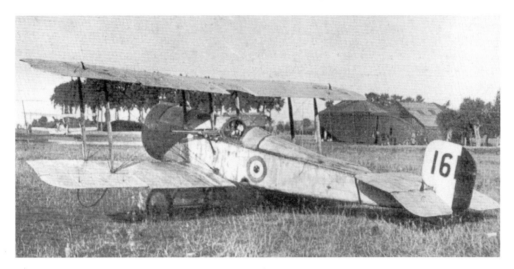

The Bristol Scout was a single-seat rotary-engined biplane. It was acquired by the RNAS and the RFC as a 'scout', or fast reconnaissance type. It was one of the first single-seaters to be used as a fighter aircraft, although it was not possible to fit it with an effective forward-firing armament, until the first British synchronisation gears became available, by which time the Scout was obsolete. It was introduced in 1914 and the final version, the Scout D entered service, November 1915. 370 Scouts were built.

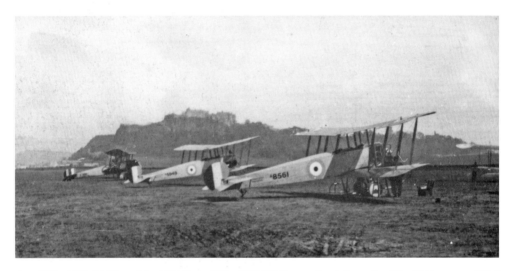

Avro 504a, 1913-14. The original 504 had a 80 hp (60 kW) Gnome Lambda engine. The 504A was modified with smaller ailerons and broader struts with 80 hp (60 kW) Gnome engine.

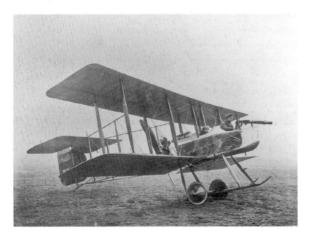

The Vickers F.B.5, (1915). Known as the 'Gunbus', the F.B.5 was a two-seat pusher biplane armed with a single .303 inch Lewis Gun operated by the observer in the front. It was the first aircraft purpose-built for air-to-air combat to see service, making it the world's first operational fighter aircraft. It came into service in February 1915 and 224 were built. .

De Havilland DH.2, of No. 24 Squadron, France, February 1916. The DH.2 eventually came into service in February 1916 and 453 were built. Geoffrey de Havilland designed the DH.2 as a smaller, single-seat development of the earlier two-seat DH.1 pusher design.

De Havilland DH.2, of No. 24 Squadron, France, February 1916. The DH.2 eventually came into service in February 1916 and 453 were built.

Royal Aircraft Factory F.E.2, two-seater, (1915). The F.E.2b was operated as a day and night bomber and fighter by the RFC. Along with the single-seat DH.2 pusher biplane and the Nieuport 11, the F.E.2b was instrumental in ending the Fokker Scourge that had seen the German Air Service establish a measure of air superiority on the Western Front from the late summer of 1915 to the following spring. A total of 1,939 were built.

Royal Aircraft Factory F.E.2b in flight. The F.E.2b epitomises the outstanding work of the Royal Aircraft Factory. It had a flexible mount for a single Lewis gun operated by the observer/gunner in the forward cockpit. A5478 was one of 50 F.E.2b built by Boulton & Paul Ltd at their Norwich factory and is a presentation 'gift', one of at least 10 from the Gold Coast (now Ghana).

Lieutenant W. C. Cambray, MC, demonstrates the 'rear guard' stance of all FE.2b gunners. Note plate camera fixed to port side of his cockpit. 20 Squadron, RFC, 1917.

F.E.2b B444 crashed Paddock Wood, Kent, 28 November 1917. *Courtesy Nick Gribble*

The Royal Aircraft Factory F.E.8 was a single-seat fighter designed at the Royal Aircraft Factory. Although a clean and well-designed little aeroplane for a pusher, it could not escape the drag penalty imposed by its tail structure and was no match for the Albatros fighters of late 1916. It was introduced to service August 1916 and 295 were built.

The Sopwith Baby was a single-seat tractor seaplane used by the RNAS from 1915. Sopwith Baby 8182 was damaged attempting to take off from the North Sea. It proved poor in anything other than a very light sea. 286 of were built.

The Sopwith 1½ Strutter was a one or two-seat biplane multi-role aircraft. It was the first British-designed two seater tractor fighter, and the first British aircraft to enter service with a synchronised machine gun. It was given the name '1½ Strutter' because of the 'one-and-a-half' (long and short) pairs of cabane struts supporting the top wing. 5,939 were built, of which 4,500 were built for France. It entered service in 1916.

Above: The Sopwith Pup was a single-seater biplane fighter aircraft. It entered service with the RFC and the RNAS in the autumn of 1916. The Pup was eventually outclassed by newer German fighters, but it was not completely replaced on the Western Front until the end of 1917. Remaining Pups were relegated to Home Defence and training units. The Pup's docile flying characteristics also made it ideal for use in aircraft carrier deck landing and take-off. Here RNAS Sopwith Pup 9927 is alongside HMS *Vindex*. 1,770 Pups were built.

Right: Catapult trials with a Sopwith Pup on HMS *Furious*.

Martinsyde G.102, (1915). The G.102 was a single-seat fighter-scout, bomber and reconnaissance biplane, powered by a 160 hp (119 kW) Beardmore engine. 171 G.102s were built.

A close view of a Martinsyde G.102.

The Royal Aircraft Factory R.E.8 was a two-seat biplane reconnaissance and bomber aircraft designed by John Kenworthy at the Royal Aircraft Factory. The R.E.8 had a speed of 103 mph and a service ceiling of 13,500 feet.

Right: An unknown pilot and observer/gunner in a Royal Aircraft Factory R.E.8. Although never a popular aeroplane, it was reasonably satisfactory for the tasks demanded of it and was even regarded with some affection, gaining the rhyming slang nickname 'Harry Tate' after a popular music hall artist of the time.

Below: The R.E.8 close-up. Although it gave reasonably satisfactory service, the R.E.8 was never an outstanding combat aircraft. Even so it served as the standard British reconnaissance and artillery spotting aircraft from mid-1917 to the end of the war and 4,077 were built. It entered service in 1916.

A pair of yoked Lewis guns on an R.E.8 of 15 Squadron, RFC. Far left can be seen the pilot's forward-firing Vickers gun. Some crews flew their R.E.8s quite aggressively; the German fighter ace Eduard Ritter von Dostler was shot down by an R.E.8 of No. 7 Squadron RFC, while No. 3 Squadron AFC was credited with 50 air victories in 12 months of operations. Lieutenants Pithey and Rhodes of No. 12 Squadron RFC were the most successful R.E.8 crew in air-to-air combat, being credited with twelve victories.

Preparing an R.E.8 for night bombing. By November 1918, the R.E.8 was regarded as completely obsolete and surviving examples were quickly retired after the Armistice. Nor was the type popular with the private owners who purchased surplus RAF aircraft after the war, and no R.E.8s came onto the civil register.

113 Squadron, Sarona, Jaffa, Palestine, 1917. *Left to right (back)*: Jenkinson; Lowrey; ?; Corporal Marly; Allen, Flight Sergeant Kelly; Marwood; Osborne. *Left to right (front)*: Wyatt; Ledger; Captain Lockyer; Tunny; Sergeant Williams.

An early form of gun mounting, in this case on a Nieuport two-seater of the RNAS, *c.* 1916. Sighting was the rifle-type of bead and range bar used by infantry gunners.

The Airco DH.4 was a two-seat day bomber designed by Geoffrey de Havilland and was the first British two-seat light day-bomber to have an effective defensive armament. It first flew in August 1916 and entered service in March 1917. The DH.4 proved a huge success and with a top speed of 143 mph was often considered the best single-engined bomber of the War. 1,449 were built for RFC and RNAS use and production was by Airco, and sub-contracted to F. W. Berwick and Co., Glendower Aircraft Company, Palladium Autocars, Vulcan Motor and Engineering, and the Westland Aircraft Works.

Flight Lieutenant R. Jope-Slade, DFC, 5(N) Squadron in DH.4 rear pit.

This picture is a mystery. The photograph is dated 8 July 1916, and yet the aircraft seems to be an Airco DH.9 which did not enter service until 1917. The assumption must be that the legend on the original photograph is incorrect. The location is outside the Thermae Palace, Ostend, with this particular DH.9 having fallen into German hands. The DH.9 was a development of the successful DH.4 and was ordered in very large numbers and 4,091 were built. The engine in the early models lacked reliability and did not generate the expected power, giving the DH.9 poorer performance than the aircraft it was meant to replace—the top speed being only 95 mph. The DH.9 suffered heavy losses.

F.2b fighter of No. 11 Squadron. The Bristol F.2 Fighter was a two-seat biplane fighter and reconnaissance aircraft. Despite being a two-seater, the F.2b proved to be an agile aircraft that was able to hold its own against opposing single-seat fighters.

Having overcome a disastrous start to its career, the F.2b's solid design ensured that it remained in military service into the 1930s. The F.2b was an important weapon in the RFC/RAF arsenal and 5,329 were built.

Bristol F.2b, D8084 of No. 139 Squadron RAF at Villa-Verla airfield, Italy, September 1918.

Above: Captain Ross-Smith (left) and observer in the front of their Bristol F.2b, 1st Squadron AFC, Palestine, February 1918. *State Library of New South Wales*

Right: A heavily armed Bristol F.2b with three Lewis machine guns. Pilots unknown.

A view of a Sopwith-Camel-F.1 from the rear. The F.1 was the main production version. Armed with twin synchronised Vickers guns. Altogether, 5,490 Camels were built during the War.

Camel F.1s of No. 45 Squadron, at Istrana, Italy, 1918. B3925, 'L'; B5152, 'M' B2494, 'S'—all of C flight. The official name was the Sopwith F.1. It gained its nickname because of the hump-shaped protective covering over its machine guns.

A fully-armed Sopwith 2F.1 Camel on the forward platform of a light cruiser.

Sopwith 2F.1 Camel at Mudros, 1918; with Major Graham Donald, RAF. Note the single Vickers gun.

Left: A Sopwith Camel pilot performing a loop over the English countryside.

Below: S.E.5a with a Lewis gun on the upper wing and a Vickers gun on the left side of the fuselage firing through propeller arc, 1918. *US Air Force photo*

Right: Royal Aircraft Factory S.E.5a's.

Below: S.E.5a of No. 1 Squadron, Lewis gun on Foster mount; Clair Marais, France, 3 July 1918.

The Admiralty, charged with coastal defence took great interest in the development of a bomber and Rear-Admiral Sir Murray Sueter (Commodore at the time, and Director of the Air Department of the Admiralty) placed an order with Handley Page saying he wanted a 'Bloody Paralyser'. On 18 December 1915 the O/100 flew for the first time. This was the forerunner of the O/400 pictured here.

More than four hundred O/400s were built by Handley Page before the end of the War. They were used principally for bombing the German Rhineland towns. The O/400 was powered by two 360 hp Rolls-Royce Eagle VIII engines. Its maximum speed was 97.5 mph and it had a range of 700 miles.

Members and staff on the Central Flying School's first course at Upavon, late 1912.

B Flight of No. 3 Squadron RFC at rest. On the formation of the RFC, on 13 May 1912, No. 2 (Aeroplane) Company, Air Battalion RE became No. 3 Squadron RFC, commanded by Major H. R. M Brooke-Popham, as one of the three founder Squadrons. In August 1914 the fighter squadron deployed to France as part of the British Expeditionary Forces on reconnaissance duties. In 1917 the squadron re-equipped with the Sopwith Camels. Note the gramophone and the pile of 78s on the far table.

THE FLIGHT THAT FAILED.

THE EMPEROR. "WHAT! NO BABES, SIRRAH?"
THE MURDERER. "ALAS! SIRE, NONE."
THE EMPEROR. "WELL, THEN, NO BABES, NO IRON CROSSES."

[*Exit murderer, discouraged.*]

Left: A Bernard Partridge cartoon for *Punch*, 27 January 1915.

Below: In an age when regular church-going was high, the Sunday service would have been of comfort to many men. Here a chaplain preaches from an unusual pulpit, the front of an F.E.2b at the depot at St Omer.

Old hand (supplying desired information to new arrival). '*Those things up there? Oh, they're canteens for the RFC.*' Cartoon from *Punch*, 5 December 1917.

No. 45 Squadron officers' Mess, at Fossalunga, Italy, 1918. No. 45 Squadron was formed on 1 March 1916. The unit was first equipped with Sopwith 1½ Strutters which it was to fly in the Scout role. Deployed to France in October of that year, the squadron found itself suffering heavy losses due to the quality of its aircraft. This did not change until it was equipped with Sopwith Camels in mid-1917. Transferred to the Austro-Italian front at the end of 1917, No. 45 Squadron there engaged in ground attack and offensive patrols until September 1918 when it returned to France.

She. '*Oh, was that a bomb?*'
He. '*Yes, I think it was. But if it was as near as it sounded it would have been very much louder.*' Cartoon from *Punch*, 5 December 1917.

No. 139 Squadron personnel on Armistice Day, 1918, Italy, possibly at Grossa airfield. No. 139 Squadron Royal Air Force was formed on 3 July 1918 at Villaverla in Italy and was equipped with Bristol F.2b fighter aircraft. It was disbanded on 7 March 1919.

Warrant officers and NCOs of No. 14 Squadron, 1918, in the Middle East theatre. No. 14 Squadron was formed on 3 February 1915. The squadron flew in support of British forces in the Third Battle of Gaza in late 1917. In November 1917 the squadron was equipped with Royal Aircraft Factory R.E.8s, which were used to perform reconnaissance duties, attacking the Turkish Seventh Army as it retreated following the Battle of Nablus. It was recalled to the UK in January 1919.

No. 113 Squadron, Sarona, Palestine, 1917. No. 113 Squadron was formed on 1 August 1917 at Ismailia as a corps reconnaissance unit. In September it began tactical reconnaissance and artillery spotting missions in Palestine flying R.E.8's against the Turkish 7th and 8th Armies where it remained until the end of the war. Returning to Egypt immediately after the war in May 1919.v

A German Holiday. *Punch*, 9 February 1916.
Child: '*Please Sir, what is this holiday for?*'
Official: '*Because our Zeppelins have conquered England.*'
Child: '*Have they brought us back any bread?*'
Official: '*Don't ask silly questions. Wave our flag*.'

A *Deutsche Flugzeugwerke* DFW C.V. This photograph is a bit of a mystery as the markings are not recognised and it appears to be in desert terrain. Accidents will happen!

A returning observation balloon. A small army of men, dwarfed by the balloon, are controlling its descent with a multitude of ropes. The basket attached to the balloon, with space for two people, can be seen sitting on the ground. Frequently a target for gunfire, those conducting observations in these balloons were required to wear parachutes for a swift descent—if necessary. (*National Library of Scotland*)

An observation balloon about to ascend, Ypres, 27 October 1917. The observation balloon most used by the Allies in the latter half of the War was the Caquot Type R Observation Balloon, named after its designer, a French engineer, Lieutenant Albert Caquot. It measured 92 feet long and 32 feet diameter and it could stay aloft in winds as high as 70 mph. The Caquot, with a capacity of 32,200 cubic ft., had sufficient lifting power for the mooring cable, basket, two passengers, and necessary communications and charting equipment when filled with hydrogen. (*Australian War Memorial Collection*)

In good weather, the balloon could ascend to over 4,000 feet with operations normally conducted between 1,000 and 4,000 feet. Depending on terrain and weather conditions, balloon observers could see as far as 40 miles. Because of their importance as observation platforms, balloons were defended by anti-aircraft guns, groups of machine guns for low altitude defence and patrolling fighter aircraft. Attacking a balloon was a risky venture but some pilots relished the challenge.

The ascent of a kite balloon on the Western Front. October, 1916. Typically, balloons were tethered to a steel cable attached to a winch that reeled the gasbag to its desired height (usually 3,000–5,000 feet) and retrieved it at the end of an observation session. Successful balloon busters, included Belgium's Willy Coppens, Germany's Friedrich Ritter von Röth, America's Frank Luke, and the Frenchmen Léon Bourjade, Michel Coiffard and Maurice Boyau. Many expert balloon busters were careful not to go below 1,000 feet in order to avoid exposure to anti-aircraft guns and machine-guns.

Right: 'The balloon's going up.' This idiom is derived from the very fact that an observation balloon's ascent likely signalled a preparatory bombardment for an offensive. The photograph here is probably training in England. (*RAF Museum*)

Below: Almost everybody has heard of Zeppelins, but few realise that Britain had a substantial RNAS fleet of airships. The S.S.Z (Sea Scout Zero) non-rigid airships or 'blimps' were developed in United Kingdom during the First World War from the earlier S.S. ('Submarine Scout') class. The main role of these craft was to escort convoys and scout or search for German U-Boats. The first S.S.7 was flown in 1916 and 77 were built.

Coastal C.12 in A-shed at RNAS Polegate, October 1916. Submarine Scout *S.S.16* is in the background. (*The Fleet Air Arm Museum*)

Above: Submarine Scout *S.S.13* being walked out of the No. 1 shed at RNAS Polegate in February 1917. A trench ran the entire length of the shed, into which the control cars of the airships could be slotted, so they did not have to sit awkwardly on the concrete floor. (*The Fleet Air Arm Museum*)

Left: S.S.Z. 37 patrolling over a ship. (*IWM*)

FRANCE
The French Military Air Service—
Aéronautique Militaire

FRENCH MILITARY AVIATION TRULY began in 1909 when the War Ministry bought an American Wright aircraft. The French War Minister ordered that French industry produce French designed and built aircraft. By 1913 the French were exporting over 400 aircraft. Two Farman biplanes, one Wright biplane and one Blériot monoplane were bought and delivered in spring 1910. Military aviation was divided into two parts—half under the Artillery, half under the Engineers.

In March 1910, ten French military officers were sent to private flying schools, and eventually, formed the nucleus of the embryo French Air Service. The first military airman to pass out as a military pilot was Lieutenant Camerman with Aero Club de France Brevet No. 33. A Military pilot's brevet came into service use in March 1911 with the first holder being Capitaine Trocornet de Rose.

The aircraft in service in late 1910 were: 11 Henri Farmans, 4 Maurice Farmans, 5 Wrights, 4 Sommers, 4 Blériots and 2 Antoinettes. In March 1912 the French Air Service was formally constituted and formed into three branches: Fighter (*Aviation de Chasse*), Reconnaissance (*Corps d' Armée*) and Bombing (*Aviation de Bombardement*). These divisions were as the French military saw the use of aircraft.

When the First World War began in August 1914 the French Air Service comprised 21 *Escadrilles* (Squadrons)—the names of each reflecting the aircraft used: Blériot BL, Henri Farman HF, Maurice Farman MF, Deperdussin D, Dorand DO, Bréguet BR, Voison V, Caudron C, Nieuport N, REP R. There were also four cavalry escadrilles making a total numerical strength of 138 aircraft. The French Navy established an Aviation Service (*Service Aéronautique*) on 12 March 1912 and when war broke out in 1914 it possed but one *Escadrille* of Borel and Nieuport floatplane fighters at Fréjus Naval Base.

The first bombing raid of the war was made by Lieutenant Ce'sari and Caporal Pindhommeau in a Voison of the French Air Service against the German Zeppelin hangars at Metz-Frescaty on 14 August 1914. At war with the German Air Service in the new dimension—the sky; the French (and the Germans) had to work out aerial combat—there was no rules laid down in a handbook yet.

The first aerial combat with firearms was on 5 October 1914 when a Voison of *Escadrille* V24, piloted by Sergent Joseph Frantz with Caporal Louis Quenault as Observer, shot down an Aviatik of Flieger Abteilung No.18, using rifle fire. It was not long before aircrew began to fit machine guns to their aircraft. Caporal Stribick piloting a Henri Farman with observer David—shot down a German spotter aircraft using a Hotchkiss heavy machine gun, fired from the rear cockpit. Both airmen were awarded The *Médaille Militaire* for this exploit.

The first French single-seat fighter to down a German aircraft, with a machine gun firing through the propeller arc, on 1 April 1915, was a Morane Salunier Type G of *Escadrille* MS 23, piloted by Roland Garros. Garros fitted deflector plates to the wooden propeller to deflect bullets from the centrally high mounted machine gun firing forward. Eventually, machine guns were fitted to fire forward through the arc of the propeller—using synchronising interrupter gear. This changed the whole tactic of air fighting and the aggressive fighter pilot came into his own—being able to fly and fire his guns at the same time.

The French Naval Air Service introduced the FBA (Franco British Aviation) flying boat in January 1915, with an *Escadrille* based at Dunkirk. Later in 1917 the Tellier flying boat came into service and during October 1917 began to arm Telliers with 37 mm cannon to combat the U Boat menace. Other Telliers could carry a 600 lb bomb load.

New developments were put to good use by the farsighted French Commanders, who began to use fighters to keep away German recce and spotter aircraft from their troop movements during the Verdun Offensive of 21 February 1916. Success was achieved by flying near continuous fighting patrols which cleared the enemy from the Front.

The same tactic was used by the French during the July 1916 Battle of the Somme—again with excellent results from the Nieuport Scouts of *Escadrilles* Nos. N3, N26, N37, N62, N65, N73 and N103. This grouping of large numbers of aircraft resulted in the formation of permanent Combat Groups (*Groupe de Combat*) each composed of four *Chasse Escadrilles*. By 4 February 1918 there were 21 Combat Groups; these began to be amalgamated into larger Units. Three Combat Groups comprised an *Escadre de Combat* with No. 1 Escadre coming into being on 4 February 1918 made up of Combat Groups 15, 18 and 19. Three weeks later another *Escadre de Combat* was formed comprised of Combat Groups 11, 13, and 17.

Bombing Groups 5, 6 and 9 (*Groupes de Bombardment*) were also amalgamated into *Escadre de Bombardment* No.12. Bombing Groups 3 and 4 were amalgamated into *Escadre de Bombardment* No. 13.

On 14 May 1918 the 1st Air Division (*Division Aérienne*) was created—consisting of the above mentioned Units—under the command of General Duval. The *Division Aérienne* was used to great effect during the Battle of the Marne—15 July 1918—great numbers of French aircraft were switched from one part of the Offensive Front to any other as directed and required. During the great US Army offensive at St Mihiel—August 1918—the French Air Division was used, again with great effect.

Opposing the Allies were the best German Squadrons—including the legendary Red Baron—von Richthofen—and his 'Flying Circus'. But by 26 September 1918 the St Mihiel offensive was won and the final push forward began. However the German Air Service still had a sting in its tail—September 1918 was the worst month for Allied air casualties since 'Bloody April' in 1917.

During the First World War the French aircraft industry produced some excellent successful aircraft as the following alphabetical list demonstrates:

FRENCH AIRCRAFT OF THE FIRST WORLD WAR

Blériot X1 aircraft
Recce unarmed single-seater , two and three seat X1-2 génie(Engineer) and X1-2 Artillerie(Artillery) marques—used until mid 1915.

Bréguet aircraft
The Bréguet biplane was a metal covered fuselage with a tractor power engine. Prior to the First World War the Bréguet was in service with *Escadrille* BR 17 only.

The two-seat recce/bomber Biplane Bréguet 14 had an advanced metal fuselage for its time. The pilot's seat was armoured to protect against ground fire. Main marks were: Bréguet A2 recce and Bréguet B2 day bomber which came into service during 1917.

The Bréguet 2, 4 and 5 were two-seat pusher propeller biplane bombers which came into service during 1915. Some 45 were bought by the British RNAS and used with success.

Caudron aircraft
Type G2 single-seat recce biplane with twin boomed tails. The G2 was followed by the improved G3 two-seater with 80 hp Gnome engine which served as an unarmed recce/bomber until 1917. When war broke out the French Air Service had but one Caudron G3 six strong Unit—*Escadrille* C11—which was used by the Army for artillery spotting. The single engined G3 was in service in Mesopotamia with the RFC and in Italy, Belgium and Russia. The United States used the G3 as a trainer. Next marque was the twin engined G4 bomber armed with one or two machine guns—used in formation in daylight bombing raids on the German Rhineland.

The more powerfully-engined G6 came after the G4 but the later (June 1915) R4 was successful as a heavily armed photo recce aircraft and *Escadrille* C46 shot down 34 German opponents. The French ace Capitaine Lecour Grandmaison—flying an R4 on the 10 May 1917—was shot down and killed as was one of his gunners Caporal Crozet. The second gunner, Sergeant Boye, took the controls and crash landed the aircraft in French territory.

The R11 was heavily armed with five machine guns—one firing downwards. This heavy firepower proved successful in a bomber escort role in July 1918 during the French bomber offensive.

Deperdussin TT aircraft
The two-seat recce shoulder wing monoplanes were used in small numbers at the beginning of the war. *Escadrilles* D4 and D6 were the only Units equipped with the TT Model—the British Royal Navy bought several for evaluation; but the aircraft was out of date, with wing warping flying controls and it was soon obsolete.

Dorand aircraft
DO 1 two-seat recce biplanes used in early part of the war by *Escadrille* DO22. It was not successful and was replaced by another Marque. Later models were the AR1 and AR2 used in 1917 to 1918—18 *Escadrilles* were equipped with the later Marks.

Farman aircraft

The British born but France-based Farman brothers—Henri and Maurice—designed and produced a series of successful two-seat pusher biplane aircraft. Each brother produced his own design of aircraft using their names independently using the same factory.

Henri Farman produced the F.20, F.21, F.22 and F.27. These were underpowered two-seat pusher type recce biplanes—which could be used as light bombers. By 1915 they were relegated to training duties. The F.27 was a metal skeletoned four wheel aircraft of which 80 were bought by the British and used in Africa, Middle East and the Dardanelles by the RNAS and RFC.

The Maurice MF.7 (Type 1913) and MF.11 (Type 1914) were early type aircraft, two-seaters with the observer in front with a Lewis or Hotchkiss machine. Power units were De Dion or Renault engines. The MF.7 was nicknamed the 'Longhorn' and the MF.11 the 'Shorthorn' due to their appearance—outriggers and frontal elevators being used on the former type.

In 1915 the Farman brothers pooled the best parts of their designs and came up with the Farman F.30, F.40, F.41, F.56, F.60 and F.61 aircraft. The F.40 was a two-seat pusher powered biplane armed with a Lewis gun—and occasionally with Le Prieur rockets fitted to the wings. A few light bombs could be carried. The F.30 was used mainly by the Russian aviation service. The F.50 Bn2. was a two-seater twin engined tractor propelled heavy night bomber—carrying 1000 lb of bombs—which saw action in September 1918, with *Escadrilles* F.110 and F.114. Early in 1917 most Farmans (Except the F50 Bn2) were made obsolete by the French Government.

Hanriot aircraft

Built by M. Hanriot the Hanriot HD-1 single-seat biplane fighter designed by Dupont—came into service in 1916. Strangely, the aircraft proved most popular with the Belgian and Italian air services. Major Willy Coppens (37 victories) was the outstanding exponent of the HD-1.

Morane–Saulnier aircraft (MS)

Morane and Saulnier began to design and build aircraft in 1911 and their Type L Parasol monoplanes were considered to be the first fighters. The first MS aircraft to come into service with the RFC in small numbers was the MS7 BB biplane in 1915

The L Type was fast and nimble and took a great toll of the German Albatros and Aviatik aircraft. The then Caporal Guynemer of *Escadrille* MS3 made his first kill in a L type with his mechanic gunner Guerder, on 15 July 1915. Flight Sub Lieutenant Warneford, RNAS, destroyed Zeppelin LZ 37 on 7 June 1915, flying MS L 3253. This exploit won him the Victoria Cross.

The Morane Saulnier N—known to the British as 'The Bullet' was a mid wing single-seat fighter monoplane. The French ace Jean Navarre used the N Type to gain kills over the Germans before he too was shot down and killed in action. Another ace—Pegoud—flew the N Type and downed six German aircraft before he too was killed in action.

Nieuport aircraft

Edouard de Nieuport began to design and produce monoplane aircraft before the First World War began. He had broken the world's air speed record on 21 June 1911, but was killed in an air crash on 16 September 1911. However his first designs of small well-built monoplanes were used in the First World War—outstanding being the Nieuport Type 6M (M meaning *Militaire*) which saw service with *Escadrille* N.12 and Italian squadrons. Some were used by the Russian Air Service.

During 1914 the Nieuport company acquired the services of designer/engineer Gustave Delage and retained them during the duration of the war. The first First World War design was the Nieuport 10 two-seat biplane—which could be flown as a single-seater as the N10 was underpowered when two guns and pilot and observer were carried. The N12 was larger with a more powerful engined version of the N10 with Lewis gun for the observer and a fixed Vickers machine gun for the pilot. The Nieuport 11 and 16 marques followed—single-seat biplane fighters. The N11—1915-1917, was known as the *Bébé*—from its small size. The N16 was bigger and better with a 110 hp Le Rhône engine.

The outstanding Nieuport was the N17 which came into service in 1916. Fitted with either the 110 hp Le Rhône rotary or 130 hp Clerget engines, the Type 17 was one of the outstanding fighter aircraft of the war. Nieuport Marks 21 and 23 were also produced. The Nieuport line continued with the 24, 27, 28C-1, and the Nieuport Delage 29 in 1918.

Letord aircraft

The Letord Marks 1, 4 and 5 recce/bombers were developed by Colonel Dorand from the Caudron R.4 twin engined biplane. The Letord 1 three seater—pilot and two Lewis gunners— went into production late in 1916 and came into *Escadrille* usage in 1917. The Letord 5 came into service in 1918 and was used for long range photography.

R.E.P. aircraft

Robert Esnault-Pelterie designed the Type N two-seat recce all red shoulder height monoplane which was used in small numbers 1914–1915 by *Escadrille* 15. Another design—the R.E.P. Parasol—was a two-seat recce aircraft—12 of which saw service use in the RNAS only. There was no French usage of the R.E.P. Parasol.

Salmson aircraft

Émile Salmson formed the Société des Moteurs Salmson in 1909 and produced the Salmson Type 2 late in 1916, with the prototype flying in April 1917. The two-seat biplane was a solid well-made machine—well liked as a reliable recce aircraft. Fitted with one Vickers and two Lewis machine guns it could give a good account of itself. One US Air Service pilot—Lieutenant W. P. Erwin—destroying eight German aircraft whilst flying the Salmson 2 A2. Some 22 French *Escadrilles* were equipped with the Salmson and 11 US Air Service Squadrons. Exactly 3,200 Salmson A A2 were produced.

Paul Schmitt aircraft

French, in spite of his German name, Paul Schmitt produced his Type 7, a big single-engined biplane heavy bomber. This type was developed from his pre-war Aerobus design of 1913 which could carry nine passengers. The Type 7 B2 had a 200 hp Renault engine, could carry 200 lb of bombs with a pilot and observer/gunner using the two machine gun defensive armament. Schmitt's Type 7/4 design had four instead of two wheels. The design quickly became obsolete and by 1917 no more were made. *Escadrilles* PS125, PS126, PS127 and PS128 were equipped with the Schmitt Type 7 and 7/4s.

SPAD aircraft

The most famous of French single-seat fighters—the SPAD. The acronym SPAD was derived in August 1914 from Société Pour L'Aviation et ses Dérivés (SPAD). The original pre-war acronym was Société Provisoire des Aéroplanes Deperdussin (SPAD). The Deperdussin TT was the generic ancestor of the SPAD—Louis Blériot having taken over the name in 1914.

The first SPAD A.2 was a two-seat biplane first flown on 21 May 1915. The machine was a tractor propeller using an 80 hp Le Rhône engine and having a forward firing machine gun. The observer/gunner was sat in a nacelle forward of the propeller! The more powerful SPAD A.4 had a 110 hp Le Rhône engine.

The famous single-seat S.7 followed in May 1916 with a 140 hp Hispano engine, and later even more powerful Hispano engines up to 200 hp were fitted. It was armed with a fixed Vickers machine gun firing forward, and some pilots had an extra Lewis machine gun fitted on the top wing. The S.7 came to the Front in late 1916 and quickly became popular with the dashing French pilots. The S.7 aircraft was the favourite of *Les Cigognes* (The Stork) *Escadrilles*—flown by aces such as René Fonck and Georges Guynemer. S.7s were used by Italy, Russia, Belgium, Britain, and the USA.

Further marques of the SPAD produced were the S.12, S.13, S.14 and S.17. By 1917 the S.7 had been replaced by the S.13. The S.14 was a seaplane type of the S.12. The S.17 was equipped with a large 300 hp Hispano Suiza engine in 1918. Twin heavy Vickers machine guns were mounted to fire through the airscrew arc. By the end of the war all but one of the French fighter *Escadrilles* were equipped with the SPAD marque.

Voison aircraft

The French used the two-seat Voison in great numbers as follows: Type 1 and 2 unarmed recce/observation aircraft, Type 3 armed with machine gun recce and observation, Type 4 ground attack, Type 8 night bomber and Type 10 heavy bomber.

The Type 8 was fitted with 220 hp Peugeot engine and was somewhat bigger than its forerunners. Unusually the aircraft was fitted with four wheels on its undercarriage—which proved remarkably effective. Almost 400 lb of bombs were carried.

In 1918 the Type 10 appeared with a bigger 300 hp Renault engine enabling it to carry some 600 lb of bombs. 26 *Escadrilles* were equipped with Voisins during the First World War and the French used them to great effect in bombing raids. By the November 1918 Armistice the French Military Air Service had 2,049 confirmed aerial victories with another 1,901 probables plus 357 balloons destroyed making a grand total of 4,307 victories. Aircraft strength had risen to 336 *Escadrilles* of which 74 were single-seat SPAD fighters. Personnel strength had risen from about 8,000 in May 1915 to 52,000 in November 1918. Aircraft losses were about 3,700, most of which, some 2,000, were during 1918.

THE FRENCH ACES AND AIRMEN

Victory totals are as accurately listed as is possible—however there is a wide difference in some totals. René Fonck is credited with 75 victories but his believed total is 127. Believed grand totals are in brackets.

French /British Rank equivalents

French Air Service	Royal Flying Corps	Royal Air Force
Colonel	Colonel	Group Captain
Lieutenant Colonel	Lieutenant Colonel	Wing Commander
Commandant	Major	Squadron Leader
Capitaine	Captain	Flight Lieutenant
Lieutenant	Lieutenant	Flying Officer
Sous-Lieutenant	2nd Lieutenant	Pilot Officer
Adjudant Chef	Warrant Officer I	Warrant Officer I
Adjudant	Warrant Officer II	Warrant Officer II
Sergent Chef	Staff Sergeant	Flight Sergeant
Sergent	Sergeant	Sergeant
Caporal	Corporal	Corporal
Soldat	Private	Aircraftman 1st & 2nd Class

Sous Lieutenant Jean Marie Dominique Navarre, (1895-1919)
15 (27) victories

Jean Navarre was born 8 August 1895 in Jouy sur Morin. He enlisted in the Army in August 1914 and gained entry into France's embryo Air Service—gaining his military pilot's flying badge No. 601 in September 1914.

He was posted to *Escadrille* MF8 then as a Caporal, to *Escadrille* MS12 Observation Unit, flying Morane Saulnier Type L parasol winged two-seat aircraft. The observation aircraft were unarmed but a variety of small arms were carried—for self defence and possible offensive action.

On 1 April 1915 at 0625 hours Navarre and his observer Lieutenant Robert attacked a German Aviatik north of Fismes—three rifle rounds were fired by the French aircrew—one round injured the German pilot forcing him to land. This was the third French Air Service victory of the war—gained by rifle fire! Lieutenant Robert was awarded *la Ordre national de la Légion d'honneur* and caporal Navarre *la Médaille militaire*.

Navarre was promoted to Sergent and transferred to *Escadrille* N.67 flying Morane Type N single-seat aircraft. When flying, Navarre always wore a lady's silk stocking instead of a flying helmet. By the 26 October 1915 his victory score stood at three—two Aviatiks and one LVG C. On 26 February 1916 he scored two more victories—a single-seat Fokker E.III and an unclassified two-seater. Two more victories were made in March 1916 followed by two more in April 1916—then two more in May 1916, making his total 11. His last confirmed victory was on 17 June 1916 bringing him up to 12, but he was also credited with another 15 probables making his score 27. On the 17 June he was shot down and badly wounded over Argonne. Navarre did not fly in combat again and did not return to active duty till November 1918 when the war ended. He flew for the Morane Company testing aircraft but was killed in an air crash on 10 July 1919.

Capitaine Paul Adrien Gastin, (1886-1976)
6 (10) victories

Paul Gastin began his aviation service on 24 February 1916, transferring from the army. He was awarded his flying brevet No. 1484 on 1 September 1915 at the age of 29 years. He was posted to *Escadrille* N49 and on 22 May 1916 he downed an Aviatik—killing both pilot and observer.

Two more victories followed in October and November 1916 and he was awarded *la Ordre national de la Légion d'honneur*. During 1917 he gained another three confirmed victories making his confirmed total six—with another four probables credited to his total. Gastin was promoted to command *Escadrille* N84 on 31 January 1917, then promotion to Capitaine on 19 April 1918. Followed by command of 23 *Groupe de Combat* on 24 August 1918. He was awarded *la Croix de Guerre* with eight palmes and a bronze star. He survived the war, reached the rank of Général and became a *Commandeur de la Legion de Honneur*. He died on 23 August 1976.

Capitaine Georges Marie Ludovic Jules Guynemer (1894-1917)
53 (88) victories

A venerated name in French aviation, Georges Guynemer was born on 24 December 1894 in Paris. When the First World War broke out he attempted to enlist but was turned down, perhaps because of his frail appearance and build. Determined to fight he persisted and on the third application succeeded in enlisting on 21 November 1914. He was posted to an aviation school to train as a mechanic, but this was not when he wanted and he applied for pilot training. He was posted to Avord to learn how to fly and on 26 April 1915 he graduated as Military Pilot No. 1832 in the rank of Caporal.

On 8 June 1915, he was posted to *Escadrille* MS3 under the command of Capitaine Brocard at Vauciennes airfield. On 15 July 1915 he brought down his first enemy aircraft—an Aviatik—which fell in flames to earth at Septmonts. This victory brought him the award of *la Médaille militaire* and on 20 July 1915 he was promoted to Sergent.

On 5, 8 and 14 December 1915 he downed another three enemy aircraft bring his total score to four victories. On his 21st birthday—24 December 1915—he was awarded *la Croix de chevalier de la Légion d'honneur*. His citation eulogy stated, 'that he had in six months taken part in thirteen aerial combats with great gallantry'.

On 3 February 1916 he engaged in aerial combat and downed two LVG C enemy aircraft within 30 minutes. Another LVG C went down on two days later—his score now stood at seven. On 15 July 1915 he was wounded over Verdun, but made a quick recovery and began to fly Nieuport Scouts. By 28 July another four LVG Cs went down—his score was now 11. By 23 September 1916 it was 17 confirmed when he shot down two Fokker E Types. At the year's end his total had risen to 25 victories and he was promoted to Lieutenant.

1917 dawned and he began to score at an incredible rate: two enemy down on 23 January 1917, two enemy down the next day and another on 26 January 1917 making his grand total 30. He was promoted to Capitaine on February 1917. His 31st victory was unusual—a Gotha G—and on 16 March 1917 he downed three enemy aircraft in the one day and another on the next day. By 14 April 1917 he had sent down 36 of the enemy. Seven more went down in May—four falling earthwards on 25 May 1917—two within one minute. On 5 June 1918 he was promoted *Officier de la Légion d' honneur* when he downed another two enemy in one day. Five more enemy were downed during July—one an Albatros shot down by 37 mm cannon fire from Guynemer's SPAD. August came and two enemy were dispatched on the 17th. His last official confirmed victory was on 20 August 1917 when he shot down a DFW C over Poperinghe. His score now read 53 kills—but—his probable total was another 35 victories.

At 0825 hours on 11 September Capitaine Guynemer took off and never returned. The French authorities issued a statement in which they said: 'Capitaine Guynemer disappeared whilst in aerial combat with a German aircraft over Belgium'.

The Germans later stated that Leutnant Kurt Weissman of *Jasta* 3 shot down Capitaine Guynemer—causing his aircraft to fall behind German Lines. The gallant Capitaine's body and SPAD aircraft were never located—a British rolling artillery barrage tore the ground into shell holes—losing his body for ever. So died one of France's greatest heroes—a truly gallant young fighter pilot. His valediction is inscribed on the wall of the crypt of the Pantheon in Paris. 'Fallen on the field of honour on 11 September 1917—a legendary hero, fallen in glory from the sky after three years of fierce struggle'.

Capitaine René Paul Fonck, (1894-1953)
75 (127–144) victories

The highest scoring Allied ace of the First World War was born on 27 March 1894 in the Vosges. When called to the Colours of France on 22 August 1914 he was sent for five months to the 11th Regiment of Engineers. However on 15 February 1915 he was posted to the famous Saint Cyr for aviation instruction. By 1 April 1915 he was at Le Crotoy learning to fly, and within two weeks he graduated as Military Pilot No. 1979.

He was posted to *Escadrille* C47 in the Vosges on 15 June 1915 flying unarmed Caudron G1Vs and clashed with an unarmed German recce aircraft on a observation mission. As both machines were unarmed it was a stalemate. On 2 July 1915 Fonck was flying again, but this time he was armed with a French issue rifle. Fonck was a crack shot and marksman, and when he came upon a German observation two-seater, he opened fire with his rifle. The German pilot turned tail and made for home as fast as he could fly. This aptitude for marksmanship was the key to René Fonck's large total of enemy aircraft sent down. Some enemy aircraft went down for the expenditure of but a few rounds of ammunition—properly placed. On the ground Fonck would practice with a Belgian-made Browning slide action rifle to enhance his prowess in aerial combat to deadly effect.

Escadrille C47 engaged in recce and bombing missions—together with hazardous gun-spotting which resulted in intense ground fire. On one occasion this resulted in Fonck making a hasty forced landing. René Fonck's first aerial victory was a Rumpler over Estrée on 6 August 1916 and his first French decoration—*la Médaille militaire* on 30 August 1916. He had been decorated with the British Military Medal on the 16 August 1916. His Caudron G1V was additionally fitted with a forward firing machine gun which improved its lethal performance.

On 14 October 1916, when on artillery spotting during the massive Somme Offensive, he shot down a rival German artillery spotter, but like many of his many victories this was unconfined.

Escadrille C47 moved base to Fismes on 17 March 1917, and Fonck had his second victory— an Albatros, one of five that he and another French pilot—Sergent Raux—clashed with.

Fonck transferred to *Groupe de Combat* No. 12—the famous *Cigognes* (Storks)—stationed at Bonnemaison on 15 April 1917. The famous Group—commanded by Commandant Brocard—comprised four *Escadrilles*: SPA3, SPA26, SPA73 and SPA103. These four *Escadrilles* were the cream of French military aviators led by some of the most illustrious pilots in the French Air Service: Guynemer, Dorme, Heurtaux, de la Tour, Garros, Auger and Deullin.

René Fonck first saw action with the Storks (SPA103) on 3 May 1917 when he and another pilot attacked two German spotter aircraft over Berry au Bac. Fonck—the superb marksman—loosed 20 rounds at one of the enemy who spun earthwards out of control—but this was yet another unconfirmed victory. His first confirmed victory with the Storks was a Rumpler on 5 May 1917 which brought his confirmed score to three. Another victory followed on 11 May 1917—the doomed enemy aircraft fell in flames onto French lines, another confirmed kill.

During July the Storks moved base to Dunkerque but began to come under German night bombing raids—also massed day attacks by swarms of Fokkers. The German attrition began to tell—the Storks losing many of their finest airmen. The French responded by putting their entire *Escadrille* into the air to give battle. On 9 August 1917 SPA103 was put into the air with Capitaine d'Harcourt in the van. Spotting a German formation of 32 Fokkers attacking French bombers—SPA 103 gave battle. René Fonck dived to the attack and put a Fokker down in flames —banking his aircraft, he shot down another Fokker. Yet again only one kill was confirmed—making his victory score seven.

By 27 October 1917 Fonck's score stood at 19 confirmed with many probables credited to him—but not on his official score. 1918 came and on 19 January Fonck began to score at a consistent amazing rate—two enemy downed; between 5 and 26 February five more victories. March—seven more kills. April three more downed making a total of 36 victories. Taking off in the afternoon of 9 May 1918, Fonck downed a enemy two-seater at 1600 hours, two minutes later another went down, three minutes later another went down—three victories in the space of five minutes, all two-seaters. Refuelled and rearmed Fonck took off again—and at 1820 hours shot down another two-seater—at 1855 hours another went earthwards and one minute later—another two-seater, this made a total of six enemy two-seater aircraft downed in one day. Confirmed victories now stood at 42 with many more probables unconfirmed. The award of *la Croix d'Officier de la Légion d'honneur* followed—the decoration being for this amazing feat of arms.

On 25 June René Fonck was back in the battle— three victories in the one day, followed by two victories on 27 June; total now 49 enemy aircraft. July 1918 was incredible—two kills on 16, two on 18 and three on 19 July; total 56 victories confirmed. Fonck's 57th victory was on the 1 August 1918—a two-seater over Hangard woods at 1100 hours. 14 August, three more victories and a grand victory score of 60 confirmed. On 26 September six aerial victories were achieved between 1145 and 1820 hours. Another seven victories were achieved between the 5 and 31 October.

Lieutenant René Fonck's last confirmed victory was on 1 November 1918—ten days before the Armistice—a Halberstadt C going down east of Vouzieres at 1420 hours making his victory total 75 enemy aircraft taken out of the air battle. Capitaine René Fonck died in Paris on 18 June 1953 aged but 59 years. He was the top scoring Allied ace with 75 confirmed victories, but with a probable total of between 127 and 144 victories. His wartime awards included: *la Croix de Guerre* with 28 palmes, Military Cross and Bar (British), Military Medal (British), Belgian *Croix de Guerre* and the Cross of St George (Czarist Russia).

Charles Eugène Jules Marie Nungesser, MC; (1892-1927)
43 victories (54)

Charles Nungesser was born on 15 March 1892 in Paris. He enlisted in 2nd Hussars and by 21 January 1915 was on ground hand to hand combat which earned him the award of *la Médaille Militaire*. Brigadier Nungesser personally accounted for four Germans in a Staff car with his rifle—then seized the car, and drove it back to French lines at speed under German fire. He was allowed to keep the seized German car as spoils of war.

Nungesser asked to be transferred to the French Air Service as he had previous flying experience—two weeks of instruction prior to the war starting. On 22 January 1915 he was sent to Avord to receive flying instruction and on 17 March 1915 was awarded Pilot's Brevet No. 1803. On 8 April 1915 he was posted to *Escadrille* VB106 stationed at St Pol near Dunkerque. A month later he was promoted to Adjudant. His first—and only—victory with *Escadrille* VB106 was on 1 July 1915 when he downed an Albatros over Nancy.

In November 1915 he was posted to *Escadrille* N65—having converted to fighter aircraft. His aircraft's fuselage was blazoned with the 'emblems of mortality'—a coffin with two lighted candles and a skull and crossbones. These symbols are Masonic and had appeared on his Voison 10 aircraft whilst in *Escadrille* VB106. He was made *Chevalier de la Légion D'honneur* in December. His second and last victory in 1915 was on 5 December when he shot down an enemy two-seater over Nomeny.

Nungesser was injured in an accident on 6 February 1916 and this kept him out of the air until 29 March. On 2 April 1916 he was airborne again and claimed a balloon downed over Septsarges. The following he shot down an LVG recce aircraft and the the day after yet another victory followed. On 14 April he was promoted to Sous Lieutenant and on 25

April another LVG C went down—making his score six victories. The next day another LVG C went down, but Nungesser was himself shot at by German fire. By 22 May 1916 his victory total stood at nine confirmed kills. His tenth kill is thought to be a German ace—Leutnant Otto Parschau, *Pour le Merite*, of FA 32.

On 22 June 1916 Nungesser was severely injured while flying his Nieuport 23. Flying over Verdun he clashed with two enemy aircraft and an hour-long furious dogfight ensued. Nungesser got the better of the two but had to crash-land his aircraft near his two downed opponents. By the 23 November Nungesser had taken his score to 18 confirmed. On 4 December he was awarded the British Military Cross and on the same day scored two more kills—his score was now 20 confirmed with many probables. His last victory of 1916 was an enemy two-seater over Touy le Grand and he ended the year with 21 victories.

Forced to go into hospital to have his broken and bruised body repaired, he had all his injuries attended to and managed to convince the Air Ministry to allow him to fly in combat again. On 1 May 1917 he was back in action—now with *Escadrille* V116—and scored two victories, both Albatros D.IIIs.

Nungesser's fame and prowess had spread to German lines—a German aircraft dropped a message on V116s airfield inviting Nungesser to a single combat duel over Douai. Taking up the gauntlet, Nungessor took off in good faith to give single combat. Over Douai he met—not one airborne knightly German pilot—but six duplicitous airborne German pilots. It was a trap in which the Germans came off worst—two of their number were sent down in flames.

Nungesser was then involved in a car accident in which his mechanic driver Soldat Pochon was killed—but the injured Nungesser returned to duty with SPA 65 on 31 December 1917 with 30 victories to his credit. He scored several victories behind German Lines but these could not be confirmed. Nungesser resumed his combat kills on 12 March 1918 and by 15 August 1918 he had 43 confirmed victories with some 11 probables to his credit. Ill health forced the gallant Nungesser to retire from combat flying.

He survived the war but disappeared over the Atlantic when he and a Capitaine Francois Coli attempted to fly to New York in a 120 mph Levasseur two-seat biplane on 8 May 1927. Charles Nungesser earned and was awarded: *Croix de Guerre* with 28 palmes and two stars, Belgian *Croix de Guerre* and *Croix de Leopold*, The US Distinguished Service Cross, British Military Cross, Portuguese *Croix de Guerre*, Serbian Cross of Bravery, Montenegro Order of Danilo, and the Russian Order of St George.

Capitaine Georges Félix Madon, (1892-1924)
41 (105) victories

Georges Madon was born in Tunisia, North Africa, on 28 July 1892, and qualified as pilot No. 595 at the Blériot School of Flying, Étampes, on 7 June 1911. He enlisted in the French Army on 12 March 1912 and transferred to the flying school at Avord on 1 January 1913. He won Military Pilot's brevet No. 231 and on 12 July 1913 was promoted to Caporal.

Madon was posted to *Escadrille* B130 as a recce pilot and on 30 October 1914 was in airborne action when he was shot out of the sky over Chemin des Dames, however he managed to land his stricken aircraft safely even though a shell had taken his Blériot's engine away.

On 20 November 1914 Madon was promoted Sergent. His unit was re-quipped with Maurice Farman aircraft and he was sent to Le Bourget to convert to the machine. On 5 April 1915 Madon and his observer/mechanic Chatelain lost their bearings in fog and inadvertently landed in neutral Switzerland. They were at once interned. Chafing at the inaction Madon and Chatelain escaped and tried to reach Italy, but were recaptured and sent back to their internment camp. The two fliers tried several times to escape and finally made it back to France 27 December 1915, where they were promptly arrested and confined to camp for sixty days—their offence was getting lost in fog and being interned!

Sergeant Madon was sent to *Escadrille* MF218 as a recce pilot but applied for—and was granted a transfer—to train as a fighter pilot. On 1 September 1916 he was posted to *Escadrille* N38 in the Champagne area flying Nieuports. On 28 September 1916 Sergeant Madon took to the air and downed a Fokker over Reims—he had his first victory. Two more Fokkers went down to Madon's remarkable marksmanship, earning him *la Médaille militare* and a reputation as a remarkable pilot. This reputation became known to the German opposition as he specialised in attacking the enemy over their own airfields. Many of his probables were gained behind German lines and were unconfirmed.

Sergent Madon was promoted Adjudant on 16 December 1916 with his victory score a confirmed four enemy downed. His fifth victory came on 31 January 1917 when he destroyed an Albatros near Suippe. On 15 February 1917 with his score at seven, Adjudant Madon was forced to land behind German lines when his engine spluttered and cut out. Landing, he repaired the fault and took off before the advancing german troops could capture him. He took off and machine gunned the Germans who had tried to capture him! On 5 May 1917 Madon was made a *Chevalier de la Légion d'honneur.*

By 20 May 1917 Madon had 12 victories but on 2 July 1917 he rammed an enemy aircraft in the heat of combat—crippling his SPAD. Madon just managed to land his stricken aircraft almost unscathed. His opponent crashed nearby. Capitaine Madon was killed in an air accident on 11 November 1924 in Tunis.

France

France was a pioneering aviation nation and was ahead of the UK before the onset of the War. The following small selection of images lists some of the French Aces and the more familiary French aircraft of the First World War.

Above: Eugène Adrien Roland Georges Garros gained his flying licence in July 1910. In 1911 he graduated to flying Blériot monoplanes and entered a number of European air races. Garros joined the French army at the outbreak of War and became the very first pilot to be referred to as an Ace. On 5 October 1918, he was shot down and killed near Vouziers, Ardennes, a month before the end of the War and one day before his 30th birthday.

Left: Colonel René Paul Fonck, Légion d'honneur, Médaille Militaire, Croix de Guerre, MC, MM and Belgian Croix de Guerre, (1894-1953). Fonck ended the War as the top Allied fighter ace. He received confirmation for 75 victories.

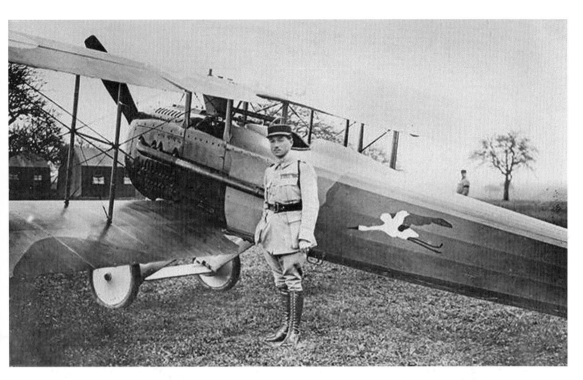

At age of 23, on 15 April 1917, Fonck received a coveted invitation to join the famous *Escadrille les Cigognes. Group de Combat* 12. He is picture here with his SPAD S.XII, with the *cigogne* (stork) painted on the side.

Fonck flew a SPAD S.XIII distinguished by the presence of a hand-loaded 37 mm Puteaux cannon firing through the propeller boss. He is apparently credited with downing 11 German aircraft with this type of armament, called a '*moteur-canon*'.

Left: Capitaine Georges Guynemer, Légion d'Honneur, Croix de Guerre, Médaille Militaire, (1894-1917). Guynemer was the first French ace to attain 50 victories and a French national hero at the time of his death. Guynemer became the first Allied pilot to shoot down a German heavy bomber, a Gotha G.III. His greatest month was May 1917, when he downed seven German aircraft.

Right: Georges Guynemer with Antonin Brocard. Felix Antonin Brocard commanded the famous Storks squadron (*l'escadrille des Cigognes*) in 1915 and recruited, among others, Georges Guynemer into the *escadrille*.

Lieutenant Georges Guynemer decorated by General Franchey d'Esperey in 1917.

Sous-lieutenant Jean Marie Dominique Navarre, Légion d'Honneur, Médaille Militaire, Croix de Guerre, (1895-1919). Navarre obtained his pilot's licence in 1911 and joined the French military in August 1914. He started with Maurice Farman aircraft and then moved across Morane-Saulnier 'parasol'. He was one of the first French 'Aces'.

On 17 June 1916, Navarre teamed with Georges Pelletier d'Oisy for Navarre's twelfth win. In the process, Navarre was shot down and sustained severe head injuries from which he never fully recovered. Navarre's younger brother was killed in a flying accident at about the same time. Navarre became close friends with fellow ace Charles Nungesser, who was as reckless and insubordinate as himself. In addition to their growing reputation as flying aces, Navarre and Nungesser also became extremely popular in Parisian nightlife for a number of colourful and unorthodox stunts.

Navarre and observer Sous-Lieutenant Jean Robert in front of their first victory, an Aviatik B.I which they captured with three rifle shots near Soissons. It was the first victory for Escadrille MS 12.

A victory parade was planned on the Champs Élysées on 14 July 1919. The high command ordered airmen to participate on foot rather than flying their aircraft. The 'heroes of the air' took this as an insult. At a meeting in the 'Fouquet' bar on the Champs Élysées, they decided to respond to this affront by selecting one of their number to fly through the Arc de Triomphe. Navarre, as the first among the aces, was considered the ideal choice despite his injuries. While practising for this stunt Navarre crashed and died at Villacoublay aerodrome on 10 July 1919.

Left: Capitaine Charles Eugène Jules Marie Nungesser, Légion d'Honneur, Croix de Guerre with 28 Palmes, Médaille Militaire, Croix de Guerre, Croix de la Couronne de Leopold (Belgium), Distinguished Service Cross (US), Croix de Guerre (Portugal), Cross of Karageorgevitch(Russia), Cross of Bravery (Serbia), (1892-1927). Despite being a decorated pilot, Nungesser was placed under house arrest on more than one occasion for flying without permission. He disliked military discipline and went to Paris for alcohol and women as often as possible. He suffered a bad car crash on 6 February 1916 that broke both his legs, and he would be injured again many times. This photograph shows scars on his face.

Right: Nungesser's silver Nieuport 17 was decorated with masonic symbols. He was rated third highest Ace in France during the War. After the war, Nungesser mysteriously disappeared on an attempt to make the first non-stop transatlantic flight from Paris to New York, flying with wartime comrade François Coli. Their aircraft took off from Paris on 8 May 1927, was sighted once more over Ireland, and then was never seen again.

Paul Gastin, Legion d'Honneur, Croix de Guerre, (1886-1976). Gastin was a French Ace who flew Nieuports. He served in four separate squadrons; *Escadrille* 23, *Escadrille* 12, *Escadrille* 49, *Escadrille* 84. By 1918 he converted to a SPAD.

Left: Georges Félix Madon, Legion d'Honneur, Medaille Militaire, Croix de Guerre, (1892-1924). Madon was the fourth ranked French ace pilot of the War with 41 victories. He served in four separate squadrons; *Escadrille* BL30, *Escadrille* MF218, *Escadrille* N38, and ended up commanding *Escadrille* Spa38 He is photographed here in flying garb leaning against his SPAD.

Right: Madon stayed in aviation after the war ended. Precisely six years after Armistice Day, Madon was killed in his native Tunisia preparing for a tribute to fellow airman Roland Garros. His aircraft suffered mechanical trouble, and he gallantly crashed it into the roof of a villa rather than hit spectators.

Very early days in French military aviation. An early Blériot monoplane is given a blessing by a Catholic priest.

Right: An airman's view, a marching infantry column.

Below: This damaged photograph shows a Caudron G.3; an early scout aircraft introduced in 1914 and designed by René and Gaston Caudron. The Caudron G.3 was a reliable reconnaissance aircraft, it could not carry a useful bomb load, and owing to its design, was difficult to fit with useful defensive armament. This particular aircraft has been captured and painted in German colours.

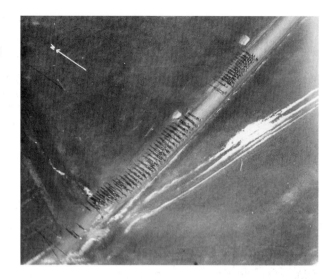

Following the outbreak of the War, Caudron G.3 was ordered in large quantities. The Caudron factories built 1,423 aircraft (2,450 total were built in France) and it was built under licence in several other countries (233 were built in England and 166 were built in Italy). The Caudron brothers did not charge a licencing fee for the design, as an act of patriotism.

This photograph is from 1918 when the G.3 was used by US pilots for initial training. 800th Aero Squadron—Flight B Caudron G.3 with Private McGowan, Wireless Operator. (*Air Service, United States Army*)

The Caudron G.4 was a French biplane with twin engines, widely used during the as a bomber aircraft. The aircraft employed wing warping for banking. The first G.4 was manufactured in 1915. Although the G.4 had a similar pod and boom layout to the G.3, it had two Le Rhône rotary or Anzani 10 radial engines mounted on struts between the wings instead of a single similar engine at the front of the crew nacelle. The wingspan was increased and the tailplane had four rudders instead of two. This allowed an observer/gunner position to be fitted in the nose of the nacelle, while the additional power allowed it to carry a bomb load of 100 kg. A total of 1,358 G.4s were produced in France, 51 in Italy and 12 were built in Britain by the British Caudron company. The gunner needed to be vigilant if he did not care to be chopped to pieces by the propellers.

Farman MF.11 *bis* of *Escadrille 62*, 1915. The chances of pilot and observer shooting each other seem frighteningly real in this photograph. The pilot, in the back, has a Hotchkiss 8 mm and the front gunner has a .30-cal. Colt-Browning. (*US Air Force photo*)

A clear photograph of a Farman MF.11 *bis* showing the overall framework of the pusher type aircraft.

A SPAD A.2 of *Escadrille* N49 at Corzieux. Early combat experience had shown it was desirable to have forward-firing machine guns. However, synchronization devices to fire a gun through the propeller were not yet available and several solutions were tested by various manufacturers. One of the most complex was that adopted by Béchereau. With this configuration—designed to combine the advantages of the tractor and the pusher types, the observer had a clear field of fire and vision to the front. However, this also seriously limited the pilot's vision, notably during landing, and made communication between the pilot and the observer nearly impossible.

Lieutenant Paul Hanciau poses in front of his Nieuport 11, the *Bébé* 'SOIT!' with its top-wing mounted Lewis machine gun.

A Nieuport 11, *Bébé* in the service of the British RNAS.

Nieuport 12 A.2. The 12 was developed from the Nieuport 10, a Gustave Delage design which had been introduced in 1914. The Nieuport 11 *Bébé*—a smaller aircraft, designed from the outset as a single-seater was developed from the 10, as also the Nieuport 12—a more powerful two-seater.

The Nieuport 80 E.2 was a later variation of the Nieuport 12. It was built in large numbers specifically as a training aircraft with the gun ring removed.

The Nieuport 17 was a slightly larger development of the earlier Nieuport 11, *Bébé* with a more powerful engine, larger wings, and improved aerodynamic form. It was at first fitted with a 110 hp (82 kW) Le Rhône 9J engine, though later versions were upgraded to a 130 hp (97 kW) engine. The 17 had outstanding manoeuvrability and an excellent rate of climb. It was introduced into service in 1916.

The Salmson 2 A2 was a reconnaissance aircraft developed to a 1916 requirement. Along with the Breguet 14, it was the main reconnaissance aircraft in use with the French army and the American Expeditionary Force's aviation units in 1918. At the end of the First World War, one-third of French reconnaissance aircraft were Salmson 2s. A total of 3,200 were built.

The SPAD S.XIII was developed by Société Pour L'Aviation et ses Dérivés (SPAD) from the earlier highly successful SPAD S.VII. It was one of the most capable fighters of the war, and one of the most-produced, with 8,472 built.

A French popular propaganda photograph, note the number plate on the motor cycle and the symbolic grave. An observation balloon being raised up adds to the imagery.

Opposite page:

Above: The Caudron R.11 was a French five-seat twin-engine bomber, reconnaissance and escort biplane developed and produced by Caudron during the First World War. This Caudron R.11 is at the Air Service Production Centre No. 2, Romorantin Aerodrome, France, 1918.

Below: A Hannover CL.IIIa, forced down near the Forest of Argonne in 1918. The German pilot was lucky to have hit nothing harder than a small tree stump.

THE UNITED STATES AIR SERVICE
1916–1918

D URING 1898, THE US Army Signal Corps operated balloons, and on 30 June the observation balloon of Sgt Ivy Baldwin was shot down by opposing Spanish gun-fire during the battle of Santiago, Cuba. On 1 August 1907, the Corps established its Aeronautical Division for aerial operations, and the US Army used aircraft for the first time on 10 August 1912. By March 1913, the first Aero Squadron had been formed.

Naval aviation had begun in 1908, when the US Navy bought and fitted an aircraft with floats. On 14 November 1910, Eugene Ely flew off the USS *Birmingham* in a Curtiss biplane, and on 17 February 1911, Glenn Curtiss flew one of his own company's floatplanes over San Diego Bay and landed alongside the USS *Pennsylvania*.

The US Aviation Section was merely part of the Army Signal Corps, with an original establishment (on 18 July 1914) of 60 officers and 260 other ranks. Late in 1915, the Chief Signals Officer—Gen. George Scriven—recommended an aviation service of eighteen squadrons consisting of twelve planes each.

The 1st Aero Squadron, comprising ten pilots, eighty-four other ranks and eight aircraft, saw service on the Mexican border in 1916 in a punitive offensive against the revolutionary leader Pancho Villa. The National Defense Act of 1916 provided an increase in the overall strength of the Aviation Section—with a new Reserve of officers and other ranks.

On 20 April 1916, the soon to be legendary *Lafayette Escadrille*—a French/American squadron equipped with seven Nieuport fighters and flown by American volunteer pilots—was formed in France, where it began to make its presence felt from its base near Luxeuil-les-Baines in the Vosges.

The squadron had begun as the *Escadrille Américaine*, but following protests from pro-Germans in the US, the name was changed to *Lafayette Escadrille*, being officially designated as *Escadrille de Chasse* Nieuport 124. It was supported by many wealthy and influential Americans—The France-America Committee—who believed that the US should be actively engaged in the war as an ally of Britain and France. The first commanding officer was Capt. Georges Thenault, with Lt Alfred de Laage de Meux as his second in command, and the seven original American members were Norman Prince, William Thaw, Elliott Cowdin, Victor Chapman, Kiffin Rockwell, James McConnell and Bert Hall. All their equipment and needs were paid for, and a bonus of $250 was given for every enemy aircraft shot down.

The only African-American aviator of the First World War was Eugene Bullard, who had transferred from the redoubtable 170th Regiment of the French Foreign Legion. He qualified as a pilot, obtained a commission and flew with *Escadrilles* Spa85 and 93, but his stay was brief. He transferred back to the iron-disciplined Foreign Legion, apparently unable to cope with the discipline of the French Air Service!

In total, 180 American pilots flew with the *Lafayette Escadrille*, their names and feats having gone into American (and other) legend. Eventually, in February 1918, the *Lafayette* was absorbed into the US Air Service as 103 Squadron.

On 6 April 1917, the United States of America entered the war on the Allied side. However, the US Aviation Section's strength was only 131 officers, 1,087 other ranks and just under 250 aircraft—none of which were considered battleworthy. In June 1917, the Aviation Section became the Airplane Division of the US Army Corps, and two months later all American air units in France were grouped into the United States Air Service (USAS).

Now at war, the US found that Britain and France were way ahead in aviation, but on 24 July the US Congress authorised $640 million for military aviation; 345 combat squadrons were envisaged, 263 of which were intended for the European war. Pilot and observer training began to get into gear, and was carried out in the USA, Canada and Europe. (By November 1918, the USAS was operating seven aviation centres in France.)

The USAS entered the European war when 1st Aero Squadron, under the command of Maj. Ralph Royce, arrived in France in August 1917. The squadron was equipped with French aircraft and trained as an observation unit at a French school. (It flew its first combat mission on 15 April 1918.) On 3 September 1917, Brig.-Gen. William L. Kenly was appointed Chief of the Air Service for the American Expeditionary Force (AEF).

The American build-up began, the Toul area becoming the centre of operations. On 14 April 1918, the 94th Squadron—the famously blazoned 'Hat in the Ring' squadron—had the honour of being the first to shoot down a German aircraft, when Lts Douglas Campbell and Alan Winslow dispatched two enemy aircraft.

The American forces came under sustained heavy attack by the Germans. Aerial battles were fought daily, and the gallant but inexperienced Americans lost heavily. The various squadrons were organised into one large group in June, the 1st Brigade, under the command of Col. Billy Mitchell at Château-Thierry, only 56 miles from Paris, and in August, Mitchell retaliated with overwhelming air power. He had eighty-nine squadrons under his control, plus nine British bombing squadrons—a total force of over 1,500 aircraft to attack the Germans at Saint-Mihiel. The assault was successful, and by 26 September the Americans had pushed forward into the Meuse-Argonne Front, again with heavy air power of over 600 aircraft. On 9 October, the heaviest blow was struck when 200 Allied bombers, 50 fighter bombers and over 100 fighter escorts attacked German troop concentration areas in two streams. USAS aircrew shot down over a hundred German aircraft and twenty-one balloons.

Among the many famous Americans who served in the war was Quentin Roosevelt, son of the 26th President of the United States, Theodore 'Teddy' Roosevelt. He fought officialdom to get into a combat unit and was posted to 95 Squadron at Villeneuve, but was shot down and killed on Bastille Day, 14 July, 1918.

By August 1918, USAS aircraft strength had risen to almost 1,500, and by the Armistice it had forty-five operational squadrons on the battlefront with a strength of 740 aircraft.

Aircrew strength was 800 pilots and 500 observers/gunners. In eighteen months of war, USAS losses were 289 aircraft and 48 balloons as opposed to enemy losses of 781 aircraft and 73 balloons.

UNITED STATES ACES

A TOTAL OF NINETY AMERICAN airmen were aces, having scored victories ranging from five to twenty-six. Four airmen were awarded the US Medal of Honor—Capt. E. V. Rickenbacker, 2Lt F. Luke, 2Lt E. R. Bleckley and 1Lt H. E. Goettler.

Captain Edward Vernon Rickenbacker, (1890-1973)
26 victories

America's top-ranking ace was born at Columbus, Ohio, on 8 October 1890. His Swiss parents' name was Reichenbacher, but this was changed to Rickenbacker when America entered the war on the Allied side.

At that time—April 1917—he was a sergeant driver for Gen. Pershing and went to France. Rickenbacker was a trained engineer and a famous racing driver, so his application to transfer to the Aviation Section was accepted and he was sent to 2 Aviation Instruction Centre at Tours. Qualifying as a pilot, he expected to get into the air war where his racing skills and quick reflexes would serve him well in split-second decision-making, but the Air Service saw another use for his skills and sent him as Chief Engineering Officer to 3 Aviation Instruction Centre at Issoudun. Not pleased, Rickenbacker learned advanced flying and gunnery skills in his own time and then bombarded officialdom with requests to fly on combat duty. Officialdom relented, and on 4 March 1918 he was sent to 94th Aero Squadron, commanded by Maj. Gervais Lufbery, on the Marne.

On 19 March, in formation with Maj. Lufbery and Lt Douglas Campbell, Rickenbacker made the first American patrol over enemy lines, his first victory coming at 1810 hours on 29 April over Baussant, when he downed a Pfalz D.III. By 30 May his victory score stood at six confirmed—another Pfalz and four Albatros aircraft. He was now officially an ace.

In June 1918, he suffered a severe ear infection and entered hospital in Paris for a mastoid operation. Returning to flying duty in September, he shot down another six enemy aircraft, and the following month he brought down eleven aircraft and three balloons, taking his total to twenty-six victories.

He was awarded the US Distinguished Service Cross, the *Croix de Guerre* and the *Légion d'honneur*, but, amazingly, America's highest award—the Medal of Honor—was not awarded to him until 6 November 1930 by President Hoover.

Eddie Rickenbacker returned to business life after the November Armistice. He undertook worldwide missions for the American Secretary of State, for which he was awarded the Certificate of Merit. On one mission his aircraft ditched in the Pacific and he and his crew had to survive in a life raft on the open ocean for twenty-one days with sparse rations.

The highly respected ace—the most successful US pilot of the First World War—finally passed away in July 1973, aged 82 years. His name will remain in aviation history for ever.

Lieutenant Frank Luke, (1897-1918)
18 victories

Frank Luke was born in Phoenix, Arizona, on 19 May 1897, of parents of German descent. Brought up in a Western-style environment, he could handle a revolver and rifle with excellence. He enlisted in the US Signal Corps on 25 September 1917 at Tucson and applied to transfer to the Corps' Aviation Section. He trained as a pilot at Rockwell Field, California, and was promoted to second lieutenant on 23 January 1918, and sailed for France from New York in the SS *Leviathan* on 4 March.

Luke was posted to 3 Aviation Instruction Centre for advanced flying training before going to Cazeau for a course in aerial gunnery, in which he excelled with his Western background. After continually badgering the authorities to get into aerial combat, on 26 July he was posted to 27th Aero Squadron and scored his first victory on 16 August. However, as he had left formation without permission, it was not confirmed.

Disappointed at not have his victory officially confirmed, he began to attack heavily defended enemy observation balloons, and his first confirmed victory was a balloon on 12 September. This was the beginning of an incredible series of victories. Two balloons were downed on the 14th, three on the 15th, and another two on the 16th. On the 18th, he dispatched two balloons and three enemy aircraft (two Fokker D.VIIs and one Halberstadt C-type)—within the space of ten minutes! On 28 September he downed one balloon and a Hannover C1, and three more balloons the following day, on his final flight, taking his confirmed score to eighteen victories.

Whilst attacking the heavily defended balloons, Luke was brought down, wounded by ground fire. Struggling out of his crashed SPAD, He was called upon by advancing German troops to surrender, but true to his Western upbringing, he refused, drew his Colt .45 revolver and gave battle. However, the odds were against him, and he fell dead from Mauser rifle fire and was buried by the Germans in Murvaux Cemetery.

He was cited for the DSC and Oak Leaf Cluster by his commanding officer, Maj. Harold Hartney, but it was felt that a higher honour was needed in recognition of his outstanding bravery. On being appraised of Luke's last moments, Maj. Hartney recommended him for America's highest honour—the Medal of Honor (not to be confused with the Congressional Medal of Honor). On 3 January 1919, his grave was found by US officials and his body was later removed to the American Military Cemetery at Romagne. Lt Frank Luke was posthumously awarded the Medal of Honor—the only wartime pursuit pilot to receive this accolade.

Major Gervais Raoul Lufbery, (1885-1918)
16 (29) victories

Gervais Lufbery was born on 14 March 1885 in central France of an American father and a French mother. At 17 years of age he travelled the world, and in 1907 enlisted in the US Army and saw active service in the Philippines, where he became an expert marksman.

When the First World War erupted, Lufbery tried to enlist in the French Aviation Service, but as an American had to join the French Foreign Legion first before transferring to the Air Service. He gained military pilot's brevet No. 1286 on 29 July 1915 at Chartres, and was posted to the Voisin-equipped *Escadrille* VB106, joining them on 7 October. For several months the Voisins of VB106 carried out daily bombing missions, but Lufbery wanted to be a fighter pilot (*pilote de chasse*) so was sent for pilot training.

On completion of his training, Lufbery was sent to N124, the *Lafayette Escadrille*, which had been formed on 20 April 1916, at Luxeuil-les-Bains. He was promoted to adjudant in June (and a year later to sous-lieutenant). On 30 July 1916, he shot down his first enemy aircraft, a two-seater, over the Forêt d'Étain. The next day he repeated the feat with another two-seater over Vaux. He became an ace on 12 October, when he shot down his fifth enemy aircraft, a Roland C.II, and was awarded a citation. His next victory was an Aviatik C over Chaulnes on 27 December.

When America entered the war, Lufbery was commissioned as a major in the USAS, and was awarded the British Military Cross on 12 June 1917—a rare honour for an American. He also brought down his tenth enemy aircraft that same day. His other decorations included the *Médaille militare*, the *Légion d'honneur* and the *Croix de Guerre*. Promotion to first lieutenant followed, and by the end of the year his score had reached sixteen victories.

He transferred to 95th Aero Squadron in January 1918, and later to 94th Aero Squadron. In spite of illness, he continued to fly with the squadron and had two further unconfirmed victories on 12 and 27 April.

Maj. Lufbery took off in a Nieuport on his last offensive combat on 19 May to engage an enemy recce aircraft. He scored hits but his Nieuport caught fire and he chose to die by jumping out of his doomed flaming aircraft rather than being burned to death. His broken body was found by French workers and immediately covered with flowers as he lay in a garden at Maron. He was buried with full military honours next day.

Captain Elliott Springs, (1896-1959)
16 (17) victories

One of the outstanding ace fighter pilots of the First World War, Elliott Springs was born in Lancaster, South Carolina, on 31 July 1896. He was educated at Culver Military Academy and Princeton University, where he learned to fly with the university flying school. In September 1917, he was posted to England to gain flying experience with the RFC, and was sent to France early in 1918, joining 85 Squadron, RAF, flying the S.E.5a. His first victory was over a Pfalz D.III on 1 June, which he sent down out of control. By 25 June he had destroyed three more enemy aircraft, but sustained injuries two days later when he was shot down and crash-landed.

After recovering from his injuries, he was sent to 148th Aero Squadron, USAS, which was flying Camels under the overall command of the RAF's 65th Wing. On 3 August 1918, he added to his score by destroying a Fokker D.VII over Ostend. This brought his total to five confirmed victories and made him an ace. Ten days later another Fokker D.VII went down under his twin machine guns, and three more Fokker D.VIIs were dispatched on one day, 22 August, for which he was awarded the British DFC and the US DSC. Other victories followed, the final one coming on 27 September, when he destroyed a Halberstadt C-type over Fontaine-Notre Dame, which brought his final score to sixteen.

Capt. Springs survived the war, entered his father's textile business and became a prolific writer on aviation themes. Recalled to the US Army Air Corps in 1941, he was promoted to lieutenant colonel. He died on 15 October 1959, aged 63 years.

Lieutenant David Sinton Ingalls, US Navy; (1899-1985)
6 victories

David Ingalls was born on 28 January 1899 at Cleveland, Ohio, where he went to school before entering Yale University. He joined the 1st Yale Unit (Flying School), graduating as naval aviator No. 85, and at the age of 18 enlisted in the 3rd Yale Unit for active service.

He was sent to France with a coastal protection squadron in November 1917, but in his own off-duty time flew Camels of 13 Naval Squadron, RNAS. (The squadron was renamed 213 Squadron on the formation of the RAF in April 1918.) He flew DH.4 bombers for two months with 217 Squadron before returning to 213 Squadron in August.

On 11 August 1918, he scored his first victory with 213 Squadron—an Albatros C-type which he destroyed over Dixmude. His excellent skills as a pilot were recognised and he was attached officially to the squadron, and on 21 August destroyed an LVG C over Zevekote. Between 15 and 24 September he destroyed three more enemy aircraft and a balloon—taking his total to six confirmed victories, which made him the only US Navy ace of the First World War.

Lt Ingalls was Mentioned in (British) Despatches and awarded the British DFC, the American DSC and the French *Légion d'honneur*. He survived the war and was recalled to duty as a lieutenant commander in the US Navy. During the Second World War he served in the Pacific and was awarded the Bronze Star and Legion of Merit. He died on 26 April 1985, aged 86 years.

Lieutenant Frank Lemon Bayliss, (1895-1918)
12 victories

Frank Bayliss was born at New Bedford, Massachusetts, on 23 September 1895. After enlisting in the US Ambulance Section he was sent to France, arriving there on 6 March 1916, and saw active duty on the Somme, at Verdun and Argonne. He was later sent to Serbia for three months and won a *Croix de Guerre* for bravery under fire. On 20 May 1917, he enlisted in the French Air service, receiving his pilot's wings on 20 September.

Bayliss joined *Escadrille* Spa73 at Dunkirk on 17 November, transferring as a sergeant to *Escadrille* Spa3—which was part of the Storks Group—on 18 December. His first confirmed victory came on 19 February 1918, when he shot down an enemy two-seater over Forges. Two more enemy aircraft were dispatched in March and another two in April, making him an ace. Between 2 and 31 May he downed seven more enemy aircraft, bringing his final total to twelve confirmed victories.

Preferring to fly and fight with the French, Bayliss refused the rank of captain in the USAS. He did, however, transfer in May with the rank of second lieutenant—but continued to fly SPADs with *Escadrille* Spa3—and on 12 June engaged in combat with four German aircraft over Lassigny. Outnumbered by the Triplanes of *Jasta* 19, he was shot down in flames onto Rollet village. The chivalrous Germans delivered an airborne message to French lines, informing his squadron of the death of the highest scoring American airman in French service. He was awarded the *Médaille militaire*, and in 1927 was reinterred at the *Lafayette Escadrille* Memorial in Paris.

Captain Wilfred Beaver, (1897-1986)
19 victories

An American serving with 20 Squadron, RAF (whose motto was 'Deeds not Words'), Wilfred Beaver flew Bristol F.2b two-seat fighters with observers/gunners Lt C. J. Angelastro, Lt H. E. Easton, Cpl M. Mather and Sgt E. A. Deighton.

Beaver and Angelastro opened their victory score on 13 November 1917 when they destroyed an Albatros D.V over Houthulst. Their squadron had been re-equipped with Bristol Fighters in August 1917 at Sainte-Marie, and Beaver and his gunners used the excellent aircraft to best advantage. They began to destroy enemy aircraft on a regular basis, with two victories in December, two more in January and five in February 1918. This took their total to ten enemy destroyed or sent down out of control.

Another two victories followed in March and April, and May saw the Bristol Fighter two-man aircrew score six more, including the downing on the 27th of three enemy aircraft—an Albatros and two Fokker Dr.Is—over Armentières within three minutes: the Albatros was sent down out of control at 1125 hours, the first Fokker Dreidecker (Triplane) was destroyed at 1127 hours, and the other at 1128 hours—and two days later Beaver and Deighton destroyed another Fokker Dreidecker. Their last victory—an Albatros D.V—came on 13 June.

Capt. Beaver was awarded the British MC on 22 June 1918. His RAF gunners/observers are credited shared victories as follows: Deighton—fifteen; Angelastro—nine; Mather—eight; Easton—seven.

Lieutenant Douglas Campbell, (1896-1990)
6 victories

Of Scottish descent, Douglas Campbell was born in California on 7 June 1896. Educated at Harvard and Cornell Universities, he learned to fly in America on a Curtiss JN-4 (Jenny). He was posted to France and completed his flying training at Issoudun, and on 1 March 1918 joined 94th Aero Squadron, serving alongside America's top ace Eddie Rickenbacker under the command of Maj. Lufbery at Villeneuve les Vertus airfield, Marne, which was awaiting its quota of Nieuport 28 fighters.

Campbell was the first American pilot of the Great War to shoot down a German aircraft—a Pfalz D.III on 14 April 1918. He and Lt Alan Winslow had taken off in a hurry at 0715 hours and closed in combat with two enemy two-seaters over Toul. Campbell opened fire and shot down in flames one of the aircraft, Winslow shooting down the other seconds later.

On 18 and 19 May, Campbell destroyed another two enemy aircraft—both Rumpler C-types—and downed a Pfalz D.III of *Jasta* 65 over Montsec on the 27th of the month. Four days later, when he shot down a Rumpler C-type of FA 242 over Lironville, he became the first American ace of the First World War. His final victory came on 5 June, when he shared victory over a Rumpler C-type over Mailly with his squadron colleague Lt James A. Meissner.

The next day, when in combat with a Rumpler, Campbell was wounded in the back by fire from the enemy gunner. In great pain from his wound, he managed to land and was taken to hospital. He convalesced in America and returned to France in November after the Armistice, being promoted to captain in spring 1919. As well as the US DSC with Four Oak Leaves, he had been awarded the French *Légion d'honneur* and *Croix de Guerre* with two palms.

When Douglas Campbell left the USAS he went into civil aviation. He died in Greenwich, Connecticut, on 16 December 1990, aged 94 years—a grand innings for a famous and gallant American ace.

Despite having been the first in flight, American technology had fallen behind. France and the UK, under the technological stimulus of war had made great strides forward. Therefore, when the United States entered the war, they commenced by buying French and British machines. Many, such as the De Havilland DH.4 were built under licence in the USA.

Prior to 1917, many Americans, seeking the thrill of flying in warfare had joined the Frech service in the *Lafayette Escadrille*. In total, 180 American pilots flew with the *Lafayette Escadrille*, their names and feats having gone into American (and other) legend. Eventually, in February 1918, the *Lafayette* was absorbed into the US Air Service as 103 Squadron. This illustration section understandably starts with the *Lafayette Escadrille*.

Left: Lieutenant Le Maitre of the French Aviation Forces in America explains the mechanism of a Nieuport biplane to an American pilot, Fort Monroe, Virginia.

Below: Escadrille Lafayette pilots with a Nieuport, 16 March1916. † = killed in action. *From left to right:* Victor Chapman†, Elliott Cowdin, William Thaw, Norman Prince†, Bert Hall, Robert Rockwell, Lieutenant Delnage, James McConnell† and Capitaine Georges Thenault.

Capitaine Georges Thenault, French Aviation Service, at Langley Field, Virginia, 4 October 1922. (*Library of Congress*)

Escadrille Lafayette, July 1917. *From left to right standing:* Robert Soubiron, James Doolittle†, Andrew Campbell†, Edwin Parsons, Ray Bridgman, William Dugan, Douglas MacMonagle†, Walter Lovell, Harold Willis, Jones, David Peterson and Antoine de Maison-Rouge. *From left to right sitting:* Dudley Hill, Didier Masson with 'Soda', William Thaw, Georges Thenault, Raoul Lufbery† with 'Whiskey', Charles Johnson, Stephen Bigelow and Robert Rockwell.

Escadrille Lafayette. Forty-three Americans volunteered to serve in the French Foreign Legion the month war was declared against France. *From left to right:* Alfred de Laage de Meux, Charles Chouteau Johnson, Laurence Rumsey, Jr., Victor Chapman†, Elliott Cowdin, William Thaw, Norman Prince†, Bert Hall, Robert Rockwell, Lieutenant Delnage, James McConnell†, William Thaw, Raoul Lufbery†, Kiffin Rockwell, Didier Masson, Norman Prince†, and standing far right, hands in pockets is Bert Hall.

Escadrille Lafayette, a final group shot. *From left to right:* Kiffin Rockwell, Capitaine Georges Thenault, behind Thénault, obscured, is Bill Thaw, Norman Prince†, Alfred de Laage de Meux, Elliott Cowdin, Bert Hall, Victor Chapman†, Elliott Cowdin, William Thaw, Norman Prince†, Bert Hall, Robert Rockwell, Lieutenant Delnage, James McConnell† and Victor Chapman†.

The French commander of *L'Escadrille de Lafayette* and four brave, young, American volunteers, all of whom gave their lives. *From left to right:* James McConnell†, Kiffin Rockwell†, the French Commander, Capt. Georges Thénault, Norman Prince† and Victor Chapman†.

Sergeant Norman Prince, Croix de Guerre, Médaille Militaire,Croix de la Légion d'Honneur, (1887-1916). Prince was a leading founder of France's Lafayette Escadrille with William Thaw II, Elliott C. Cowdin, Frazier Curtis, and Greeley S. Curtis, Jr. On 12 October 1916 Prince flew as an escort for a bombing raid on the Mauser rifle works at Oberndorf during which he shot down an enemy plane. Returning to base, his landing wheels hit telegraph cables near his air base and his plane flipped over and crashed. He was severely injured and died on 15 October.

Kiffin Yates Rockwell, Médaille Militaire, Croix de guerre, (1892–1916). Kiffin Rockwell was a member of *L'Escadrille de Lafayette*. On 18 May 1916, Rockwell attacked and shot down a German plane over the Alsace battlefield. For this action he was awarded the *Médaille Militaire* and the *Croix de Guerre*. On 23 September 1916, during a fight with a two-man reconnaissance plane, Rockwell was shot through the chest and killed instantly.

Kiffin Rockwell was first buried in the cemetery at Luxeuil-les-Bains, but his remains were later moved to the *Escadrille Lafayette* Memorial at Marnes-la-Coquette. He became the second American airman to die in combat in France.

Weston Birch 'Bert' Hall, (1885-1948). Bert Hall was not quite an Ace, as he had only four confirmed victories. He was one of the seven original members of the *Escadrille Lafayette* but supposedly he was greatly disliked by his comrades. Upon joining the French Air Service, he claimed to have flying experience, but when he was asked to prove it, he rolled a training aircraft down the runway and crashed into a barn, wrecking the airplane. He then confessed he had never flown before. Nonetheless, the French were greatly impressed by his audacity and kept him.

Bert Hall standing in front of his Nieuport 11. He was an outrageous adventurer, he did get four confirmed kills, several medals and was the squadron adjutant. He was a good poker player who could read his opponents and usually cleaned the table.

Gervais Raoul Lufbery, Légion d'Honneur, Médaille Militaire, Croix de Guerre, MM (UK), (1885-1918). Lufbery, a French-American fighter pilot volunteered for French service and became an early member of the *Escadrille Lafayette*. He joined the unit on 24 May 1916 and was assigned a Nieuport fighter. Lufbery spoke English with a thick French accent and had little in common with his comrades, most of whom were from wealthy families and were Ivy League educated. Once in combat, though, his dogged determination and success earned him the respect and admiration of his peers.

One night while the squadron was resting in Paris, Lieutenant-Colonel William Thaw bought a lion which had been born on a boat from Africa. After taking him around Paris, the pilots took him back to Luxeuil. He was named 'Whiskey', as he had a taste for a saucer full of whiskey. Here Whiskey is with Lufbery. He followed him around the base like a dog.

Lieutenant-Colonel William Thaw, who had been responsible for the acquisition of Whiskey. Whiskey, later joined by Soda, was popular with the men of the *Escadrille*, and the cubs were afforded a great deal of freedom to roam as they pleased. (*US Air Force photo*)

Lufbery raised Whiskey for several years. Later, Whiskey was given a playmate, named Soda since she got on so well with Whiskey. Soda was wilder than Whiskey and would spit and claw at anyone who came near with the notable exception of Lufbery. In this photograph Whiskey is gnawing on the ace Raoul Lufbery as Soda and pilot Douglas MacMonagle watch.

Officially, all but one of Lufbery's 17 combat victories came while flying in French units. After the US entry into the War he was commissioned into the United States Army Air Service in late 1917. Lufbery was chosen to become the commanding officer of the yet-unformed 94th Aero Squadron with the rank of major. His principal job was to instruct the new pilots such as Eddie Rickenbacker in combat techniques. On 19 May 1918, Lufbery took off in his Nieuport 28 in an attempt to intercept a Rumpler near to the 94th's home airfield. Closing in to attack, the German gunner's fire hit the Nieuport. What happened next has been a matter of debate, but Lufbery died and was buried with full military honours.

Captain Edward 'Eddie' Vernon Rickenbacker, Medal of Honor, Distinguished Service Cross (9), Légion d'Honneur, Croix de Guerre, (1890-1973), 26 victories.

'Eddie' Rickenbacker received the Medal of Honor and was America's most successful fighter ace in the War. Rickenbacker was placed in one of America's air combat units, the 94th Aero Squadron, informally known as the 'Hat-in-the-Ring' Squadron after its insignia, partially visible in this photograph.

Before the War Rickenbacker was well known as a race car driver, competing in the Indianapolis 500 four times and earning the nickname 'Fast Eddie'.

Captain Edward V. Rickenbacker of the 94th Aero Squadron with his SPAD S.XIII. The 'Hat-in-the-Ring' Squadron insignia is more visible in this photograph.

Lieutenant Frank Luke Jr., Medal of Honor, Distinguished Service Cross (2), Croce al Merito di Guerra (Italy), (1897-1918) was ranked second among US Army Air Service Aces after Eddie Rickenbacker. His official score was 18 and he was the first airman to receive the Medal of Honor.

Because of his arrogance and his occasional tendencies to fly alone and to disobey orders, Luke was disliked by some of his peers and superiors. But the 27th was under standing orders to destroy German observation balloons. Because of this, Luke, along with his friend Lieutenant Joseph Wehner, continually volunteered to attack the balloons notwithstanding the anti-aircraft guns. The two pilots began a remarkable string of victories together, with Luke attacking the balloons and Wehner flying protective cover. Wehner was killed in action on 18 September 1918. On the same day Luke was photographed with his 13th official kill.

On 28 September 1918 Luke made his final flight. He was killed by a single bullet, fired from a hilltop machine gun position. Eddie Rickenbacker said of Luke: 'He was the most daring aviator and greatest fighter pilot of the entire war. His life is one of the brightest glories of our Air Service. He went on a rampage and shot down fourteen enemy aircraft, including ten balloons, in eight days. No other ace, even the dreaded Richthofen, had ever come close to that.'

Captain Elliott White Springs, (1896-1959). Springs enlisted in the autumn of 1917.and was sent to England to train with the RAF, and was selected by Billy Bishop to fly the S.E.5 with 85 Squadron over France. After claiming three destroyed, Springs was himself shot down on 27 June 1918, but survived. After recovering from wounds received, he was reassigned to the US Air Service's 148th Aero Squadron, flying the Camel under the operational control of the RAF's 65th Wing. By 24 September 1918 Springs had claimed 10 victories destroyed, 2 shared destroyed and 4 driven down 'out of control'. He had shared three wins with such squadron mates as Lieutenants Henry Clay and Orville Ralston; all in all Springs achieved a total of 16 victories.

Captain Harvey Weir Cook, Distinguished Service Cross with Oak Leaf Cluster, (1892-1943). 'Weir', as he was known, left Washington and Jefferson University to drive an ambulance in France early in 1917. When the US entered the war, Cook enlisted in the aviation section of the Army Signal Corps. After flight training, he was assigned to Captain Eddie Rickenbacker's famous 'Hat in the Ring' 94th Aero Squadron. Incredibly aggressive in combat he was twice cited for singly attacking formations of multiple German fighters. Captain Weir Cook was credited with seven victories, including four enemy balloons and was promoted to captain in 1919.

A SPAD XVI with two Lewis guns in the rear and a Vickers forward-firing gun. (*National Museum of the USAF*)

De Havilland DH-4 with two Lewis guns for the observer and two Marlin guns firing through the propeller arc. Wright-built DH-4s rolled off the assembly line. By October 1918, production reached 1,000 aircraft a month. A total of 4,846 of the British-designed DH-4s were built by Dayton-Wright through to the middle of 1919. (*National Museum of the USAF*)

An American built DH.4 which possessed lower performance than its British counterpart. While the British DH.4 was powered by the Rolls Royce Eagle engine, Dayton-Wright used the ubiquitous American-made 400-horse-power Liberty 12. The two engines provided top speeds of 143 miles per hour and 124 miles per hour, respectively. Service ceilings were listed at 23,500 feet and 19,500 feet. Even so, it remained a successful aircraft for both services.

A French-built Salmson 2A2 with a Vickers forward-firing gun and two flexible Lewis guns, 1918. (*National Museum of the USAF*)

Members of the 12th Aero Squadron standing in front of a Salmson 2A2-2.

1st Aero Squadron Salmson 2A2, in France, 1918. The 1st Reconnaissance Squadron is the United States military's oldest flying unit, first established on 5 March 1913.

1st Aero Squadron pilot and observer next to their Salmson 2A2 with American Flag squadron emblem.

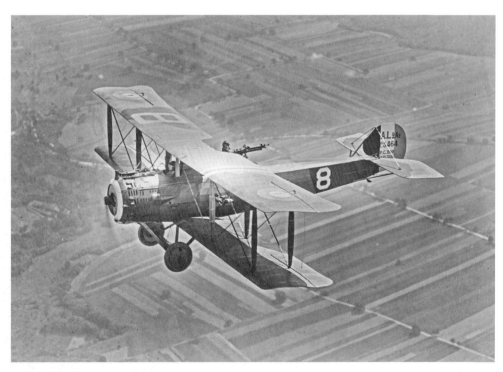

1st Aero Squadron Salmson 2A2, flying over France, 1918. The Salmson 2A2 was a French-built biplane developed to a 1916 requirement. Along with the Breguet 14, it was the main reconnaissance aircraft in use with the French Army and the American Expeditionary Force's aviation units in 1918.

United States Air Service Nieuport 17 training unit in France. The Nieuport 17 was a slightly larger development of the earlier Nieuport 11, with a more powerful engine, larger wings, and improved aerodynamic form. Later versions (as here) were upgraded to a 130 hp engine. The American Expeditionary Forces purchased 75 Nieuport 17s for training.

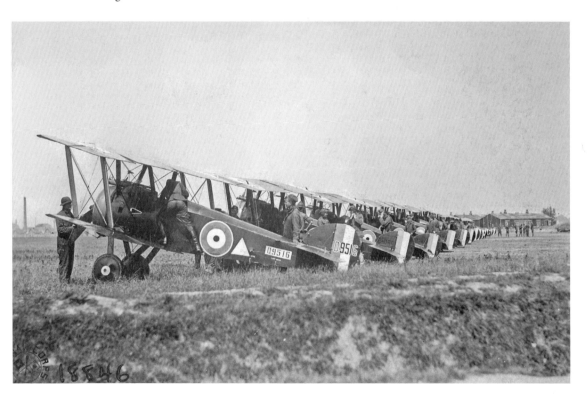

Sopwith Camels of the US 148th American Aero Squadron at Petite-Synthe, Dunkerque, on 6 August 1918. Camel D9516 at the front was lost on 28 August with its pilot, G. V. Siebold killed in action.

Planes of the 135th Aero Squadron line up on 7 August 1918, for the first mission flown over the Front by US-built DH-4s. (*National Museum of the USAF*)

The first US-built DH-4 flew in France on 17 May 1918, and by the Armistice, 3,431 had been delivered, of which 1,213 had been received in Europe. (*National Museum of the USAF*)

American Airmen and a captured Fokker D. VII with two fixed Spandau guns, September 1919. (*National Museum of the USAF*)

Breguet 14 of the 96th Aero Squadron with two Lewis guns on a rotating Scarff ring mount (named for its British inventor, F. W. Scarff), 1918. (*US Air Force photo*)

Nieuport 28 of the 95th Aero Squadron with two Vickers guns, 1918. (*US Air Force photo*)

Breguet 14 of the 96th Aero Squadron with Vickers gun mounted on the side of the fuselage, 1918. (*National Museum of the USAF*)

24th Aero Squadron, Vavincourt Aerodrome, November 1918. The observation unit had initially deployed to England after the US entry into the war on 9 January 1918, and after a training period moved onwards to France on 18 July 1918, positioned first at St Maxient and later at Ourches.

ITALY
Aeronautica de Regio Esercito—
(Royal Army Air Service)

I TALIAN MILITARY AVIATION BEGAN when a flying school was created at Centocelle outside Rome in the spring of 1910, which catered for both military and civil aircrew, and by December of that year thirty-one Italian military pilots had qualified. During 1911, the Italians enthused over aviation, and flying schools began to proliferate. The airfield at Aviano opened in April and became the hub of Italian aviation. (During the 1999 Balkans War, it was the base of NATO operations.) On 22 October 1911, Capt. Carlo Piazza flew the first aeroplane in their war against Turkish forces.

Only ten aircraft were in use at this time—a motley collection of Blériots, Henri Farmans, a Nieuport and an Etrich. A *Battaglione Aviatori* (Air Battalion) was created on 27 June 1912, and a year later expanded into the *Servizio Aeronautica Militare* (Military Aviation Service). By 1913, thirteen military airfields were in service with twelve squadrons.

The Italian Navy formed a naval aviation branch, the *Sezione Aviazione Marina*, in 1913. A year earlier, a naval flying school had been set up at Venice to train pilots. The Naval Branch expanded into a Service a year later.

With war looming on the horizon in 1914, the far-sighted Italians had fourteen military airfields and thirteen squadrons with two military flying schools. The *Aeronautica della Regia Marina* (Naval Aviation Service) possessed two airships and twenty-nine seaplanes and flying boats, plus several land aircraft. When war with Austria-Hungary broke out on 23 May 1915, the *Corpo Aeronautico Militare* (Military Aviation Corps)—as it had been renamed on 7 January—had fifteen squadrons and some eighty-six aircraft in service, and the Navy had some twenty-seven seaplanes in serviceable condition.

Italy had a thriving aircraft industry, which began to produce excellent aircraft.

ITALIAN AIRCRAFT OF THE FIRST WORLD WAR

Ansaldo
Ansaldo produced the A.1 Balilla (Hunter) single-seat biplane fighter late in 1917.

Caproni
The Ca.22 biplane three-engine heavy bomber was produced in 1915, and the Ca.3 in 1917, followed by the Ca.4 triplane night and torpedo bomber. The Ca.5 was a successful day/night biplane bomber used during 1918.

Macchi
The company produced L.1, L.2, L.3, M.3, M.5, M.7 and M.8 flying boats, used from late 1915 onwards for coastal patrol and combat. The L-types were copied from the successful Austro-Hungarian Lohner flying boats. The Parasol was an observation monoplane used when war broke out but soon replaced by the French Caudron G.3.

Pomilio
The Pomilio PC, PD, PE, and PY two-seat observation aircraft were initially not very effective, although the later PD, PE and PY types were extremely successful. The company was taken over by Ansaldo in 1918.

SAML (Società Anonima Meccanica Lombardo)
The SAML Aviatik was copied from the Aviatik B.I two-seat observation biplane and was used mainly for training. This was followed by the SAML Types 1 and 2 observation biplanes.

SIA (Società Italiana Aviazione)
The SIA 7B1 and 7B2 two-seat reconnaissance biplanes operated during 1917–18, but were taken out of service early in 1918. The SIA 9B was used by the Navy as a bomber. The company became Fiat Aviazione in 1918 and produced the Fiat R.2—derived from the SIA 7B2—as an observation/light bomber.

SP (Savoia-Pomilio)
The SP.2 and SP.3 were two-seat pusher reconnaissance/bomber biplanes which their aircrews detested, labelling them two-seater coffins because of their lumbering low speed and heavy handling. The SP.4—a twin-engine bomber with a three-man crew—was used from December 1917 to the summer of 1918.

SVA (Savoia-Verduzio-Ansaldo)
The company designed and produced the successful 220 hp SVA.5 biplane fighter in the summer of 1917. However, it was found that it was more suitable as a very long range recce, bomber and observation aircraft. During 1918, it made an amazing flight (for the time) of 625 miles. A seaplane version—the SVA Idro-AM—was made and allocated to one squadron. A total of 1,245 SVA.5s and about fifty Idro-AMs were made, which testifies to the quality of the machines.

Although the Italians had excellent aircraft of their own make and design, they were not averse to using other countries' makes. The standard Italian fighter was the Franco-British Hanriot, but Nieuport 10s, 11s and 24s, SPAD S.7s and even a German Taube were employed. Blériots XIs, Voisins, Caudron G.3s and Farman MFs and 5Bs were also put to good use.

The Italian Air Service was reshaped early in 1916, with a strength of thirty-five squadrons equipped with Caproni Ca.32s and 33s, Caudron G.4s, Italian-engined Voisins, Farmans, several Aviatiks and Nieuport *Bébé* fighters equipping Nos 70a and 71a squadrons. Italy declared war on Germany on 27 August 1916, and there were sixty-two squadrons in service by the spring of 1917, and fifteen fighter squadrons, fourteen Caproni bomber squadrons and thirty recce and observation squadrons by November that year.

To bolster the strength of the Air Service, three RAF squadrons (Nos 28, 45 and 66)—ninety aircraft, of which fifty-four were Camels—were detached to Italy. By November 1918, Italian air strength stood at sixty-eight squadrons plus four British and three French squadrons—twenty of which were fighter units.

The Italian Navy comprised forty-six squadrons made up of nine fighter units and thirty-seven recce and observation units, with fifteen airships and a small unit—*Squadra San Marco*—of SVA.5s, odd Capronis and a few SIA 9Bs. There were ten main naval air bases.

ITALIAN ACES

Maggiore Francesco Baracca, (1888-1918)
34 victories

Francesco Baracca was born near Ravenna on 9 May 1888, the son of a farmer. Not relishing such a life, he decided to go to the military school near Modena in October 1907. Two years later, in September 1909, he passed out as a second lieutenant (sottotenente) before joining the 2nd Cavalry Regiment.

On 28 April 1912, he applied for and was granted entry into the embryo Italian Aviation Service and was sent with several other officers to Reims in France to learn to fly. Within nine weeks he qualified on a Hanriot two-seater aircraft and was awarded brevet No. 1037.

Baracca was initially posted to the *Battaglione Aviatori*, and on 25 July to Somma Lombardo airfield flying Nieuports. He qualified for his full military brevet on 8 December 1912 and continued to gain experience flying various aircraft types throughout 1913.

After Italy declared war on Austria-Hungary in 1915, Baracca was soon in the air war and early in September over Udine he saw his first enemy aircraft. Closing with the Austrian two-seater, he opened fire but to no avail due to repeated stoppages of his machine gun. At the turn of the year, No. 70a *Squadriglia* (Squadron) was equipped with Nieuports, and Baracca flew a Nieuport 11 *Bébé* single-seat fighter.

He scored his first victory on 7 April 1916 over an Austrian Aviatik, forcing it down by determined, accurate bursts of machine-gun fire. Baracca landed his aircraft and approached the downed adversary, engaging the pilot and wounded observer in conversation until Italian troops arrived. The observer died from his wounds; the pilot went to a PoW camp.

Baracca continued in his aerial combat war but his aircraft continued to suffer machine-gun stoppages and he did not score again until 16 May, when he and his squadron fought an aerial duel with fourteen Austrian bombers over Udine. Baracca scored another victory, bringing the enemy aircraft down over Gorizia. On 25 November he scored his fifth victory, an Albatros, making him an ace. He had a prancing horse (*cavallino rampante*) emblazoned on the fuselage of his Nieuport, indicating his cavalry roots. This prancing horse insignia badge was given by Baracca'a mother to the Italian motor racing driver Enzo Ferrari, who later put the badge on his racing cars.

On 11 February 1917, Baracca—climbing to 12,000 feet—shot down an Albatros over Ozzano and was promoted to captain the next day and awarded his third Silver Medal. With his score standing at ten victories on 1 May, Baracca was among a battle-hardened Flight of pilots that formed No. 91a *Squadriglia* flying the SPAD S.7. The new fighter proved popular with the pilots, and Baracca shot down three enemy aircraft in three weeks.

Baracca was placed in command of the squadron in June and moved base to Istrana. He continued to score victories, and by September his total had risen to nineteen. Airborne in a SPAD on 21 October, he gave battle to five Albatros D.IIIs. Breaking off the unequal contest, he flew off and then engaged two enemy two-seater aircraft over San Gabriele, shooting down both—his first double victory.

Four days later he and his squadron engaged in no fewer than five aerial combats with the enemy, destroying an Albatros himself. On 26 October he scored his second double victory when he downed two German Aviatiks, making his total twenty-four victories.

The Italian Army retreat at Caporetto caused Baracca's squadron to move to Pordenone airfield where it was re-equipped with new aircraft—the excellent SPAD S.12—but the aerial battles grew harder as his squadron was opposed by the Austrian fighter ace Hauptmann Godwin von Brumowski and his squadron.

Nevertheless, Baracca continued to up his score—on 6 November he downed two Aviatiks within thirty minutes and next day shot down another. Within a short time, his total had reached thirty victories and he was sent test flying at Ansaldo's factory in Turin.

On 6 February 1918, Baracca was invested by King Albert I of the Belgians with a decoration and, in March, he and two of his pilots were awarded Italy's highest honour—the *Medaglia d'oro al valor militare* (Gold Medal for Military Valour)—at La Scala, Milan. Back with his squadron on 3 May, Baracca was soon in action. He clashed with six Austrian Albatros D.IIIs, shooting one down. His next victory came on 22 May, and his final two on 15 June.

Baracca and two other aircraft of his squadron took off on a patrol and ground support mission on 19 June 1918. Flying low, at 100 feet, over the ground enemy at Montello, the three Italian aircraft machine-gunned Austrian troops below. The enraged enemy returned fire with heavy machine guns, and all three Italian aircraft were hit. In the mêlée, Baracca disappeared from his comrades' view and was never seen alive again. His body was found—with a bullet hole in his forehead—next to his burned out SPAD aircraft. So died the gallant Capt. Baracca, Italy's highest scoring ace, with thirty-four victories. His prancing horse fuselage badge is still carried by all Ferrari motor cars around the world—a fitting memento of a redoubtable and dashing fighter pilot.

Tentente Silvio Scaroni, (1893-1977)
26 victories

Silvio Scaroni first served with No. 4a *Squadriglia*, flying Caudron G.4s on recce and artillery spotting missions. It was not until the summer of 1917 that he applied for, and was granted, training as a fighter pilot. By November that year he had qualified as a pilot and was sent to No. 76a *Squadriglia* at Istrana. The squadron had both Nieuport and Hanriot fighters on charge and Scaroni was soon in action—on 15 November he closed with an Albatros two-seater and shot it down in flames onto Colberstadio. Two days later he shot down another Albatros, and on 19 November yet another.

Scaroni became an ace in December 1917 after shooting down three Albatros C.IIIs on the 5th, 10th and 19th. On 26 December, the airfield at Istrana was attacked by a strong force of Austrian aircraft—almost thirty bombers protected by swarms of fighters—and Scaroni's squadron gave battle with the raiders. He made Italian aviation history when he shot down three of the enemy—two WKFs and a Gotha—in one sortie. Several other pilots accounted for more Austrian aircraft—making a total of eight enemy aircraft shot out of the sky. Two days later Scaroni dispatched two Albatros recce aircraft over Montello—again on one sortie.

During January 1918, Scaroni destroyed two Brandenburg two-seaters, bringing his victory total to eleven. By 3 April he had increased his total to sixteen enemy aircraft, and by 15 June it was nineteen. On 7 July, with his score at twenty-one victories, and with Sgt Romolo Ticconi as wingman, he attacked a formation of Austrian aircraft, knocking out a Brandenburg within minutes. Ticconi shot down two Phonix aircraft, and Scaroni another Brandenburg and then a Phonix—five enemy aircraft downed by the two pilots.

On 12 July 1918, No. 76a *Squadriglia* was giving fighter protection umbrella to three Italian observation aircraft when they were engaged by a strong formation of enemy Phonix and Albatros fighters. A classic dogfight ensued, with both sides trying to shoot each other out of the sky. More Italian aerial reinforcements arrived and joined the battle, followed by a RAF Camel Flight. Still outnumbered, the Allied aircraft began to give a good account of themselves, Scaroni shooting down an Albatros and then a Phonix. He was hit by a machine-gun bullet and passed out, but luckily came round and regained partial control before his Hanriot crashed. As his machine hit the ground at speed, Scaroni was thrown clear from the wreckage badly wounded.

Lt Scaroni convalesced after treatment in hospital, and some six months later was returned to his squadron—but the war was over and he did not fly in anger again. He was awarded the *Medaglia d'oro al valor militare* for his twenty-six victories and remained in the Italian Air Force, attaining the rank of general.

Tenente Colonnello Pier Ruggero Piccio, (1880-1965)
24 victories

Pier Piccio was born in Rome on 27 September 1880 and joined the Italian Army as a regular officer, rising to the rank of captain. He gained his flying badge, No. 256, on 12 July 1913, which made him one of the first aviators in Italy.

In 1914, still in the rank of captain, he was placed in command of No. 5a *Squadriglia* at Arsizio. (Italy's top ace, Francesco Baracca, was in the same squadron at the time.) Piccio was an enthusiast in aviation and had set an Italian altitude record of 3,800 metres. He also specialised in long-distance endurance flying, setting some remarkable records for the time. Thus, when Italy entered the First World War on the Allied side, Piccio was an experienced pilot and officer, and flew with Nos 70a and 91a *Squadriglie* as a fighter pilot in spite of his promotion to lieutenant colonel. He was awarded the *Medaglia d'oro al valor militare* in 1916.

By 30 September 1917, Piccio had twelve confirmed victories, adding two more on 25 October—both Albatros aircraft, shot down in flames. Flying with No. 91a *Squadriglia*—known as 'The Squadron of Aces'—in a SPAD S.XIII, he undertook many offensive strafing missions against the ground enemy and also several recce operations, sometimes flying with Baracca and Calabria as wingmen.

Piccio ended the war with a victory total of twenty-four. In March 1918, together with Baracca and Calabria, he was invested with his country's highest honour—the *Medaglia d'oro al valor militare* —a much deserved accolade for three of Italy's aces.

Tenente Flavio Torello Baracchini, (1895-1928)
21 victories

Flavio Baracchini was born at Villafranca in Lunigiana on 28 July 1895. He was educated at technical schools in La Spezia. On joining the Italian Army he was assigned to the 3rd Engineer Battalion, but in the autumn of 1915, he reported to the SIT School in Torino for pilot training. After qualifying on Voisins in December 1915 he was posted on 28 February 1916 to 7a *Squadriglia*, later redesignated 26a *Squadriglia*, and piloted a Voisin there until 20 November 1916. In December 1916, he was commissioned as a Sottotenente. Baracchini had no success as a fighter pilot until May 1917, when he was assigned to the newly formed 81a *Squadriglia*. His very first claim of 15 May went unconfirmed, but he got his initial official victory five days later, when he shot down an Albatros south of Marco. He scored again on the 23rd and 25th. He scored once more on 6 June 1917 while flying a Nieuport 11, before upgrading to a Nieuport 17. He used his new plane to tally four more triumphs that month. By the 22nd, he had scored eight victories by fighting in the air on 35 occasions in 39 days. For this extraordinary display of zeal, Flavio Baracchini became the first Italian fighter pilot to win the *Medaglia d'oro al valor militare*.

Baracchini transferred to 76a *Squadriglia* and a Hanriot HD.1 on 14 July 1917. He had one more victory in July and two more in August on the on the 3rd and 8th. He was so seriously wounded in the left jaw on 8 August 1917 that he was out of action for nine months.

Upon his return, he again had an unconfirmed credit on a balloon, on 3 April 1918. Then he was transferred back to 81a *Squadriglia*. He had four confirmed and four unconfirmed kills in May and began his final month of combat with a double victory on 15 June, with a third claim going unconfirmed. On the 21 June he finally became a balloon buster, for his nineteenth credit. He scored again on both 22 and 25 June to bring his total to 21 confirmed and nine unconfirmed. On the 25th, he was again severely wounded, this time when he was shot down by machine gun fire. He survived the war, and quit flying in 1921.

After the war be experimented with new signalling device for communicating with aircraft, which was adopted by Italian aviators. He then began development of an explosive mixture in a laboratory. It ignited accidentally and burned him severely on 29 July 1928. He lingered a short while, before dying of his injuries on 18 August 1928.

Capitano Fulco Ruffo di Calabria, (1884-1946)
20 victories

Fulco di Calabria was born in Naples on 12 August 1884. He was a member of No. 70a *Squadriglia* and became the fifth highest scoring Italian ace. Cool in combat, he was an outstanding pilot and an excellent marksman.

He scored his first victory on 23 August 1916, with Baracca and Olivari (with whom he usually flew), when he shot down an Austrian observation aircraft over the Tolmino part of the Front. His next victory came on 16 September—again on combat patrol with Baracca and Olivari—when he shot down an Austrian Lohner two-seater near Villach. The pilot of the Lohner was killed and the observer wounded. On 1 January 1917, di Calabria scored another victory—an Austrian two-seat observation aircraft.

Selected to join Baracca in forming No. 91a *Squadriglia*, he continued to score victories with this squadron until his grand total reached twenty aircraft downed. He was promoted to captain and awarded the prestigious *Medaglia d'oro al valor militare*.

Italy

Italy had its own aircraft industry and was at the forefront of aircraft development. Nominally allied with the Central Powers of the German Empire and the Empire of Austria-Hungary in the Triple Alliance, the Kingdom of Italy refused to join them when the war started in August 1914. Instead in May 1915, almost a year after the war's commencement, after a period of wavering and after secret negotiations with France and Great Britain in which Italy negotiated for territory if victorious, Italy entered the war on the side of the Allies.

Giovanni Battista Caproni founded Società de Agostini e Caproni in 1908. Here he is at the front of a Ca.3 standing next to an officer of the *Corpo Aeronautico Militare*. This was formed as part of the part of the *Regio Esercito* (Royal Army) on 7 January 1915.

Caproni Ca.33 'Cannoncino", with a 450 hp engine and a machine gun. The Caproni Ca.33 was a re-powered version of the earlier Ca.32, annd became Italy's most widely used bomber.

Caproni Ca.33 Bomber No. 4229, *Corpo Aeronautico Militare* Service.

The later development of the Ca.33 was designated Ca.36, and remained in service until the second half of the 1920s. The Caproni Ca.36 had removable wings for easier hangar storage.

Caproni Ca.42 No. 3388 'bombed up'. The Ca.4 was a three-engine, twin-fuselage triplane of fabric-covered wooden construction. An open central nacelle was attached to the under-surface of the centre wing. It contained a single pusher engine, pilot, and forward gunner. The remaining engines were tractor-mounted at the front of each fuselage. Armament consisted of four (but up to eight) Revelli 6.5 mm or 7.7 mm machine guns in front ring mounting and two boom ring mountings. Bombs were suspended in a bomb bay.

Ca.4s were tested by the *Corpo Aeronautico Militare* in 1917 and began operations in 1918. They were used for attacking targets in Austria-Hungary. In April 1918, six Ca.42s were issued to the British RNAS (No. 227 Squadron) but were never used operationally and were returned to Italy after the war. The Ca.4 was well designed. Its size, without regards to its height, was not any larger than that of other foreign heavy bombers. With American Liberty engines, it had a fast speed, similar to other heavy bombers, while its bomb load had one of the largest capacities of that era, 3,200 lb (1,450 kg).

The Hanriot HD.1 was a French single-seat fighter aircraft. Rejected for service with French squadrons in favour of the SPAD S.7, the type was supplied to the Belgian and the Italian air forces where it proved highly successful. Of a total of about 1,200 examples built, 831 were produced by Italian companies under licence. This example is of the *76a Squadrigilia* at Casoni, 1918.

A Caproni Ca.3 coming in to land. It was a bomber and first saw service in 1916. It was powered by three Isotta-Fraschini V.4B six-cylinder water-cooled in-line piston engines, each developing 150 hp and had a maximum speed of 85 mph with a range of 372 miles carrying 1,764 lb (800 kg) of bombs.

Ca.763 crashed. This appears to be an early Ca.3.

The Nieuport 11 was basically a smaller, simplified version of the Nieuport 10—designed specifically as a single-seat fighter. Nicknamed the *Bébé*, it was flown by *Aéronautique Militaire* in France, the RNAS in Britain and air services in Belgium, Russia and Italy. 646 were produced by the Italian Macchi company under licence. This photograph is of the production line of the Macchi-Nieuport at Aermacchi's factory.

From top to bottom:

Nieuports 11s, *Bébés* of the *83a Squadriglia* lined up in 1917.

The Pomilio brothers first armed reconnaissance biplane was the Pomilio PC1 which appeared in 1917. It was a conventional biplane of mixed construction with a fixed tailskid landing gear. It was the first Italian armed reconnaissance biplane. Powered by a 260 hp Fiat A.12 engine it proved to be difficult to handle which led to the improved Pomilio PD.

The PC1 was succeeded by an improved design the Pomilio PD. The PD had a revised engine cowling and to help with the stability a ventral fin. Production of both the PC and PD was 545 aircraft, mainly PDs. A further improvement was the Pomilio PE which had a re-designed tail unit with an increase in area of both the fin and tailplane. It was also fitted with a more powerful variant of the Fiat A.12. Changes were made throughout the production run of 1,071 aircraft with later aircraft fitted with synchronized forward-firing machine-guns as well as the observer's Lewis machine gun.

The Savoia-Pomilio SP.2 was a reconnaissance and bomber aircraft. It was a refined version of the SP.1, and like it, took its basic configuration from the Farman MF.11; a biplane with twin tails and a fuselage nacelle that accommodated the crew and a pusher-mounted engine. The SP.2 entered mass production with SIA, and with co-designer Ottorino Pomilio's own firm that he had recently established. About 300 SP.2s were built and it entered service in 1917.

A Caproni Ca.42 sea plane of the *Regia Marina*.

Left: Tenente Silvio Scaroni, Medaglia d'oro al valor militare, Medaglia d'argento al valor militare (plus many more medals), (1893-1977) was the second ranking Italian ace of the war with 26 victories. He was forced down by machine gun fire on 13 July 1918 and saw no further combat in the war.

Right: Tenente Gabriele D'Annunzio, (1863-1938), Prince of Montenevoso. D'Annunzio was an Italian writer, poet, journalist, playwright and soldier. He is pictured with his pilot, Capitano Beltramo.

Tenente Gabriele D'Annunzio in the front seat of the Ansaldo SVA flown by Capitano Natale Palli ready for the raid on Vienna. On 9 August 1918, as commander of the *87a Squadriglia La Serenissima*, he organised one of the great feats of the war, leading nine aircraft in a 700-mile round trip to drop propaganda leaflets on Vienna. This is called in Italian *il Volo su Vienna*, 'the Flight over Vienna'.

Tenente Giuseppe Miraglia, Medaglia d'argento al valor militare (and five other medals), (1883-1915). Miraglia was an early pilot in the Italian Royal Navy, *Regia Marina*, and was shot down and killed on 21 December 1915. He was a close friend of the poet Gabriele D'Annunzio who dedicated sixty pages of his poem *Nottorno* to the memory of Giuseppe Miraglia.

Pietro Massoni, one of the pilots of *87a Squadriglia La Serenissima* who took part in the flight to Vienna in his Ansaldo SVA SN 6846.

Maggiore Francesco Baracca, (1888-1918), was Italy's top fighter ace, credited with 34 aerial victories. Baracca scored his first victory on 7 April 1916 in a Nieuport 11 *Bébé*, holing the fuel tank of an Austrian Hansa-Brandenburg C.I and wounding its two-man crew. This was also Italy's first aerial victory in the war.

It was around this time that Baracca adopted as a personal emblem a black prancing horse on his personal mount, in tribute to his former cavalry regiment. After his death this prancing horse insignia badge was given by his mother to the Italian motor racing driver Enzo Ferrari, who later put the badge on his racing cars.

Another striking pose by Baracca by the side of one his victories. He always appears stiff in his poses with his walking stick in his right hand. Baracca remained a modest, sensitive man conscious of his duty and compassionate to both his squadron comrades and to his defeated enemies. He would try to visit his victims in hospital afterwards, to pay his respects, or he would place a wreath on the grave of those he killed.

Baracca saw little action in 1918, but he added more victories, for a total of 34, before failing to return from a strafing mission on 19 June. Baracca and an inexperienced pilot Tenente Franco Osnago were hit by ground fire and split from one another. A few minutes later, both Baracca's home airfield and Osnago saw a burning aircraft fall. Some days later, on 24 June, after an Austro-Hungarian retreat, Baracca's remains were recovered from where they lay, four metres from the burnt remnants of his SPAD VII.

Pilots and Airmen of the *91a Squadriglia* with their Nieuport 17 aircraft, showing the badge of the unit, the winged griffin.

Left: Tenente Colonnello Pier Ruggero Piccio, (1889-1965).

Right: Tenente Colonnello Pier Ruggero Piccio was one of the principal Italian air aces behind only Count Francesco Baracca and Tenente Silvio Scaroni. Count Piccio rose in the ranks and in later years was appointed a Senator in 1933 by King Emmanuel III and served Benito Mussolini as a member of the Fascist Party. In 1940, while living in Geneva, Piccio met his former enemy and long-time friend, Belgian ace Willy Coppens. Coppens mentioned that they must be enemies again. Piccio continued to live in neutral Switzerland. He helped Italian soldiers who sought sanctuary after the mid-war armistice.

Capitano Bartolomeo 'Meo' Costantini joined the Italo-Turkish War (1911), and later became a flying ace with six victories flying a SPAD in the *Squadriglia degli Assi,* (Aces) of *91a Squadriglia,* a fighter squadron of the *Corpo Aeronautico Militare.*

Pilots of the Italian *91a Squadriglia* (91st Fighter Squadron), 1917-1918. *From left to right:* Sergente Mario D'Urso, Sergente Gaetano Aliperta, Tenente Gastone Novelli, Tenente Cesare Magistrini, Capitano Bartolomeo Costantini, Capitano Fulco Ruffo di Calabria, Colonnello Pier Ruggero Piccio, Tenente Guido Keller, Maggiore Francesco Baracca, Tenente Ferruccio Ranza, Tenente Mario de Bernardi, Tenente Adriano Bacula, Sergente Guido Nardini and Sottotenente Eduardo Olivero.

A victim of *91a Squadriglia* , this Hansa Brandenburg CI 27-59 was forced down in Italian territory.

The SPAD SVII fighter planes of *91a Squadriglia* lined-up at the airfield of Quinto di Treviso, where the unit was sent on 11 March 1918.

Nieuports Ni.17s of the *91a Squadriglia degli Assi* (Aces Squadron). The first is Poli's aircraft (blue star), the second is Fulco Ruffo's (skull and crossbones) and the last is Baracca's (black stallion).

Right: Maggiore Francesco Baracca in the cockpit of his Nieuport-Macchi 11.

Below: Legendary pilots of 'The Aces Squadron'. *From left to right:* Gastone Novelli (8 victories), Ferruccio Ranza (17), Fulco Ruffo di Calabria (20), Bartolomeo Costantini (6) and Francesco Baracca (34).

Capitano Fulco Ruffo, (1884-1946). Here he is standing by the side of his Nieuport Ni.17. His aircraft had a skull and crossbones painted on the fuselage.

Ruffo climbing into the cockpit of his Nieuport Ni.17. He came from an aristocratic family and was Fulco VIII, Prince Ruffo di Calabria, 6th Duke of Guardia Lombarda. He was later a Senator under the fascist regime of Benito Mussolini for which he was convicted after the war. He was also posthumous father-in-law of King Albert II of the Belgians, and grandfather of the current King, Philippe of Belgium.

Right: Fulco Ruffo di Calabria checking the engine of his SPAD. After Baracca's death on 18 June 1918, Fulco assumed command of the renowned 'Squadron of Aces'. He relinquished command of *91a Squadriglia* on 18 September to Ferruccio Ranza, after suffering a nervous breakdown. After recovery, he was handed command of 10th Gruppo, on 23 October 1918, but was shot down by artillery fire near Marano on 29 October 1918. In the end, he shot down 20 enemy airplanes in 53 combats, making him the fifth highest scoring Italian flying ace.

Below: Tenente Luigi Gori, (1894-1917) and Tenente Maurizio Pagliano, (1890-1917). The details of their main missions are painted on the nose of their Caproni Ca.3. They were both killed in action on Piave Front on 30 December 1917.

Tenente Maurizio Pagliano (*left*) and Tenente Luigi Gori (*right*) and the commander of the VIII Squadron Capitano Govi and Capitano Aurelio Barbarisi, observer and leader of the Caproni Ca.2 (300) 'S. Giorgio' SN.1151, the first with the 'Ace of Spades'. La Comina airfield, 1916.

Tenente Luigi Gori (*right*) and Maurizio Pagliano (*left*). The four aircraft lined-up in the *8a Squadriglia* of the *4° Gruppo*, were characterized by the four aces from the card pack: Hearts, Diamonds, Clubs and SPADes.

BELGIUM
Belgian Air Arm — Compagnie des Aviateurs/ Aviation Militaire

T HE *COMPAGNIE DES AVIATEURS* had been founded on 16 April 1913, and with the First World War looming, Belgium mobilised its small air arm on 1 August 1914. Only Nos 1 and 2 *Escadrilles* became fully operational, with Nos 3 and 4 working up. Thirty-seven military pilots were on strength, eight more civilian pilots volunteering their services to their country, and three pilots brought their own aircraft to fight the coming battle.

On 4 August 1914, Germany invaded Belgium and the Belgian Air Arm went to war. In 1915 it was reorganised as *l'aviation militaire*, and during the next three years fought well and produced five aces.

The Belgian Navy did not have any aircraft of its own and used four Short 827s (Nos 3093-95 and No. 8219) acquired from Britain late in 1915. These were sent in crates to the Belgian Congo and assembled on the slipway at Lake Tongwe in May 1916. One of the Short 827s was used to good effect in the Belgian Congo on 9 June, when Belgian aircrew bombed the German 800-ton *Graf von Götzen* on Lake Tanganyika. Five FBA flying boats, plus the four Short 827s, which had returned from the Congo and were used by the Belgian Navy out of Calais during 1917–18.

BELGIAN ACES

Sous-Lieutenant Willy Coppens de Houthulst, (1892-1986)
37 victories

Belgium's top ace was born in Brussels in 1892. After army service, Willy Coppens joined the Belgian Air Arm as a trainee pilot in early September 1915, training at Hendon in England and graduating as a pilot in December before returning to Belgium. He continued with flying training and had qualified as a fighter pilot by July 1916. His first posting was to 6th *Escadrille* at Houthem, flying British B.E.2c and Farman aircraft, but the recce squadron soon re-equipped with ex-Royal Navy Sopwith 1½ Strutters.

On 1 May 1917, when flying a Sopwith, he was bounced by four German fighters. He retreated from the unequal dogfight and managed to land his bullet-riddled aeroplane safely, this first brush with the enemy bringing him a Mention in Despatches. On 15 July he was posted to a Nieuport Scout fighter squadron based at Les Moëres airstrip, Dunkirk, and six days later was in air action but failed to open his victory score. The squadron was re-equipped with small but agile Hanriot HD.1 single machine-gun fighters, which Coppens flew and liked, but during the winter of 1917–18 he failed to score a single victory.

Three Belgian squadrons were combined to form a fighter group in March 1918 in the hope that a large force would be able to take on the rampant German Air Service. On 18 March, Coppens attacked a German observation balloon, but his machine gun did not have incendiary bullets and he failed to set the balloon on fire. However, the resourceful Coppens obtained standard British .303 incendiary bullets and renewed his attack against enemy balloons, albeit without result.

On 25 April, Coppens was flying his blue-painted Hanriot, with his commanding officer on his wing, when he sighted a gaggle of enemy aircraft being pursued by other Belgian aircraft. He came to close quarters with a German fighter and, seizing his chance, poured a burst from his machine gun into the enemy machine, which turned over and went down—crashing to earth near the village of Ramscapelle. Coppens had at last scored his first victory. Between then and October 1918 he destroyed no fewer than thirty-four German observation balloons and two other enemy aircraft.

The following month saw Coppens devise a method of ammunition loading. Inserting four incendiary bullets into the normal gun feed belt to his machine gun, he would then close to short range against a target balloon for maximum effect. He scored a balloon victory with this method—and then another over Houthulst Forest. Time after time he shot down German observation balloons in the forest zone, which was his favourite combat area. On one occasion he downed a balloon with just one incendiary bullet—an amazing feat.

A dawn take-off on 14 October to attack balloons above Torhout and Praet Bosch led to Coppens shooting down one balloon, but he was hit by flak when attacking another and received a wound to his leg. Having managed to control his aircraft and crash land, he was taken from the mangled wreckage by ground troops and rushed to De Panne hospital where his wounded leg had to be amputated.

The loss of a leg was the end of Willy Coppens' war, although he stayed in the Belgian Air Arm until the outbreak of the Second World War, when he went to Switzerland after the Belgian surrender. He was knighted as a *Chevalier of the Légion d'honneur* and awarded the British DSO among many other decorations.

Lieutenant André de Meulemeester, (1894-1973)
11 victories

Known as 'The Eagle of Flanders', André de Meulemeester volunteered for the embryo Belgian Air Arm and trained as a pilot at the Blériot Flying School at Étampes. Late in 1916 he was assigned to a top unit—the Nieuport-equipped 1st *Escadrille*—whose squadron crest was a Scottish thistle with the Scottish national motto *Nemo me impune lacessit* (No one injures me with impunity, or in the Scots tongue, Wha daur meddle wi' me).

De Meulemeester proved to be a natural pilot and opened his victory total on 30 April

1917, when he shot down an enemy two-seat recce aircraft over the German front line at Lecke. On 11 June he dispatched another enemy machine over Beerst, and three days later he shot down an Albatros in no-man's land between the opposing front lines. Another Albatros was downed five weeks later, but de Meulemeester was wounded in the dogfight and taken to hospital.

The following month he was back on squadron and promoted to flight commander, which entitled him to a wingman—Willy Coppens—and by October de Meulemeester was flying a new Hanriot HD.1 which he had painted a glaring yellow. On 2 November he shot down another Albatros over Dixmude.

On Sunday 4 November, de Meulemeester and two wingmen were airborne in their yellow Hanriots when they came on a dogfight between five German and four British aircraft. The Belgians joined the battle with gusto and de Meulemeester immediately shot down an Albatros, which flamed into the German front line. However, it was not until 17 March 1918 that he increased his score, when he shot down another Albatros over Houthulst whilst leading a finger-five formation. On 3 May he dispatched another Albatros, and by the November Armistice his victory score stood at eleven.

Sous-Lieutenant Edmond Thieffry, (1892-1929)
10 victories

Edmond Thieffry was conscripted into the 14th Regiment of the Belgian Army in 1912. Two years later he was at Louvain University studying to be a lawyer, but he was back in the Army in July 1914 with the 10th Regiment at Liège and in battle with German invaders. He applied to join the new Belgian Air Arm and trained as a pilot at Étampes in July 1915, gaining his pilot's brevet the following February, when he was sent to a recce squadron equipped with Voisin Canons and Farman F.20s. Unfortunately, Thieffry was prone to accidents caused by pilot error and was transferred to single-seat fighters. It was thought that he was less of a risk if he flew alone!

Arriving at Houthem airstrip in December 1916, he joined 5th *Escadrille* equipped with Nieuport *Bébé* fighters. His first victory came on 15 March 1917, when he shot down a German recce biplane, which was seen to crash behind German lines, and eight days later he clashed with a Fokker D.V, bringing it down behind Belgian lines. Flying again the next day he fought a duel with two enemy fighters but came off worst, crashing between Belgian and German lines.

In May 1917, Thieffry's squadron was re-equipped with SPADs, and when flying a SPAD on the 12th of the month he shot down an Albatros. On 20 June he made it four victories when he dispatched an Albatros in a dogfight. However, next day Thieffry was himself shot down, but walked away unharmed. He had an amazing record of emerging unscathed from crashes.

When acting as protection for slow observation aircraft on 3 July, and flying a powerful 220 hp SPAD, Thieffry and his squadron clashed with the enemy over German lines. Within a few minutes he shot down two Albatros aircraft, which brought him a commission from King Albert I. On 16 August he fought two Albatros aircraft over Houthulst and sent one crashing earthwards, followed by another victory six days later and another on the 26th, bringing his victory score to nine. He had also shot down several enemy aircraft behind German lines, which were not confirmed. Thieffry's final victory came on 16 October against an enemy scout over Merckem.

On 23 February 1918, Thieffry was again in action but was shot down and went missing, believed killed in action. Weeks later it was found that he had been wounded and had then become a PoW. He remained interned until the November Armistice. After the war he went into civil aviation but was killed on 11 April 1929 during a flight to the Belgian Congo.

Capitaine Fernand Jacquet, (1888-1947)
7 victories

Fernand Jacquet was born at Petite-Chapelle in November 1888 and enrolled at the Brussels Military Academy in 1907, graduating as an officer on 25 June. He was allocated to the 4th Regiment but requested flying training and was sent to flying school early in 1913. By the autumn of that year he had graduated as a pilot and was posted to 2nd Escadrille equipped with Henri Farman aircraft.

By August 1914 his squadron was stationed at Namur, but the Farman engines were underpowered and Jacquet was unable to fly. Eager to be at the enemy's throat, he undertook a ground attack in an 'armoured car' and accounted for a squadron of German cavalry. His squadron then relocated to France and was re-equipped with Farman F.20s by the French and, by October, it was based near Dunkirk as the German advance drove the Belgian Army back. The Belgian Air Arm began using the Farmans to drop bombs, Jacquet taking part in a raid on a railway station.

Posted to 1st *Escadrille* in January 1915, Jacquet flew a Maurice Farman equipped with a Lewis machine gun. However, it was not until 17 April that he brought the gun into action, when he shot down a German Aviatik over Beerst. This was his first victory—and was also the first victory for the Belgian Air Arm.

His method of operating was to fly with his observer as a single aircraft intruding into German airspace. In this way he shot several enemy aircraft, but as they were behind enemy lines they could not be confirmed. By February 1917, Jacquet was an ace, having shot down five enemy aircraft, and by the following January he was in command of three squadrons and flying a SPAD S.11. He had shot down two more enemy aircraft by November 1918, bringing his official victory score to seven, although his unconfirmed score was many more.

During the Second World War, Fernand Jacquet was an active member of the Resistance and was imprisoned by the Germans, but survived the war and died in October 1947.

Lieutenant Jan Olieslagers. 1883-1942)
6 victories

Jan Olieslagers was born in Antwerp in May 1883 and at 17 years of age became a motor-cycle racing ace, gaining wealth and fame in the process. He bought his own Blériot aircraft, taught himself how to fly it, and took part in the first Belgian air display in 1909. He then took his aircraft to Algeria, Spain and Italy to give displays. He again became an ace—this time in the air.

When the First World War broke out, Olieslagers offered his aircraft and personnel in defence of his country. He joined the Belgian Air Arm as a corporal and a year later was made a second lieutenant. By March 1915, he was flying Nieuport Scouts—his beloved Blériot was no match for the new German fighters. Like Capt. Jacquet, he preferred to fly deep into his opponents' territory and take the fight to the enemy, shooting down several German aircraft which were unconfirmed and not claimed.

Lt Olieslagers came through the war safely with six victories confirmed, although his actual score was much more. He died in Antwerp in March 1942, aged 58 years.

Aviation Militaire *Victory Totals*

2Lt W. Coppens—37
Lt A. de Meulemeester—11
2Lt E. Thieffry—10
Capt. F.Jacquet—7
Lt J. Olieslagers—6

All of the above aces survived the war.

Adjt G. K. de Lettenhove—4
Lt L. Robin—4
Sgt E. Hage—3
Lt M. Benselin—2
Lt P. Braun—2
2Lt J. Goethals—2
2Lt L. Ledure—2
Adjt G. Medaets—2
Adjt M. Medaets—2
Sgt-Maj. C. Montigny—2
Adjt R. Rondeau—2

Twenty-seven other pilots scored one victory each.

By September 1918, *l'aviation militaire* had built up to a strength of eleven squadrons. Nos 9, 10 and 11 *Escadrilles* were fighter squadrons equipped with Hanriot HD.1s, SPAD S.13s and Camels. No. 8 *Escadrille* was a night bombing unit equipped with Farman F.40s. Nos 2 to 7 *Escadrilles* were used for observation and were equipped with Breguet 14 A2s, SPAD S.11s and Farmans. No. 1 *Escadrille* had a maintenance role. Total aircraft strength was sixty-nine single-seat and fifty-eight two-seater aircraft.

Four members of Belgium's air force, 37 pilots strong when the War began, rest beside their French-designed Farman HF20 biplane in October 1914.

Sous-Lieutenant Willy Coppens de Houthulst, (1892-1986). Coppens was the top Belgian ace with 37 victories. Coppens devised a method of ammunition loading. Inserting four incendiary bullets into the normal gun feed belt to his machine gun, he would then close to short range against a target balloon for maximum effect. He scored a balloon victory with this method—and then another over Houthulst Forest.

For his successes Coppens was ennobled, Coppens de Houthulst. Here he is being decorated by King Albert I. Willy Coppens' war ended on 14 October 1918 when he was hit by flak when attacking another and received a wound to his leg. Having managed to control his aircraft and crash land, he was taken from the mangled wreckage by ground troops and rushed to De Panne hospital where his wounded leg had to be amputated.

Willy Coppens is pictured in front of his 1917 Hanriot-Dupont HD.1. In June 1918, he was promoted to sous lieutenant, thus becoming an officer. His royal blue plane with its insignia of a thistle sprig wearing a top hat became so well known that the Germans went to special pains to try to kill him. Coppens remained in the *l'Aviation militaire belge* until just before the Second World War.

In March 1915, the Army air arm became *l'Aviation militaire belge* (Belgian Military Aviation). It was credited with a first official aerial victory on 17 April 1915 when Captain Fernand Jacquet and his observer Lieutenant Hans Vindevogel of *Escadrille I* shot down a German Albatros. They were flying a Maurice Farman MF.11.

After purchasing 10 French Farman F 40s in 1916, the Belgians decided to produce their own pusher. Re-designed by Lieutenant Georges Nélis. Here, Capitaine-Commandant Fernand Maximillian Leon Jacquet, (*right*) and Georges Nélis give last minute advice to pilot Sub-Lieutenant René Vertongen before a test-flight with the Farman-Nélis GN-1 at Calais Beaumarais aerodrome. Jacquet went on to become one of Belgium's aces with 7 victories.

A Belgian B.E.2c, its crew positions reversed to place the observer/gunner I the rear cockpit, crewed by Capitaine Walter Gallez (*left*) and Lieutenant Marcel De Crombrugghe, (1894-1978). The *9ème Escadrille de Chasse* was originally the *1ère Escadrille de Chasse*, which was founded in February 1916 as the first dedicated fighter squadron of *l'Aviation militaire belge*. *9ème Escadrille* was headed by Walter Gallez, but little is known of him.

Sous Lieutenant Edmond Thieffry, (1892-1929). One of Belgium's most successful fighter pilots, posing next to the battered remains of his Nieuport XVI after what must have been quite a heavy landing. Thieffry was an ace with 10 confirmed victories. Thieffry joined the army but was soon captured by the Germans. He escaped on a stolen motorcycle and was interned when he entered the Netherlands. Employing all his legal skills, he successfully argued for his release and was promptly back on the stolen motorcycle, heading for home. In July 1915, Thieffry transferred to the Belgian Air Service where he crashed more aircraft during training than any other Belgian pilot. As a result, his superiors were reluctant to assign him to a two-seater squadron for fear he would kill the observer in a crash. Instead, he was assigned to fly single-seat fighters.

Right: Thieffry soon crashed his first Nieuport scout and as he attempted to extract himself from the wreckage, he inadvertently fired his machine gun, scattering the onlookers who were rushing to his aid. His skills as a pilot eventually improved and Thieffry went on to become an ace. In February 1918, he was shot down in flames but survived and was captured.

Middle: Fighter ace Lieutenant André 'Mystère' De Meulemeester in front of Hanriot HD-1 H-30 at De Moeren (les Moëres) airfield in 1918.

Below: Jan Olieslagers, (1883-1942). A modest man and a pre-war motor cycle champion, Olieslagers purchased a Blériot monoplane in 1909, receiving Pilot's Brevet No. 5 in October. In 1910, he competed at the Meeting d'Aviation de Rheims. By 1913, he had set seven world aviation records. In June 1914, he proved himself as good an aerobaticist as Roland Garros. He was indifferent at claiming victories, so his official tally of 6 is probably considerably understated.

IMPERIAL RUSSIA
Imperial Russian Air Service

THE IMPERIAL RUSSIAN ARMY began training its first military pilots in 1910, and two years later the Imperial Russian Air Service became a separate branch of the Army. Before the outbreak of the First World War there were some 200 military airmen in the Russian forces, and in 1914 the Imperial Russian Air Service comprised both Navy and Army Divisions.

In 1912, aircraft designer D. P. Grigorovich designed his first successful flying boat—the M-1 (Naval No. 1). This was followed by various marques, up to the M-5, which was bought by the Imperial Russian Navy and put into large-scale production. Others in the M series were the M-7, M-9, M-11, M-15 and M-16. The latter two were delivered in small numbers only. Several M-9 flying boats survived the war intact—probably because they were built in such large numbers by Shchetinin, the first Russian aviation company, at St Petersburg.

Germany declared war on Russia on 1 August 1914, followed by Austria-Hungary four days later. (Russia declared war on Turkey on 2 November 1914.) The Grigorovich flying boats were used as part of the Russian Baltic Fleet and carried out many offensive missions against German forces in the Baltic, flying from their base at Libau. The Navy also acquired three FBA flying boats from France, as well as ten Curtiss flying boats.

The Russian Black Sea Fleet had Grigorovich M-class flying boats, a few Curtiss flying boats and two fighter aircraft. The main naval base, at Sevastopol, had hangars for forty-two seaplanes, while two other bases, at Odessa and Krugla, could accommodate seventeen seaplanes.

For its air war against Turkey from the Black Sea, Russia had to use three aircraft tenders, owing to the limited range of its flying boats. Raids were carried out, with some small success. During 1917, before the Revolution, the Black Sea Fleet had ninety-seven flying boats on strength.

At first the Imperial Russian Air Service's strength comprised some 224 aircraft, twelve airships and forty-odd kite balloons, but during the following three years aircraft strength increased to 1,039 in 1917. A copied and modified Voisin biplane—designated the V.1 after its modifier Lt V. Ivanov—was built at the Anatra factory at Odessa but was plagued by a series of crashes and declared unfit for use in 1917.

The St Petersburg Aviation Company was founded by Vladimir A. Lebedev prior to the First World War and built aircraft for the Imperial Russian Air Service. In 1915, a captured German Albatros reconnaissance two-seater was copied for Russian production. Designated the Lebed XI, the aircraft underwent a satisfactory air test on 28 December and 225 were ordered in April 1916, ten entering service in August. Two more models were produced—the XII and XIII—and about 214 Lebed XIIs were produced.

Russia designed no successful fighter aircraft and mainly relied on foreign imports, mostly French, and licence-built aircraft—of which it is estimated that some 4,700 were built. Where Russia did excel, however, was in the production of heavy bombers.

The Sikorsky Ilya Muromets was the first four-engine aircraft in the world. The Escadra Vozdushnykh Korabley (Squadron of Flying Ships), abbreviated to EVK, was equipped with these giant heavy bombers and used them to great effect—they could carry 1,120 lb of bombs. Bombing raids on East Prussia by the EVK commenced in February 1915. The German seaplane station on Lake Angern and Courland in Latvia, the German Army HQ at Shavli in Lithuania, and the towns of Willenberg, Soldau and Neidenburg were all heavily bombed. Long-range strategic bombing had arrived.

The massive armoured Muromets was hard to shoot down. Only one was ever downed—on 12 September 1916—and that was after the EVK crew had dispatched three attacking German aircraft. The bomber carried three machine gunners, and some had 50 mm cannon. Way ahead of its time, it also had fire-proof petrol tanks. Two other Muromets aircraft crashed, but these were the only casualties out of the EVK Squadron's strength. In total, eighty Muromets bombers were made by the Russo-Baltic Wagon factory.

After the Russian Revolution in November 1917, thirty Muromets aircraft were lined up at Vinnitsa by their crews, on 17 February 1918. Each heavy bomber was systematically wrecked by the crews so that the invading Germans could not seize and use them.

RUSSIAN ACES AND AIRMEN

As the varieties of spellings of Russian personnel are so varied and open to argument about which may be the most appropriate Anglicisation, the Cyrillic version is also given as an anchor point for readers who wish to seek additional information.

Staff Captain Alexander Alexandrovich Kazakov,
[Александр Александрович Казаков],(1889-1919)
20 victories

Alexander Kazakov, the leading Russian air ace, was unofficially credited with a total of thirty-two victories and held sixteen decorations, including the British DSO, MC, and DFC, and the French *Légion d'honneur*.

Kazakov began his formal pilot training in 1913, graduating at the start of the war. Over the next three years he increased his tally of victories and was promoted to lead a group of four fighter squadrons. In March 1915, he used his aircraft's undercarriage in flight to rip off the wing of his adversary, causing it to crash. Kazakov then had to crash land his Morane.

During 1916, he downed four Fokker monoplanes, an Albatros and a Brandenburg. The following year he shot down several more aircraft, including an Albatros D.I, a Rumpler and a Brandenburg—his last victory of the war—which ended with the Russian Revolution. Kazakov joined the British forces in Russia with the rank of major and fought in command of the Slavo-British Squadron. He died in an aircraft accident in August 1919, aged 30 years.

Ensign Vasili Ivanovich Yanchenko, [Василий Иванович Янченко], (1894-1959)
16 victories

Vasili Yanchenko was born on 4 January 1894 and joined the Imperial Russian Air Service on 22 November 1914. He learned to fly at Sevastapol, going solo on 4 September 1915. Two months later he went to Moscow Air School to convert to Morane-Saulnier Type H fighters.

In March 1916, he joined 7th Fighter Detachment in the rank of sergeant. He opened his score on 25 June by shooting down an Austro-Hungarian Aviatik No. 33.30 when flying with Ens. Ivan Orlov. This earned him the Soldier's Cross of St George 2nd Class, and later the rank of warrant officer. On 21 August he was promoted to the rank of ensign.

Yanchenko had scored three victories and been awarded further decorations by 18 October. In early February 1917, he scored his fourth victory and two more followed on 13 April. By 27 June his score was seven. Four more victories came during July, and on 5 August he downed his twelfth aircraft. By 5 October, his score had increased to fifteen. His final victory came on 14 October—an Albatros C.III over the battlefront at Gorodok. A few days later the Russian Air Arm was under Bolshevik control and Yanchenko deserted, joining the Volunteer Army in 1918. He later moved to America and worked for Sikorsky as an engineer.

Captain Paul d'Argueeff, [Павел Владимирович Аргеев], (1887-1922)
15 victories

Born in the Crimea in March 1887, Paul d'Argueeff was in France when the First World War broke out and enlisted in the 131st Infantry Regiment of the French Army. Wounded in action, he left the infantry and enlisted in the air arm and in 1917 was sent to Russia with *Escadrille* Spa 124. He scored six victories with the squadron, earning two Russian decorations—the Orders of St George and St Vladimir. He returned to France in 1918 and shot down nine German aircraft, and during his French air service gained seven Mentions in Despatches (Citations). He died in France in 1922.

Captain Ivan Vasilyevich Smirnov, [Иван Васильевич Смирнов], (1895-1956)
11 victories

Ivan Smirnov was born in Vladimir in January 1895 and joined the 96th Infantry Regiment in 1914, being awarded the Cross of St George whilst with the regiment.

In 1915, Smirnov moved to 19th Corps Air Squadron where during the next two years he shot down twelve enemy aircraft and was commissioned as a first lieutenant. Further promotion to captain followed.

Following the Revolution, Smirnov left Russia and went to England and, enlisting in the RAF for a short time. In 1922, he joined the Dutch airline KLM, retiring from flying in 1949. Smirnov died in Majorca in 1956.

Ensign Grigory Eduardovich Suk,
[Григорий Эдуардович Сук Григорий Эдуардович Сук], (1896-1917)
9 victories

Born in Lithuania on 12 December 1896 of Russo-Czech parents, Grigory Suk trained at Moscow Flying School, graduating in 1916. He was then posted to No. 9 Fighter Squadron. By 1917 he had shot down nine enemy aircraft and had been decorated with all four classes of the Order of St George. Suk died on 28 November 1917, when he was shot down in air combat over the Romanian Front.

Captain Vladimir Ivanovich Strzhizhevsky,
[Владимир Иванович Стрижевский], (1894-1940)
8 victories

Vladimir Ivanovich Strzhizhevsky was born 26 December 1894. He attended St Petersburg Technical Institute until volunteering for military service on 14 October 1914. Four days later, he began training in the theory of aviation at the Saint Petersburg Polytechnical Institute. He graduated on 2 January 1915, and was forwarded to Gatchinsky Military Air Force School for practical training. After aviation training, he graduated from Flying School in Sevastopol on 29 July 1915. His initial posting was to the 16th *Korpusnoi Aviatsionniy Otryad* (Corps Aviation Detachment) on 10 August 1915. He arrived at the 16th KAO on 5 September; on 14 September 1915, he was promoted to 2 Lt. By January 1916, Strzhizhevsky had flown 43 combat sorties and during this period, he was awarded all four classes of the Cross of Saint George and promoted.

On 9 March 1916, while on patrol, Strzhizhevsky's aircraft engine failed and he crash-landed suffering serious injuries to his right leg and face. He was hospitalized and not able to return to battle until 24 August 1916, when he joined the 9th *Aviatsionniy Otryad Istrebitlei* (Fighter Aviation Detachment). Over the next three months, he gradually flew a slowly increasing number of missions as his health improved. When the combined Austro-Hungarian and German forces broke open the Romanian front in early 1917, the 9th Fighter Aviation Detachment moved its base to Săucești. From this airfield, only 13 kilometres behind their own fighting lines, Strzhizhevsky gained his aerial successes and was awarded the Fourth Class Order of Saint George for his bravery. On 17 March 1917, he scored his first aerial victory. He would score three more times in April 1917, twice while on escort missions and once while on patrol. On 17 May 1917 while flying SPAD

VII 1446 he brought down a Hansa-Brandenburg D.I. On 17 June 1917, still in his SPAD Vii he brought down his sixth victim, a Fokker Eindekker. The following day in Nieuport 17 N1448 he brought down a Hansa-Brandenburg C.I 67.54. His victory tally ended on 18 July 1917, when he was hit in the right leg by two bullets while engaging the enemy and shooting down his 8th and final enemy, a two-seater Hansa-Brandenburg C.I 67.52.

As the October Revolution threw the Russian war effort into chaos, Strzhizhevsky was co-opted into the Red Air Force as the commander of the First Voronezh Aviation Group. However, on 4 November 1918, he deserted across the lines to join the White Russian Army; he also served in the Armed Forces of South Russia. On 21 July 1920, he was promoted to Captain. In November 1920, he left Russia with the fleeing White Army. From the Crimea, he found his way to the Kingdom of Yugoslavia and joined their air force. Vladimir Ivanovich Strzhizhevsky died in Belgrade on 22 August 1940.

Donat Aduiovich Makijonek, [Донат Адамович Макеёнок], (1890-date of death unknown)

8 victories

Donat Makijonek was born into a peasant family in the village of Dambovka, Osvedskoy volost, the province of Vitebsk. He was ethnically Polish and on 7 November 1911, he was conscripted into the 97th Infantry Liflandsky Regiment for his military service. At the time he joined, the Imperial Russian Air Service planned to expand greatly the following year. In 1912, he was accepted for pilot training and trained on the Nieuport IV monoplane. He graduated from training on 7 March 1914 being granted brevet number 239. He was quickly promoted to senior sergeant).

On 27 April 1915, Makijonek was flying reconnaissance in Morane-Saulnier G serial number MS107 when a bullet hit his engine. After the motor stopped, he barely stretched his glide over enemy lines to safety with Russian troops near Nida. He pulled his observer from the overturned aircraft and hustled them both in a crawl into a nearby trench as enemy artillery rained in on the wreckage. The feat won the young pilot the Third Class Cross of Saint George, awarded 28 April 1915. On 16 June 1915, Makijonek and his observer saw a bridge was being built across the San River to convey an attack into Russian territory. His report of this to Russian headquarters gained him a Second Class award of the Cross of Saint George, and a promotion to *Podpraporshchik*—senior NCO on the 19 June. On 13 January 1916, Donat Makijonek was deemed experienced enough to be appointed as a fighter pilot by Imperial Order. He trained on Nieuport 11s at Odessa. He graduated on 12 August 1916, and in December 1916 was assigned to the 7th *Aviatsionniy Otryad Istrebitlei* (Fighter Aviation Detachment), which was based near Tarnopol and commanded by Ivan Orlov. Makijonek fought several furious engagements during February 1917, though without success. He realized that an experienced wingman would improve his chances. He struck up both a working partnership and a close friendship with Vasili Yanchenko. On 13 April, Makijonek shared a pair of triumphs with both Yanchenko and Juri Gilsher. On 16 April and 29 June, he scored clean solo victories. On 4 July 1917, his commander,

Ivan Orlov, was killed in action; Gilsher assumed command. On both the 6th and the 11th, Makijonek and Yanchenko once again shared victories. On 20 July, Makijonek, Gilsher, and Yanchenko flew an evening sortie to intercept eight enemy fighters. Makijonek was waylaid en route by an enemy fighter, and engaged it. Gilsher and Yanchenko flew into a lopsided battle against 16 enemy aircraft. Juri Gilsher died in action when his aircraft fell apart in midair. After his commander's death, Makijonek stepped into the vacant command slot.

There are confusing accounts after this, but it appears Makijonek was severely wounded while scoring his eighth victory on 5 August 1917. He was sent to St Petersburg to work in the Aviation and Aeronautic Department, but its work had ground to a halt because of the Revolution. In the ensuing chaos he left the Russian Air Service after almost 600 combat missions and more than 30 aerial battles. In the process, he had operated 14 types of aircraft. After the War Makijonek helped found the 1st Polish Aviation Detachment, and became its deputy commander. By the time the Polish–Soviet War began in 1920, Makijonek commanded the 3rd Polish Squadron. He was still in command in 1921, after the war's end. After that, little is known of him. He is believed to have died in Auschwitz concentration camp during the Second World War.

Captain Yevgraf Nikolaevich Kruten, [Евграф Николаевич Крутень]. (1890-1917)
7 victories

Yevgraf Kruten was born in Kiev in December 1890 and was commissioned as a second lieutenant in the Army in 1912. The following year he joined the 11th Corps Air Squadron as an artillery spotter and trained as a pilot. In September 1914, he began flying Voisins on night bombing missions.

Kruten's first aerial victory came in May 1916, when he shot down a German Albatros. Three months later he forced an Albatros two-seater to land at Nesvizh where the crew were captured by Russian soldiers. He shot down another Albatros over the same town on 14 August. Kruten became a squadron commander and then commander of Fighter Group 2, his personal aircraft emblazoned with the head of a Russian medieval knight.

During the harsh Russian winter of 1916–17 he was sent to France to learn British and French aerial battle tactics, later becoming a successful author of seven small books on aerial fighting and bombing. Returning to operational combat flying in the summer of 1917, he dispatched several more enemy aircraft over the Galician front, taking his final victory total to seven confirmed, although his true total is believed to be fifteen. (The other eight were not confirmed, as they were downed behind enemy lines.)

Capt. Kruten died on 19 June 1917, when his aircraft spun into the ground on landing approach returning from a combat mission.

Lieutenant Alexander Nikolaivich Prokofiev de Seversky,
[Александр Николаевич Прокофьев-Северский], (1894-1974)
6 victories

Born in Tiflis (Tbilisi) in June 1894, Alexander Seversky was destined for a career in the Imperial Russian Navy. After graduating from the naval academy he took a flying course at the Military School of Aeronautics and graduated as a pilot on a Farman F.40. He then obtained a commission as a second lieutenant in the Imperial Russian Naval Air Service and was sent to the Baltic 2nd Bombing Squadron base at Oesel Island. On 2 July 1915, whilst flying a two-seater seaplane on a night mission, his aircraft was shot down in the Gulf of Riga. His observer was killed and Seversky's right leg was blown off. Six months later he was back in the air, and shot down thirteen German aircraft in fifty-seven sorties.

His final combat came on 31 July 1916, when he and another pilot flying seaplanes fought off seven German aircraft. During the two-hour combat—outnumbered seven to one, as his fellow pilot's machine guns had jammed—Seversky took on the enemy single-handed, shooting down two and driving off the other five. For this superb action he was awarded the exclusive Gold Sword of St George.

Seversky went to America in 1917, became a test pilot and founded the Seversky Aero Corporation in 1923.

Lieutenant Viktor Georgiyevich Federov,
[Виктор Георгиевич Фёдоров], (1885-1922)
5 victories

Born on 11 November 1885, Viktor Federov studied at Kharkov University where he developed revolutionary social democratic views. He was in France when the First World War broke out and enlisted in the Russian Battalion, being wounded in February 1915. In July he transferred to the French Air Arm and learned to fly at Dijon. He was posted to *Escadrille* Spa 3 in December in the rank of sergeant, flying with the same observer/mechanic, Pierre Lanero, for the duration of the war.

In the spring of 1916, Federov shot down five enemy aircraft over the Verdun battlefront within a period of sixteen days and became known as 'The Russian Air Cossack of Verdun'. Promotion to lieutenant followed, together with the award of the *Croix de Guerre* and the *Médaille militaire*.

On 2 April 1916, he was wounded in an air battle and after recovering was sent, with Lanero, to Romania, and then to Russia as a flying instructor. He returned to action in France in April 1918, and shot down his fourth aircraft on 29 September. His last victory was on 9 October, when he downed an enemy fighter over Argonne. Seven days later he was wounded and his military service came to an end. Lt Federov died in Paris in March 1922.

Ensign Ivan Alexandrovich Orlov, [Иван Александрович Орлов], (1895-1917)
5 victories

When the First World War began, Orlov joined Russian military aviation as a private. He was posted to the 5th Corps Air Detachment, and brought his personal Farman S.7 to the new unit, which consisted of six Farman F.22 biplanes. On 20 August 1914, Orlov flew a reconnaissance mission over Stalupepen, the first of 18 military sorties he would fly that month. His dash and courage flying these hazardous scouting missions in Voisins soon earned him both promotion and honors. After being decorated on 2 September 1914, Orlov was promoted to corporal on 14 September. On 3 October, he was promoted again. Orlov moved to staff duty with the 5th Air Corps Detachment; on 21 November 1914, he was decorated for organising communications with the 2nd Army. He had not ceased flying however; on 18 November 1914, he was decorated for bombing a railway. On 19 December, he was sent for advanced training on Voisins. On 4 February 1915 and was assigned to the First Army Aviation Detachment. He left Warsaw on 13 April in a Voisin to join the unit near Snyadovo, adding aerial combat to his skills. He made his first aerial victory claim on 26 May 1915, but it was unconfirmed.

On both 11 and 28 August 1915, Orlov flew hazardous reconnaissance duties under intense ground fire; he won medals for valor for both sorties. In September 1915, he was entrusted with picking up new aircraft from the factories in Petrograd and Moscow and did not return to front line duty until October and on 10 December 1915, he moved to Odessa Flying School to undergo fighter conversion training there on Nieuports.

Orlov graduated from Nieuport training on 10 January 1916 and joined the new dedicated fighter units, making the new 7th AOI unit's first operational flight on 28 April 1916. Orlov scored his first two confirmed aerial victories in June 1916. On the 8th, he closed to 35 metres before shooting the enemy observer in the chest and downing the Austro-Hungarian craft. On the 25th, on his tenth sortie for the day, Orlov and Vasili Yanchenko wounded the aircrew with close-range fire and drove them and their aircraft down into captivity. On 13 November, he was posted on exchange duty to the Western Front to study French aerial tactics. He sailed on a week-long voyage from Murmansk to Brest to join the famous Stork Squadron, *Escadrille* 3 joining experienced figher pilots such as Georges Guynemer and Alfred Heurtaux. On 24 January 1917, while flying a SPAD VII with *Escadrille* 3, Orlov drove down an enemy aircraft north of Fresnoy for his fourth victory. He exited the dogfight by purposely spinning his aircraft to escape two enemy Halberstadt fighters.

At the end of January, Orlov was one of a party of six Russian pilots who returned home. He reached St Petersburg on 20 March 1917 and submitted hs report and had a nine page brochure on air tactics published by the Aviation and Aeronautics Field Department Bureau; ways of Conducting an Air Combat principally encapsulated from tactical advice received from Guynemer and Heurteaux, and enumerated 16 main points. A key recommendation was the use of an induced spin to escape a losing situation, as he had done at Fresnoy.

Orlov returned to take up his duties with the 7th AOI in the wake of the February Revolution. The political turmoil in Russia was undermining the Russian military's combat capabilities; however, Orlov kept his unit in the fight. In April, he flew 13 combat missions from his unit's airfield near Markovtse. He used a Nieuport 11 to shoot down an Albatros two-seater on 21 May. By June, the 7th AOI had moved to Kozova, then on to Vikturovka; by now, it was reduced to six pilots and eight Nieuports. As his detachment flew intensive operations, Orlov personally flew 13 sorties in June. On the 20th, Orlov and Yanchenko tangled with two of a flight of five enemy planes; Orlov reported one of them as gliding down near Leśniki. On the 26th, he saved Yanchenko from a rear attack, driving off the attacker but being foiled of a victory by a blownout cartridge case jamming his gun. Then, on 4 July 1917, he unsuccessfully engaged attacking enemy fighters, using his new Nieuport 23, serial no. N2788. After combat manoevring, the lower right wing of his Nieuport ripped loose, and Ivan Aleksandrovich Orlov fell 3,000 metres to his death in the Russian front line trenches near Kozova.

Lieutenant Commander Victor V. Utgoff, [*born in Poland no Cyrillic version given*], (1889-1930)
5 victories

Victor Utgoff was born on 14 July 1889 in Novoradomsk (now Lodz, Poland). He became a naval cadet and joined the Imperial Russian Navy, serving with the Black Sea Fleet. In 1912, the Fleet established an air arm and Utgoff underwent flying training, gaining his pilot's wings on 21 July. Promoted to naval lieutenant in December 1913 and awarded the Order of St Stanislaus, he became the Russian Navy's first wartime pilot flying seaplanes with the Black Sea air arm.

In March 1915, Utgoff began flying offensive sorties against Turkey from a seaplane carrier. He was decorated with the Order of St George, promoted to captain and made second in command of the air arm. Utgoff was flying M-9 seaplanes in August 1916, and bombed the Bulgarian port of Varna to such good effect that he was awarded the Golden Sword of St George.

When the Russian Revolution began in 1917, Utgoff and his family went to America, initially on a temporary basis, but decided to stay there when the Bolsheviks seized power. In 1920 he was working as a naval attaché at the Russian Embassy in Washington DC.

Yuri Vladimirovich Gilsher, [Юрий Владимирович Гильшер], (1894-1917)
5 victories

Yuri Gilsher was a remarkably resilient person. He was born in Moscow in 1894. After graduating from commercial school he planned to study civil engineering, but on the outbreak of war he enrolled in the Army, joining the Nikolayevsky Cavalry school in December 1914. After a short period of training with the 13th Dragoon Regiment he requested a transfer to the new air service—the Emperor's Military Air Fleet—and entered flight school in Gatchina, near St Petersburg on 16 June 1915. He graduated on 21 October 1915, and was posted to the 4th Army Air Detachment. Nine days later, he was designated as a military pilot. On 9 November, the new unit moved forward into combat. However, Gilsher's career suffered a setback on 20 November when a propeller fractured both bones in his right forearm while he was starting an aircraft engine. He was removed from the unit and assigned to Moscow's Dux aircraft factory as a quality control inspector until he healed. After recovery, he underwent advanced flight training on fighters in Odessa during February 1916 and returned to active service on 21 March 1916, posted to the 7th Fighter Aviation Detachment. The unit transferred to combat duty at Tarnopol. On 12 April 1916, Gilsher was promoted to Kornet.

On 10 May 1916, Gilsher and his aerial observer flew a sortie in Sikorsky S-16 serial no. 201. They attacked a German Aviatik B.III and downed it. Upon their return to base, the fighter plane went into a spin at 1,200 metres because the left elevator jammed. Both Gilsher and his observer survived the crash with serious injuries; Gilsher's left foot was amputated.

Despite calls to step down from active duty he asked to resume his service in the Air Force and six months later he was able to fly with a prosthetic leg. Remarkably, the medical commission stated that the Air Force service 'does not require a serious physical effort', so his request, submitted to the Command on 29 October 1916, was granted.

His first two successes were scored in a single day, 13 April 1917, with subsequent victories following on 15 May, 17 and 20 July. His final victory was on 20 July 1917 when he and Vasili Yanchenko shared a victory near Tarnopol. However, Gilsher's Nieuport, in his combat with at least 10 German planes, was hit by enemy fire and broke up, resulting in his death. Yanchenko wrote to Gilsher's father: 'Attacking the second airplane, your son closed the distance to 70 metres. But the enemy fired first. Nieuport engine fell out from the frame, its wings collapsed and like a stone it fell...'

Boris Vasilievich Sergievsky, [Борис Васильевич Сергиевский], (1888–1971)
2 victories

Boris Sergievsky was born in 1888 and learned to fly in 1912. This earned him a captain's commission in the Imperial Russian Air Service and command of 2 Fighter Squadron. During his military career he shot down two enemy aircraft and was awarded ten medals and decorations, including the Cross of St George.

Fleeing the Russian Revolution, he went to England and served with the RAF before returning to White Russia in 1920. Three years later he emigrated to America and became an engineer and test pilot.

Imperial Russian Air Service Victory Totals

Russian military records are somewhat sparse regarding their pilot's victory totals, but the following list is reasonably accurate. Pilots shared in kills and had some unconfirmed—all of which distorts true victory totals.

S/Capt. A. A. Kazakov—20
Ens. V. I. Yanchenko—16
Capt. P. V. d'Argueeff—15

Capt. I. V. Smirnov—11
Ens. G. E. Suk—9
Lt G. M. Lachman—8
Lt D. A. Makijonek—8
Capt. V. I. Strzhizhevsky—8
Capt. Y. N. Kruten—7
Capt. Louis Coudouret—6
2Lt Ivan Alexandrovich Loiko—6
Capt. Konstantin Konstantinovich Vakulovsky—6
Lt Alexander Nikolaivich Prokofiev de Seversky—6
Lt Viktor Georgiyevich Federov—5
2Lt Yuri Vladimirovich Gilsher—5
Capt. Maurice Roch Gond—5
Ens. Nikolai Kirillovich Kokorin—5
Ernst K. Leman—5
Ens. Ivan Alexandrovich Orlov—5
Lt Eduard Martynovich Pulpe—5
Lt Alexander Mikhailovich Pishvanov—5
Capt. Mikhail Ivanovich Safonov—5 (known as 'The Eagle of the Baltic')
Lt Cdr Victor Utgoff—5
Adjt Charles A. Revol-Tissot—5

Mention must be made of a pilot who scored just one victory but was regarded as a national hero. Flying an unarmed Morane M-type monoplane, S/Capt. Petr Nikolaevich Nesterov attacked three enemy machines and rammed the leading aircraft, bringing it down but killing himself in the process. He was buried with full military honours and had a town named after him.

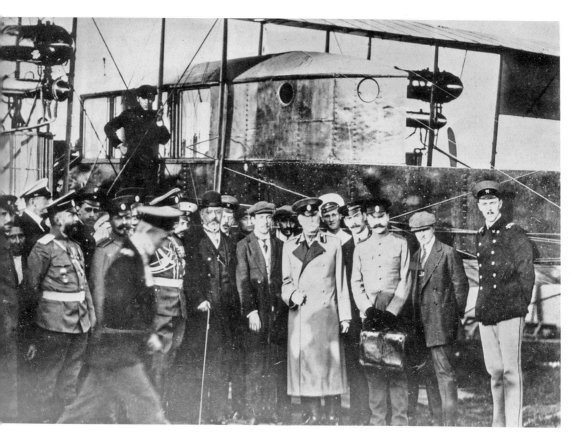

Igor Sikorsky with an assembly of senior Russian officials, who are being shown his proposed bomber prototype with a view to building the aircraft for official service.

The Sikorsky Ilya Muromet large four-engine aerplane was designed by Igor Sikorsky. The Ilya Muromet first appeared in 1913 and was a revolutionary design, intended for commercial service with its spacious fuselage incorporating a passenger saloon and washroom on board. During the War it became the first four-engine bomber to equip a dedicated strategic bombing unit and was unrivalled at the time. It was slow at just 68 mph but it could carry 12,000 lb (4,600 kg) of bombs.

From top to bottom:

Igor Sikorsky was not the only innovator in Russia, in 1913, Dmitry Grigorovich designed Russia's first seaplane. The flying boat, called the M-1, participated in the Russian war effort.

Alexander Alexandrovich Kazakov, (1889-1919). Alexander Kazakov, the leading Russian air ace, was unofficially credited with a total of thirty-two victories and held sixteen decorations, including the British DSO, MC, and DFC, and the French *Légion d'honneur*. His official tally was 20 Victories. Kazakov flew on Morane-Saulnier, SPAD SA2, Nieuport 11 and Nieuport 17 aircraft.

Below near left: Staff Captain Peter Nikolaevitch Nestorov, (1887-1914). Nestorov scored just one victory but became a 'Hero of Russia' by ramming the Austrian Baron von Rosenthal in aerial action and saving the town of Sholkiv. After using a pistol to fire unsuccessfully at the Austrian Albatros B.II he used his Morane-Saulnier Type G to ram it. He probably intended a glancing blow but damaged his own aircraft as much as the enemy's and both planes crashed. Nesterov was not strapped in and he fell from his plane.

Far left: Captain Evgraph [Yevraf] Nikolaevich Kruten, (1890–1917). Kruten was credited with 7 Victories. He began the War as an observer. He rose through the ranks, to be appointed as his unit's commander on 6 June 1916. With his victory tally at three, he was forwarded to service with the French *Aéronautique Militaire*. While learning French aerial tactics, Kruten shot down a German aircraft during February 1917. He died in a landing accident on 19 June 1917.

Above left: Alexander Nikolaevich Prokoffief de Seversky, (1894-1974). 6 victories. During the 1917 Revolution, Seversky was stationed in St Petersburg and remained in uniform at the request of the commander-in-chief of the Baltic Fleet. In March 1918, he was selected as an assistant naval attaché in the Russian Naval Aviation Mission to the United States. Seversky departed via Siberia and while in the USA, decided to remain there rather than return to a Russia torn apart by the Revolution.

Above right: In the USA Seversky invented a gyroscopically stabilized bombsight which was sold to the US Government for $50,000. With the money Seversky founded the Seversky Aero Corporation in 1923. This was financially insecure requiring bail-out money. When Seversky left for Europe on a sales tour in the winter of 1938-39, the Board reorganized the operation on 13 October 1939, renamed as Republic Aviation Corporation which became an industrial giant during the Second World War designing and producing the Republic P-47 Thunderbolt .

Right: Yuri Vladimirovich Gilsher, (1894-1917). Gilsher scored 5 victories. On 20 November 1915, in his early days in the air service, he fractured both bones in his right forearm after being hit by the propeller while he was starting an engine.

On 10 May 1916, Gilsher's Sikorsky S-16 went into a spin at 4,000 feet due to the left elevator jamming. Both Gilsher and his observer survived the crash, but Gilsher's left foot was amputated. This photograph was taken six months later on his return to duty with Gilsher sitting near his Nieuport 10, Galicia, December 1916.

Like Douglas Bader later, Yuri Gilsher was provided with a prosthetic leg.

Left: In March 1917 Yuri Gilsher designed and tested a 'swinging training set' to improve aiming and shooting skill of his fellow trainee pilots.

Right: Donat Aduiovich Makijonek, (1890-date of death unknown). Makijonek was the only ace of Polish ethnic heritage to fight against the Central Powers. In later life, he helped found Polish military aviation immediately after the First World War, and fight in the Polish-Soviet War of 1919-1921.

Captain Paul d'Argueeff, (1887-1922). At the outbreak of the War Argueeff was in France where he worked in the Russian military mission to armaments. After initial service there he returned to Russia, but returned to France after the Revolution. Argueeff had 15 victories, 6 in Russia and 9 in France.

Grigory Eduardovich
Suk, (1896-1917). Suk
had 9 victories, flying
a Nieuport 11, Vickers
F.B.19 and a SPAD VII.

A French built Caudron G4
in the Imperial Russian Air
Service, (Императорскій
военно-воздушный флотъ,
literally *Emperor's Military Air
Fleet*).

An aerodrome at the front,
c. 1915 with a Russian-built
reconnaissance Deperdussin.

Tsar Nicholas II in the Royal bomber with the Royal Crest on the Bow.

Victor V. Utgoff, (1889-1930). in flying helmet in Curtiss 1913 Model F, Sevastapol, October 1915. Utgoff served as lieutenant in the Imperial Russian Navy Black Sea Fleet. In 1914 became the Navy's first wartime pilot flying seaplanes. Utgoff became one of Russia's aces with 5 victories. Following the February Revolution, he travelled to the United States with his family in 1917, initially temporarily and then—once the Bolsheviks seized power in October 1917—permanently.

Above: A French-built Nieuport in service with the Imperial Russian Air Force.

Left: Yankovsky Georgy Viktorovich, (1888-1944). Viktorovich was a Polish-born pilot in Imperial Russian service. He was a former pilot of the famous 'Ilya Muromet; bomber. After the civil war in Russia he emigrated to the kingdom of Yugoslavia and from 1941 fought in the Croatian air service where he died at the hands of Tito partisans in 1944.

Most of the aircraft used by the Imperial Russian Air Service were of French or other western designs such as the Farman F.30 and F.40 pusher two-seat biplanes. There were of both French and Russian build, and 400 of F.30 and F.30bis were built at the Dux factory in Moscow. They were armed with a machine gun and bombs, and used in reconnaissance and bomber roles in the War. This particular Farman with Bolshevik insignia came to an unfortunate end.

A Russian Polikarpov R-1 with officers and ground crew. The Polikarpov R-1 was an unlicensed version of the British Airco DH.9A, a single-engined light bomber designed and first used shortly before the end of the War. Over 2,400 examples of the pirated Polikarpov R-1 were built by the Bolsheviks.

IMPERIAL GERMANY
Fliegertruppen des deutschen Kaiserreiches Luftstreitkräfte

I N ORDER TO UNDERSTAND the complexities of the various German kingdoms, principalities and states at this time, and their unified approach to the First World War, it
may help to explain the way they developed and also kept, to a certain degree, their
own identities.

The Second Reich (the first Reich was deemed to be the ancient Holy Roman Empire)
followed the Franco-Prussian War of 1870–71, the German states continuing their process
of unification in order to counterbalance the power of Russia, France and Austria-Hungary.
The then King of Prussia became the first Kaiser (Emperor) and the new German Empire,
with its federal constitution, was created in January 1871 and proclaimed in the Hall of
Mirrors at Versailles. For the first time since the Middle Ages, the mass of German-speaking
people of Europe were united in a single state.

The new empire was a confederation of twenty-six states: the kingdoms of Prussia, Bavaria,
Saxony and Württemberg; the grand duchies of Baden, Hesse, Mecklenburg-Scherwin,
Mecklenburg-Strelitz, Saxe-Weimar and Oldenburg; the duchies of Anhalt, Brunswick,
Saxe-Altenburg, Saxe-Coburg-Gotha and Saxe-Meiningen; the principalities of Lippe,
Ruess-Greiz, Ruess-Schleiz, Schaumburg-Lippe, Schwarzburg-Rudolstadt, Schwarzburg-
Sondershausen and Waldeck; the territory of Alsace-Lorraine; and the cities of Bremen,
Lübeck and Hamburg. By 1910, the population of Germany had risen to 65 million, with
Prussia having over 40 million.

The first Kaiser, Wilhelm I, ruled over Germany from 1871 to 1888, followed by
Friedrich III during 1888, and finally Wilhelm II from 1888 until 1918. They were all
members of the aristocratic Prussian Hohenzollern dynasty and were descendants of
Frederick the Great.

Within the federal constitution some armies were under the control of the Prussian Army,
but others—such as the royal armies of Saxony and Württemberg—retained their own war
ministries, HQ staff and establishments. The Royal Bavarian Army remained autonomous
under the command of its king, again with its own HQ staff and establishment, but the
various military forces of the smaller states and provinces became integrated with the
Prussian Army. At the outbreak of the First World War, however, the forces of the German
Empire were under a unified command, only Bavaria maintaining a separate establishment.

Each state had its own range of decorations and medals. During the First World War, the Order of *Pour le Mérite* with Oak Leaves was Prussia's highest award for individual gallantry in action. Not one was awarded to any member of the Imperial German Air Service, but the *Pour le Mérite* was given to eighty-one aviation personnel during the conflict. The award, which had been founded in 1740 by Frederick the Great, was discontinued after the defeat of Germany in 1918.

Friedrich Wilhelm III of Prussia instituted the famous Iron Cross in 1813 as an award for gallantry in combat. The 1st and 2nd Classes of the award were reinstated for the Franco-Prussian War and continued to be conferred until the end of the First World War. Between 1813 and 1918, there were 219,300 awards of the Iron Cross 1st Class, and some 5,500,000 of the Iron Cross 2nd Class. The award consisted of a cross pattée in black iron edged with silver, with the imperial crown and royal cipher on the upper limb and the dates '1813', '1870' or '1914' on the lower limb. The Iron Cross 1st Class was fixed to the uniform jacket like the Star of an Order, whereas the 2nd Class award was worn on the left breast from a black ribbon with white edges.

The Imperial German Air Service was regarded until 1916 as part of ground communications troops, although a separate command had been established in March 1915 but had not been unified. At first, the individual armies to which they were attached controlled aviation units. For example, Württemberg insisted that its aviation units were to be staffed only with its citizens.

Politics and local pride created confusion. This situation reigned until 8 October 1916, when Gen. Ernst von Hoeppner was appointed Officer Commanding the Imperial German Air Service and immediately began to reorganise its command structure, creating fighter units of eighteen aircraft each, ground attack units of six to twelve aircraft, and bomber units with about twenty-four aircraft each, as well as reconnaissance units, artillery units and single-seat aircraft for home defence. However, the Imperial German Naval Aviation Service remained independent, operating flying boats from some thirty-two bases on German and occupied coasts and land-based aircraft for coastal defences.

In Germany there was a certain social attitude towards flying aircraft in the early years. Prior to 1914, gentlemen of means employed chauffeurs to drive their cars, and the piloting of an aircraft was regarded in the same manner. The first pilots were drawn from the ranks of NCOs, while the commissioned officers—usually cavalrymen, some with the rank of freiherr (baron)—acted as observers. This sometimes caused great problems, as in the early years most of the cavalrymen insisted on being properly dressed—and that included wearing swords. As the aircraft were made of wood and fabric, this caused holes to be torn in the fuselage areas so the practice of carrying a sword was very soon dropped. However, it was not long before these frustrated cavalrymen were drawn into the excitement of the chase and quickly grasped the chance of individual combat in the air—to symbolically tilt the lance at their enemies, as the knights of medieval times had done.

IMPERIAL GERMAN AIR SERVICE—*LUFTSTREITKRÄFTE*

T HE ORIGINS OF THE Imperial German Air Service—*Die Fliegertruppen des deutschen Kaiserreiches*—date from 1909, when the German Army used aircraft for the first time and Hauptmann de la Roi of the Prussian War Ministry was appointed to head up an aviation test project, with a technical section under the control of Major Hesse. The results were so encouraging that Generalleutnant Freiherr von Lyncker was put in charge of the Inspectorate of Transport Troops, under which umbrella the Imperial German Air Service flourished.

In the ensuing years both civil and military pilots were licensed by the German Aviation Association and the Inspectorate of Military Transport (military only). The first pilot's certificates were issued to August Euler and Hans Grade on 1 February 1910. Euler, an engineer, went on to become an aircraft designer. During the spring of 1910 the first flying schools were set up and, by December, ten officers had completed their flying training and had been awarded their certificates.

The German War Department—*Allgemeines Kriegsdepartement*—encouraged by the results of the pilot training—allocated the sum of 110,000 marks for the purchase of military aircraft. The future Imperial German Air Service was slowly coming into being, and at the outbreak of war on 4 August 1914, Germany had a strength of 228 aircraft plus a small reserve. Aircrew strength stood at 600 officer pilots and 220 NCO pilots, and 500 officers had qualified as observers—a total of 1,320 flying personnel. This complement was allocated to forty-one *Flieger Abteilungen* (Flying Units), of which thirty-three were *Feldflieger Abteilungen* (Field Aviation Units). Eight were designated Fortress *Flieger Abteilungen*, whose role was to defend strategic towns.

German Army aircraft were placed under the control of the military, whilst the large fleet of airships was placed under the control of the Navy. At this time German thinking was that aircraft and airships were to be used for reconnaissance—aircraft for short-range missions, such as artillery spotting and photo reconnaissance, and airships for long-range reconnaissance duties. The tactical use of aircraft as fighters and bombers was to come shortly.

The first long-range bomber units—*Kampfgeschwader* (KG)—were formed in October 1914 and came under Army command. The first such unit was a clandestine one code-named *Brieftauben-Abteilung Ostende* (BAO), Ostend Carrier Pigeon Flight, under the command of Maj. Wilhelm Siegert.

Early German aircraft—such as the Aviatik C.I—were two-seaters, with the pilot and observer firing machine guns sidewards and rearwards from their cockpits. The airmen were unable to fire forward through the propeller arc, as no firing interrupter gear had as yet been perfected. Some aircraft had machine guns mounted on the upper wing to fire over the propeller arc but this was not very successful.

However, it was not long before a reliable firing interrupter mechanism was developed. It was said to have been invented by Anthony Fokker after seeing the French pilot Roland Garros's design on his Morane Parasol after it had been shot down, but it is now accepted that it was probably the brainchild of Heinrich Luebbe, a member of Fokker's design team. On 23 May 1915, the Fokker Eindecker—equipped with a machine gun firing through the propeller—entered front-line service with FA 62 at Douai. German fighter aircraft now came into their own, attaining air superiority over the Allies, at least for a time.

This development attracted the attention of Hauptmann Oswald Boelcke and Oberleutnant Max Immelmann—both already famous in Germany as pilots. Boelcke and Immelmann immediately went into combat with the new Eindeckers of FA 62, Boelcke shooting down a Morane Parasol on 4 July and Immelmann a B.E.2c on 1 August 1915.

Shrewdly, the German War Ministry realised the propaganda value of casting its pilots and observers as national heroes by awarding honours and decorations for the number of enemy aircraft shot down. At first, four victories were needed to give Ace (Kanone) status, six kills were rewarded with the Knight's Cross of the Royal House Order of Hohenzollern, and eight for the award of the *Pour le Mérite*.

Famous airmen began to emerge. Both Boelcke and Immelmann would earn Prussia's highest decoration—the *Pour le Mérite*—on 12 January 1916, as did Kurt Wintgens later that year, and the men were immortalised on Sanke cards. These postcards carried portraits of airmen in various heroic poses and were avidly bought and collected by an admiring German public.

During the winter of 1916 the tempo of aerial conflict increased, and the number of victories required for high honours increased. To gain the *Pour le Mérite*, sixteen kills were now needed. This later rose to twenty, and to thirty by the end of the war. Strangely, some pilots with high scores—including Leutnant Paul Billik with thirty-one kills, and Josef Mai with thirty kills—were never awarded the 'Blue Max'. Thirty-five other pilots scored between fourteen and twenty-six victories but were not decorated with the *Pour le Mérite*. Nineteen known pilots were actually awarded the decoration but never received it for various reasons, including death, as the decoration could only be awarded to a living officer. Non-commissioned ranks received the Golden Military Service Cross, of which there were eighty awards.

By now the new Albatros D.I and D.II scouts were in service and could outfly most of the Allied aircraft, the British Pup and the French Nieuport being the best the Allies could put in the air. By the end of 1916, the German Air Service had twenty-four fully staffed operational fighter squadrons (*Jastas*) and these started to take an even higher toll of Allied aircraft. Many fighter pilots began to rise to prominence, including Hartmut Baldamus, Otto Bernert, Erwin Böhme, Albert Dossenbach, Wilhelm Frankl, Heinrich Gontermann, Hans Müller, Max Müller and Werner Voss.

Fate, however, took a hand. Hauptmann Oswald Boelcke died in combat with DH.2s of 24 Squadron RFC on 28 October 1916, his aircraft colliding with one of his former flying pupils, Erwin Böhme. Boelcke's death brought the pilot who was destined to become legendary— Manfred Freiherr von Richthofen—to the fore. His Albatros was painted bright red—hence his nickname, the Red Baron. By the end of the year he had fifteen confirmed victories to his credit.

In January 1917, Manfred von Richthofen took command of *Jasta* 11 and under his inspired leadership it became the second highest scoring *Jasta* in the German Air Service. During April, known to the Allies as 'Bloody April', *Jasta* 11 shot down eighty-nine aircraft with their Albatros D.IIIs. More and more fighter pilots rose to national fame, including Karl Allmenröder, Lothar von Richthofen (the Red Baron's brother), Karl Schäfer, Adolf von Tutschek and Kurt Wolff.

The German Air Service, though outnumbered, now had air superiority over the Allies, with the RFC taking heavy casualties. To counteract their numerical inferiority, the *Jastas* were combined into groups—*Jagdgeschwader* (JGs)—in June. *Jastas* 4, 6, 10 and 11 were combined as JG I under the command of Manfred von Richthofen. Being highly mobile, JG I soon became known as the 'Flying Circus' from its ability to move quickly from battlefront to battlefront.

However, the RFC—aided by Sopwith Triplanes of the RNAS—were beginning to regain control of the air. New aircraft, such as the Bristol F.2b, the Sopwith Camel, and the S.E.5 were coming into front-line service and restoring the balance. The French Air Service squadrons of SPAD S.VIIs and SPAD S.XIIIs also entered service and scored many successes.

The Allies' objective was to overwhelm the enemy in the air by numerical superiority, but the Allied airmen were, to a certain extent, not so skilled as the Germans at this time. However, the RFC were soon to change this and gain the edge. Tactical bombing, first by DH.4s and then by DH.9 day bombers, was increased. Fighting back, the German Air Service took delivery of the Albatros D.V and the Pfalz D.III, but these fighters made little impact in spite of the superior flying skills of the German pilots.

The Fokker Dr.I Dreidecker came into service in the autumn of 1917 but had to be withdrawn with wing root problems. It re-entered service later, and Kurt Wolff was killed in action flying the new aircraft on 15 September. The high-scoring Werner Voss, also flying a Triplane, fell in action against S.E.5s of the elite 56 Squadron RFC, and another ace, Heinrich Gontermann—destroyer of seventeen balloons—was killed on 30 October when his Triplane's top wing folded in flight.

Meanwhile, the Imperial German Naval Air Service, with its own seaplane fighters and land-based aircraft, was duelling with its British counterparts over the North Sea. Oberleutnant Friedrich Christiansen won his *Pour le Mérite* on 11 December 1917. His exploits included an air-to-surface battle against a British submarine, the C25, at the mouth of the River Thames. Two other naval fliers—Oberleutnant Gotthard Sachsenberg and Leutnant Theo Osterkamp—scored many kills and both were awarded the *Pour le Mérite*.

The German Naval Airship Division flying Zeppelins also made many raids over England. Kapitänleutnant Horst Treusch Freiherr von Buttlar-Brandenfels won his *Pour le Mérite* for flying nineteen missions, and *Fregattenkapitän* Peter Strasser won the supreme award in 1917 but lost his life in Zeppelin L 70 when leading a mass attack against England.

German airmen continued to die in combat. Karl Schäfer, Eduard Ritter von Dostler and Erwin Böhme fell, and the Red Baron himself was wounded and hospitalised. New airmen appeared in the sky—Fritz Rumey and Otto Könnecke of *Jasta* 5 took up the challenge, and many Allied aircraft fell beneath their guns. At the start of 1918, famous names continued to fall in aerial combat. Walter von Bülow-Bothkamp died on 6 January, and Max Ritter von Müller three days later, under the guns of the RFC. The brave Müller jumped to his death from his blazing aircraft—a quick death rather than the agony of dying in the flames of his fighter.

January 1918 also saw the Fokker Triplane come into its own when Manfred von Richthofen discovered the agility of the machine in a dogfight. Again he had his aircraft painted bright red. Some *Jastas* were fully equipped with the Triplanes, others only partly so, and it was the Triplanes of von Richthofen's 'Flying Circus' that scored the most victories during March and April. However, the Red Baron met his end on 21 April, shot down in action by Australian ground forces on the Somme.

With the United States of America now in the war, the German Government realised that it would have to increase the size of its air arm in order to compete with America's industrial might. Forty new *Jastas* were created and two new *Jagdgeschwader*. Hauptmann Adolf von Tutschek commanded JG II, and Oberleutnant Bruno Loerzer JG III. Aircrew reinforcements became available from the now defunct Russian Front, and these battle-hardened pilots and observers provided a valuable pool of new blood.

Other pilots began to show their worth. Oberleutnant Ernst Udet—who ended the war with sixty-two victories and was the highest surviving ace—was posted to *Jasta* 11. Oberleutnant Hermann Wilhelm Göring—later to become Reichsmarschall of Nazi Germany—was appointed to command von Richthofen's JG I, but scored only one more kill to bring his total to twenty-two victories.

During April, JG I began to receive one of Germany's best First World War fighters—the Fokker D.VII—which went on to become the outstanding German fighter of the war. By the end of May most of the German Air Service was battling against its French and American counterparts on the Aisne Front. The RFC had established air superiority over the British section of the Front and was flying sorties without opposition over and behind the German lines.

As the Allies' war of attrition began to tell, the German Air Service started to run out of experienced aircrew, the last of their air aces taking to the sky in the summer of 1918, flying their Fokker D.VIIs. The Germans were also engaged in aerial combat on other fronts—Palestine, Italy and the Dardanelles—where Hauptman Hans-Joachim Buddecke had gained the third *Pour le Mérite* of the war on 14 April 1916. In Italy, the German Air Service had been assisting its Austro-Hungarian allies with three *Jastas*, but with the big German offensives in France, these *Jastas* were withdrawn and the Austro-Hungarians fought on unaided.

The last three months of the war saw the German Air Service still hard at battle. On 8 August 1918, the RAF suffered its highest casualty total of the conflict, its pilots going down to aces Otto Könnecke, Erich Löwenhardt, Lothar von Richthofen, Ernst Udet and Arthur Laumann. The following month, the Germans inflicted the most aerial casualties sustained by the Allies since April 1917.

However, the ground war was not going well for the Germans. Although the Russian exit helped Germany and although very few of the German troops were attracted to Communism, the Bolshevik appeal for an end to the war met with a powerful resonance and was the direct cause of a wave of strikes beginning in Vienna in January 1918 and spreading to Germany. Despite these problems, and although a number of senior commanders were exceedingly sceptical about the chances of success, German expectations were high that the 'Michael' offensive across the old Somme battlefields in March would end the war, with Germany victorious. The German Army made astonishing advances in the first few days of the offensive, advancing up to 60 kilometres and destroying the British Fifth Army. But the campaign soon became bogged down and degenerated into a series of limited attacks with no clear operational goal. The French counter-attacked in July, the British in August, and it was now clear that the Central Powers could not possibly win the war. Germany had lost the initiative, Austria-Hungary was on the verge of collapse and there was a chronic shortage of manpower.

Kaiser Wilhelm was at the Imperial Army headquarters in Spa, Belgium, when uprisings in Berlin and other centres took him by surprise in late 1918. Mutiny among the ranks of his beloved *Kaiserliche Marine*, the Imperial Navy, profoundly shocked him. After the outbreak of the German Revolution, Wilhelm could not make up his mind whether or not to abdicate. Up to that point, he accepted that he would likely have to give up the imperial crown, but still hoped to retain the Prussian kingship. However, this was impossible under the imperial constitution. While Wilhelm thought he ruled as emperor in a personal union with Prussia, the constitution actually tied the imperial crown to the Prussian crown, meaning that Wilhelm could not renounce one crown without renouncing the other. Internal revolution brought about primarily from hunger forced the Kaiser to abdicate and brought the war to an end. Germany eventually capitulated—but not through decisive military defeat, and the First World War ended at 11 a.m. on 11 November 1918.

The Imperial German Air Service was bruised, battered and bloodied but unbowed. It had fought a good fight—largely with honour—but had succumbed to the overwhelming material power and resources of the Allies. Not many German air aces survived the war. Some of those who did, died between the wars by murder, revolution and accident, whilst others survived to serve again in the Second World War for their fatherland—Nazi Germany.

Glossary of German Terms

AFP	*Armee Flug Park*	Supply Depot
Bogohl	*Bombengeschwader*	Bomber Unit
FA	*Flieger Abteilung*	Flying Section
FA(A)	*Flieger Abteilung Artillerie*	Flying Section (Artillery)
FEA	*Flieger Ersatz Abteilung*	Pilot Training Unit
FFA	*Feldflieger Abteilung*	Field Aviation Unit
Fr	*Freiherr*	Baron
Jasta	*Jagdstaffel*	Fighter Squadron
JastaSch	*Jagdstaffel Schule*	Fighter Pilot School
JG	*Jagdgeschwader*	Jasta Group (Permanent)
JGr	*Jagdgruppe*	Jasta Group (Temporary)
Kagohl	*Kampfgeschwader der OHL*	Combat Squadrons
Kanone		Pilot with ten or more victories
Kasta	*Kampfstaffel*	Fighter Unit or Section
Kek	*Kampfeinsitzerkommando*	Fighter Group
Kest	*Kampfeinsitzerstaffeln*	Home Defence Squadron
KG	*Kampfgeschwader*	Bomber Squadron
Kofl	*Kommandeur der Flieger*	Commanding Officer
Kogenluft	*Kommandierender General der Luftstreitkräfte*	Air Force Commander

MFJ	*Marine Feld Jasta*	Marine Fighter Squadron
OHL	*Oberste Heeresleitung*	High Command
Ritter von		Knight of (awarded by royal decree)
Schlasta	*Schlachtstaffel*	Ground Support Unit
SFA	*Seefrontstaffel*	Marine Unit
SflS	*Seeflug Station*	Naval Air Station
SSt	*Schutzstaffel*	Ground Support Unit

German/British Rank Equivalents

GERMAN	BRITISH
Generaloberst	N/A
General der Kavallerie	General
Generalleutnant	Lieutenant General
Generalmajor	General
Oberst	Colonel
Major	Major
Rittmeister	Cavalry Captain
Hauptmann	Army Captain
Obertleutnant	Lieutenant
Leutnant	Second Lieutenant
Fähnrich	Officer Cadet
Offizierstellvertreter	Warrant Officer or Acting Officer
Vizefeldwebel/Wachtmeister	Sergeant Major
Feldwebel	Sergeant
Unteroffizier	Corporal
Gefreiter	Lance Corporal
Flieger	Private

German Navy

Kapitänleutnant	Naval Captain
Leutnant zur See	Naval Lieutenant
Oberflugmeister	Naval Aviation Senior NCO
Vizeflugmeister	Naval Aviation Junior NCO
Flugmeister	Naval Airman

Classification of German Aircraft

A	Unarmed monoplane
B	Unarmed biplane—observation and training
C	Armed biplane—reconnaissance and bombing
CL	Light C plane
CLS	*Schlachtflieger*—C plane for ground attack
D	Single-seat armed biplane fighter
DJ	Single-seat ground attack
Dr	Single-seat armed triplane
E	Single-seat armed monoplane
F	Fokker Dr.I
G	*Grossflugzeug*—twin-engine biplane bomber
J	Two-seat ground attack/infantry support aircraft
R	*Riesenflugzeug*—multi-engine armed biplane long-range bomber
S	*Schlachtflugzeug*—ground attack aircraft

The serial numbers on the sides of the fuselage or fin(s) showed the maker, type, number and year of production, e.g. Udet's Fokker D.VII 4253/18. Germany's ally Austria-Hungary used a slightly different system:

A	Monoplane
B	Older biplane of up to 150 hp
C	Two-seat biplane of 150 hp to 250 hp
D	Single-seat fighter
F	Single-engine biplane of 350 hp upwards
G	Twin-engine bomber
R	Giant bomber

Added to this was a manufacturer's number code, each manufacturer being allocated an identifying letter and number abbreviation.

GERMAN ACES AND AIRMEN

AIRMEN ARE LISTED IN alphabetical order, with the exception of Germany's premier aviator of the Great War—Rittmeister Manfred Freiherr von Richthofen—who must take pride of place.

Manfred Freiherr von Richthofen, (1892-1918)
80 victories

The legendary Red Baron was born at Breslau on 2 May 1892 into the aristocratic Prussian family of Albrecht von Richthofen, a major in the 1st Regiment of Cuirassiers, and his wife Kunigunde von Richthofen. Blue-eyed, blond-haired and of medium height, he was destined to leave his mark on aviation. At the age of 11, he attended the military school at Wahlstatt before entering the Royal Prussian Military Academy. Easter 1911 saw him join a famous regiment of lancers—Uhlan Regiment No. 1 'Kaiser Alexander III'—and in the autumn of 1912 he was commissioned as a lieutenant in the 1st Uhlans.

On the outbreak of war the Uhlans were sent into Russian Poland, but within two weeks the regiment was transferred to the Meuse in France, where it was allocated to the Crown Prince's German 5th Army. Von Richthofen, attached to 6th Army Corps, was awarded the Iron Cross 2nd Class for active service with the Uhlans, but trench warfare ended his cavalry unit and he transferred to the German Air Service in May 1915. After four weeks of training as an observer at FEA 7 Cologne and FEA 6 Grossenhain he was posted to FA 69 on the Eastern Front as an observer in an Albatros B.II. His pilot, Lt Georg Zeumer, was dying from tuberculosis and had a death wish to die in action. In August 1915, von Richthofen was posted to the so-called Mail Carrier Pigeon Unit at Ostend, the innocuous title being a cover for a long-range unit training to bomb England.

Von Richthofen's first taste of aerial combat came on 1 September 1915, when flying as an observer in an AEG with Zeumer he spotted an RFC Farman flying nearby and ordered Zeumer to close for combat. Armed with a rifle, von Richthofen opened fire on the Farman but missed with his four shots. The observer in the Farman replied, scoring several hits on von Richthofen's machine.

A week later he was flying as an observer in an Albatros piloted by Lt Osteroth when he sighted a solitary Farman flying over French lines. Ordering his pilot to the attack, von Richthofen opened fire with his machine gun and poured 100 rounds at the enemy aircraft. The stricken Farman plunged to earth, crashing nose-first behind French lines. However, the victory was unconfirmed, so von Richthofen was not credited with his first aircraft downed.

En route to Metz on 1 October to join another bomber unit, von Richthofen met the already legendary Oswald Boelcke on a train. Fired by Boelcke's example, he decided to become a pilot and asked Lt Zeumer to teach him to fly. However, his first attempt ended in disaster when he crashed on landing, but he persisted and on Christmas Day 1915 qualified as a pilot. He was posted to Russia, and it was not until March 1916 that he returned to the Western Front and was ordered to fly a two-seat Albatros—not a single-seat fighter.

He adapted the Albatros by fitting a machine gun on the upper wing, which he could fire from the pilot's seat.

On 26 April 1916, he brought his machine gun into action against a French Nieuport. Riddled with bullets, the Nieuport crashed behind French lines at Douaumont—but again his victory was unconfirmed. Von Richthofen was yet to open his score officially.

He joined Boelcke's Jasta 2 on 1 September 1916, flying new Albatros D.IIIs, and on the 17th of the month Boelcke led his eight-strong Jasta into action, sighting eight B.E.2c aircraft of 12 Squadron RFC and six F.E.2bs of 11 Squadron bombing Marcoing railway station. Von Richthofen, flying Albatros D.III 491/16, chose an F.E.2b as his target, opened fire, but missed, his opponent returning Lewis machine-gun fire. Banking out of range before coming back under and behind the F.E.2b, von Richthofen closed to point-blank range and, unseen by the enemy aircraft's crew, discharged a burst of fire on the machine's engine and cockpit, wounding the pilot, 2Lt L. B. F. Morris, and his observer, Lt T. Rees. The doomed F.E.2b plunged downwards, the dying pilot managing to land the crippled aircraft behind German lines. Von Richthofen followed it down and landed nearby, where he found the pilot mortally wounded and the observer dead. He had scored his first officially confirmed victory, and to commemorate the event he had a cup made by a Berlin silversmith. It was to be the first of many such cups.

By the end of October, von Richthofen had six confirmed victories to his credit. On the 28th, Boelcke was killed in an aerial collision with Erwin Böhme and Jasta 2 was renamed Jasta Boelcke (Royal Prussian) with Oberleutnant Stefan Kirmaier in command.

Von Richthofen's victory score continued to increase, and by 20 November he had ten confirmed kills. Two days later he shot down the RFC's leading ace, Maj. Lanoe Hawker flying a DH.2 of 24 Squadron, in a dogfight. On learning who his opponent had been, he flew over British lines and dropped a message to inform the squadron of Hawker's death. Jasta Boelcke arranged a military funeral for Hawker, but von Richthofen did not attend. It was not the done thing.

After being promoted to flight commander with Jasta Boelcke, von Richthofen had his Albatros aircraft painted bright red so that his aerial opponents would know with whom they fought—hence his most famous title, the Red Baron. When he scored his sixteenth victory on 4 January 1917, the Kaiser awarded him, by special citation, the *Pour le Mérite*. He was just 24 years old and was now Germany's national hero. With the award came promotion to Rittmeister and command of Jasta 11.

On 11 April 1917, von Richthofen had taken his victory score to forty confirmed kills, and by the end of the month it had risen to fifty-two. Over Drocourt on 30 April, he crossed swords with the Canadian ace William Bishop. Try as he might, von Richthofen could not best Bishop, who outflew him and riddled his Albatros with bullets. The Red Baron was forced to break off the duel and retreat eastward towards safe territory.

After the German High Command grouped *Jastas* into *Jagdgeschwader* (JGs), von Richthofen took command of JG I, comprising *Jastas* 4, 6, 10 and 11, and continued to increase his score. When flying his red Albatros with Jasta 11, he attacked six F.E.2d aircraft of 20 Squadron RFC. In the ensuing dogfight the observer of one of the F.E.2s wounded the Red Baron in the head, causing him to break off combat and make a heavy landing near Wervicq. After being hospitalised, von Richthofen returned to duty but was plagued with headaches and dizziness. Nevertheless he managed to fly and score victory after victory, and by 30 November he had shot down sixty-three enemy aircraft.

During March 1918, von Richthofen shot down eleven aircraft, taking his total to seventy-four, and on 2 April was awarded the last of his twenty-six decorations—the Order of the Red Eagle with Crowns and Swords. By 20 April, he had achieved what was to be his final score—an unprecedented eighty confirmed victories.

On Sunday 21 April, the Red Baron took off from his base at Cappy, France, with Jasta 11 on what was to be his final flight. His squadron engaged the enemy over Le Hamel and a huge dogfight ensued, with von Richthofen in the thick of it. He swung onto the tail of a Camel of 209 Squadron flown by a young pilot, Lt Wilfrid May, and gave chase. Capt. A. Roy Brown, flying above, saw May's perilous position and dived to the rescue. Coming up on von Richthofen's aircraft from behind, Brown fired a long burst at the all-red Triplane, but the Red Baron, apparently unharmed, continued to chase and machine gun May's Camel.

As von Richthofen flew low over Morlancourt Ridge he came under fire from Australian ground gunners. His aircraft side-slipped and glided into the ground nose-first. The Red Baron had been killed in action.

The following message was dropped by a British aircraft:

To

The German Flying Corps.
Rittmeister Baron Manfred von Richthofen
was killed in aerial combat
on April 21st, 1918.
He was buried with full
military honours.

From British Royal Air Force.

Manfred Freiherr von Richthofen was buried at Bertangles, his coffin draped with the Imperial German Flag. Pilots of the Imperial German Air Service flew unhindered over his grave and dropped wreaths. His remains were removed to Berlin in 1925 and reburied at the Invaliden Cemetery.

Leutnant Paul Bäumer, (1896-1927)
43 victories

Paul Bäumer was born on 11 May 1896 at Duisburg and spent most of his childhood fascinated by the giant Zeppelins that operated from Friedrichshafen near his home. He learned to fly at his own expense, gaining his pilot's licence, and tried to enlist as a naval airman when war broke out but was turned down. He then volunteered for the 70th Infantry Regiment at Saarbrücken and, after training, saw combat at Saint-Quentin in France.

In the early part of 1915 he was posted to the XXI Army Corps on the Russian Front, where he was badly wounded in the left arm. Whilst recovering in hospital he applied for transfer to the German Air Service but was refused. He then saw vacancies for technicians in the air arm and, using his experience as a dental assistant, persuaded the authorities to agree to his transfer. At the beginning of 1916, he was accepted for 'general duties' in the German Air Service and posted to Döberitz. Within a few months he had asked his commanding officer to look at his previous flying experience and put his name forward for flying training.

The spring of 1916 saw Bäumer at flying school. After qualifying, he was posted in October to Armee Flug Park No. 1 as a ferry pilot and flight instructor. He was promoted to the rank of gefreiter on 19 February 1917 and posted to FA 7 on 26 March. Three days later he was promoted to unteroffizier.

On 15 May, Bäumer was awarded the Iron Cross 2nd Class and two days later was sent for fighter pilot training. On completion of training he was posted to *Jasta* 2 (Boelcke) on 28 June for two days, and then to *Jasta* 5. On 12, 13 and 15 July he scored his first three victories when he shot down three reconnaissance balloons, for which he was awarded the Iron Cross 1st Class. Bäumer was posted back to *Jasta* 2 in August, and by the end of the year his victory score had risen to eighteen. On 12 February 1918, he was awarded the Golden Military Merit Cross. His nineteenth victory, a Sopwith Camel shot down whilst on patrol north of Zonnebeke on 9 March, was recognised by granting him a commission to the rank of leutnant in April.

The 200th victory of *Jasta* 2 on 23 March was Bäumer's next kill, and was made even more remarkable by his shooting down of two R.E.8s and one Camel in under three hours. Nine days later, whilst trying to land a badly shot-up Pfalz D.VIII, Bäumer was injured in the crash landing, sustaining a broken jaw amongst other injuries.

In September he was given the nickname of 'Der Eiserne Adler' (The Iron Eagle) after being awarded the Silver Wound Badge, and by the end of the month his score had increased to thirty-eight, having dispatched new fewer than eight Allied aircraft in less than a week. His thirtieth victory brought the nation's highest award—the *Pour le Mérite*—on 2 November, making him one of only five people to receive both the *Pour le Mérite* and the Golden Military Merit Cross.

After the war, Bäumer worked briefly in the dockyards before he became a dentist, and reportedly one of his patients, Erich Maria Remarque, used Bäumer's name for the protagonist of his antiwar novel *All Quiet on the Western Front*.

Hauptmann Rudolf Berthold, (1891-1920)
44 victories

Rudolf Berthold was born at Ditterswind, near Bamberg in northern Bavaria on 24 March 1891. At 19 years of age he joined the Army and was assigned to 3rd Brandenburg Infantry Regiment No. 20. Berthold decided to learn to fly at a private flying club, and after gaining licence No. 538 on 26 September 1913, he applied for transfer to the newly formed German Army Air Service. At the outbreak of war, Berthold was posted for flying training as an observer on Halberstadt two-seat aircraft with FFA 23, and by the end of 1914 had been awarded the Iron Cross 2nd Class for a number of reconnaissance flights and been promoted to the rank of feldwebel.

In 1915, Berthold transferred to DFW aircraft and carried out a large number of observation flights over enemy lines. He was awarded the Iron Cross 1st Class in the autumn of that year and applied for transfer to a fighter *Jasta*. He went to *Jasta*schule in December, and on graduating was posted to Kek Vaux, flying single-seat Fokkers.

On 2 February 1916, Berthold opened his victory score by shooting down a Voisin whilst on patrol over Chaulnes. By the end of April his score stood at five and he had been awarded the Bavarian Military Merit Order 4th Class and the Knight's Cross of the Military Order of St Henry. Returning from a mission on 25 April, he suffered severe injuries during a seriously misjudged crash landing in a Pfalz E.IV. He returned to his unit before his wounds had properly healed and was commissioned to leutnant.

Berthold was given command of *Jasta* 4 in August 1916, after forming the *Jasta* from Kek Vaux. On 27 August came another award, the prestigious Knight's Cross with Swords of the Royal House Order of Hohenzollern, and on 14 October he handed *Jasta* 4 over to Hans-Joachim Buddecke and took command of *Jasta* 14. Berthold increased his score by shooting down a Farman of Escadrille F 7 on 24 March 1917. In May his patrol was attacked and he was shot down by a British fighter. His aircraft crashed within German lines and he sustained a fractured skull, pelvis and thigh, and a broken nose. After two months in hospital, he again discharged himself and returned to his squadron.

On 12 August 1917, he was given command of *Jasta* 18 and promotion to oberleutnant. He shot down a SPAD nine days later, bringing his score to thirteen. During September he bagged a further fourteen victories, and another kill came on 2 October when he shot down a DH.4 of 57 Squadron RFC. Eight days later, during a dogfight with a British patrol, his right upper arm was smashed by a bullet. Whilst in hospital he was awarded the *Pour le Mérite*, and promotion to hauptmann came ten days later. Yet again he discharged himself early to return to combat.

Berthold took charge of JG II in March 1918, taking with him nearly all the best pilots of *Jasta* 14 and exchanging them with pilots of *Jasta* 15. His aircraft, with its distinctive livery of red and blue (red from the nose to the cockpit, then blue to the tail) and its winged sword painted on the fuselage, was well known to the Allies.

On 10 August, Berthold's patrol became involved with a patrol of DH.4s and during the ensuing dogfight he dispatched two Allied aircraft but collided with one of his victims, badly damaging his Fokker D.VII. He struggled to keep control but crashed into a house. He survived, but the crash effectively ended his combat career.

On his release from hospital the war was over. In 1919 he joined the 'Eisern Schar' (Iron Horde) of the Freikorps and fought during the post-war German Revolution. On 15 March 1920, he was attacked by rioters in Harburg, and it is said that he was beaten and then strangled with the ribbon of his *Pour le Mérite*.

Hauptmann Oswald Boelcke, (1891-1916)
40 victories

One of six children, Oswald Boelcke was born in Giebichenstein, near Halle in Saxony, on 19 May 1891. After leaving school, he decided on a military career and in March 1911 joined the Prussian Cadet Corps and was posted to No. 3 Telegraph Battalion at Koblenz. After completing his initial training, he was posted to Metz War School to complete his officer training.

After graduating, Boelcke successfully applied for transfer to the German Army Air Service for training as a pilot and was posted to the flying school in Halberstadt, completing his flying training in October 1914. Initially assigned to Trier, two weeks later he was posted to FA 13 near Montmédy where his older brother Wilhelm was an observer. The two brothers became a team, flying observation missions over the Argonne region. Boelcke received the Iron Cross 2nd Class for his work flying reconnaissance missions.

He continued flying these missions into the first quarter of 1915, receiving the Iron Cross 1st Class on 4 February, and at the beginning of May, Boelcke was transferred to FA 62, which was equipped with LVG C.Is. On 4 July, together with his observer Lt Heinz von Wühlisch, he went on patrol over Valenciennes and encountered a Morane Parasol. After a brief action, the Parasol was shot down—and Boelcke had opened his tally. His enthusiasm for engaging enemy aircraft prompted his squadron commander to transfer him to single-seat fighters.

The single-seat Fokker Eindeckers had been allocated to the squadron for scouting and protection of reconnaissance aircraft. Early in July, Boelcke saved the life of a 14-year-old French boy and was awarded a life-saving medal.

Flying in a Fokker Eindecker from Douai on 19 August, Boelcke shot down a Bristol biplane over the front line. (It was whilst at Douai that he met Max Immelmann, both learning tactics from each other.) By the end of the year, Boelcke had increased his victory score to six and had been awarded the Knight's Cross with Swords of the Royal House Order of Hohenzollern. In the first two weeks of January 1916, he shot down three more Allied aircraft, bringing his total to nine, and was awarded the *Pour le Mérite*.

Every month Boelcke was mentioned in communiqués to the German High Command as he steadily increased his score. By the end of June, he had nineteen victories to his credit and had become a household name in Germany. When Max Immelmann died that month, the High Command decided to send Boelcke on an inspection/public relations tour of Vienna, Budapest, Belgrade and Constantinople (Istanbul). This gave him the chance to study the way aerial combat was developing, and he wrote a thesis, 'Air Fighting Tactics', which he submitted to the High Command and was to become the 'bible' of German fighter pilots.

In July 1916, Boelcke was recalled from his tour and given command of *Jasta 2*, with promotion to the rank of hauptmann. Among the pilots he chose for the squadron were Manfred von Richthofen, Max Müller and Erwin Böhme. On 2 September, Boelcke scored his twentieth victory when he shot down a DH.2 of 37 Squadron RFC, and by the end of the month he had downed nine more. By 26 October he had shot down a further eleven enemy aircraft, taking his final victory total to forty.

On 28 October 1916, whilst on patrol with von Richthofen and Böhme, he attacked a flight of seven Allied aircraft. Flying in tandem, Boelcke and Böhme chased a British fighter, but just as they closed on it, another British fighter, being chased by von Richthofen, cut across in front of them. Böhme rolled out of the way at the same time as Boelcke and the two aircraft collided. Böhme managed to control his machine, but Boelcke's Albatros D.II spun into the ground, killing the ace.

Leutnant Franz Büchner, (1898-1920)
40 victories

Franz Büchner was born on 2 January 1898 in Leipzig. At the onset of war in 1914, at only 16 years of age, he joined up with the 106th Saxon Infantry Regiment. In March, the regiment moved to the Russian Front, and five months later Büchner was commissioned. Moving back to France in September with his regiment, he was awarded the Iron Cross 2nd Class after being involved in a number of actions. On 3 April 1916, he was wounded during a battle on the Western Front.

Büchner decided to apply for a transfer to the German Army Air Service, was accepted and posted to FFA 270 for training as a pilot. On graduating in July of 1916, he was posted to *Jasta* 9 flying single-seat aircraft. He had one success in the period from July 1916 to August 1917—a Nieuport fighter over Chappy on the 17th of the month — and was posted to *Jasta* 13 in October.

On 10 and 11 June 1918, Büchner increased his score by shooting down two SPADs over Vauxaillion. Such was the high regard in which he was held that he was made squadron leader on 15 June, despite having scored so few victories. However, his scoring rate started to improve rapidly in July, and by the end of the month it had risen to twelve. Büchner was awarded the Iron Cross 1st Class in August, followed by the Knight's Cross with Swords of the Royal House Order of Hohenzollern and the Saxon Albert Order 2nd Class with Swords.

By the end of August he had downed another eight Allied aircraft. On 12 September, Büchner shot down a DH.4 of 8th Aero Squadron, USAS, whilst on patrol over Hattonville, in one of the first contacts between the Germans and the Americans. The same day he shot down another DH.4 and a Breguet 14 bomber, and by the end of September had dispatched eighteen USAS aircraft, taking his victory score to thirty-seven. For this achievement he was awarded Saxony's highest award—the Military Order of St Henry.

Büchner later shot down a Salmson 2 A2 bomber, but a collision with one of his fellow pilots on 10 October nearly ended his life. Both aircraft were attacking an Allied bomber when they collided in mid-air. The pilots took to their parachutes and, fortunately for them both, the parachutes opened—a rarity in those early days—taking them safely to the ground.

Before the war ended, Büchner managed to add another two kills to his score. On 25 October, at the age of 20, he was awarded the *Pour le Mérite*—the highest award given to a fighter pilot, whose record of victories at the end of the conflict numbered forty.

Although the war may have ended in Europe for the Allies, it still continued within Germany as the post-war revolutionaries attempted to take over. Büchner fought on with the Reichswehr, but was shot down and killed on 18 March 1920 whilst on a reconnaissance flight near his home town of Leipzig. Like Rudolf Berthold, he was killed by his own countrymen.

Kapitänleutnant Horst Julius Freiherr Treusch von Buttlar-Brandenfels, (1885-1962)

Horst Julius Treusch von Buttlar-Brandenfels was born on 15 June 1885 in Hanau, Darmstadt. After finishing high school, he followed the family tradition and joined the

Imperial German Navy in 1903 as a sea cadet. On completion of his initial training, Buttlar-Brandenfels was commissioned to the rank of leutnant zur see and sent on a radio-telephony course. On graduating he was posted as R/T officer to the staff of the Commander of Reconnaissance Ships. Zeppelins at this time were beginning to show their worth, and flight trials were begun in 1910 with the intention of using the Zeppelin as an aerial scouting ship for the Navy.

The first air-to-ship radio test flight was with the L 2 airship, but because of the extra equipment aboard, some of the crew, including Buttlar-Brandenfels, were scratched from the flight. The Zeppelin crashed during trials, killing all on board. Buttlar-Brandenfels successfully applied to become an airship pilot, and at the age of 26 was in command of airship L 6.

His first contact with the enemy was on Christmas Day 1914, when, whilst on patrol off Heligoland, he sighted three mine-layers accompanied by two cruisers and eight destroyers. He attempted to send a radio message, but his equipment was out of order, and he decided to attack, dropping three 110 lb bombs from a height of over 4,000 feet. However, the bombs did no damage and L 6 came under heavy and accurate fire from accompanying cruisers. Buttlar-Brandenfels withdrew his craft into cloud-cover and then came in low, strafing the enemy ships with machine-gun fire from the two gondolas and the upper gun platform. The ships returned fire, puncturing the L 6 repeatedly, so Buttlar-Brandenfels abandoned his attack and turned for base. He received the Iron Cross 2nd Class for the mission and was promotion to kommander.

On 19 January 1915, Buttlar-Brandenfels, again with L 6, awaited orders to carry out the first attack on England. Later that year, on 17 August, he was to undertake his first successful raid with airship L 11, and by the end of the war had flown more than nineteen missions against England. He was awarded the Iron Cross 1st Class and promoted to kapitänleutnant, and after his fifteenth mission received Prussia's highest award—the Pour le Mérite. His airship crew each received the Iron Cross 1st Class.

At the end of the war, Buttlar-Brandenfels was one of those responsible for destroying the entire airship fleet at Nordholz in defiance of the Treaty of Versailles. He died in September 1962 in Berchtesgaden.

Kapitänleutnant zur See Friedrich Christiansen, (1879-1972)
13(?) victories

The son of a sea captain, Friedrich Christiansen was born at Wyk-auf-Föhr on 12 December 1879. In 1913, he decided to learn to fly, and after graduating and gaining licence No. 707 he became an instructor at a civilian flying school. In August 1914, Christiansen was called up and posted to Zeebrugge as a naval aviator, and for a year flew Brandenburg W.12 seaplanes on missions over the North Sea and Britain. He even carried out a bombing mission on Dover and Ramsgate, for which he was awarded the Iron Cross 2nd Class. Further decorations followed on 27 April 1916, when as a lieutenant of naval artillery he received the Iron Cross 1st Class and the Knight's Cross with Swords of the Royal House Order of Hohenzollern.

Christiansen claimed his first victory on 15 May 1917, when he shot down a Sopwith Pup off Dover. On 1 September he took command of the naval air station at Zeebrugge and was promoted to oberleutnant, and on the same day shot down a Porte FB2 Baby off Felixstowe. He continued to carry out reconnaissance, rescue and bombing missions, and by December that year had completed 440 missions, including the downing of British airship C 27, for which he was awarded the *Pour le Mérite.*

On 15 February 1918, Christiansen increased his victory tally when he shot down a Curtiss H-12B flying boat from Felixstowe. This was followed by two more Curtiss H-12Bs on 24 and 25 April, and in June and July he claimed three more flying boats—all Felixstowe F.2As. On 6 July, when on patrol over the Thames estuary, he surprised British submarine C25 cruising on the surface, killing the captain and five crewmen. He thought that he had sunk the submarine, but in fact it managed to limp back to harbour.

By the end of the war, Christiansen had raised his victory score to thirteen—but this is speculative because there are possible shared victories. He returned to the merchant marine for a while, before taking a post as a pilot for the Dornier Company. It was whilst with Dornier that he flew the largest seaplane in the world at that time—the Dornier Do X—on its maiden Atlantic crossing to New York in 1930.

In 1933, Christiansen joined the German Aviation Ministry as it attempted to rebuild its air force. He was appointed Korpsführer of the National Socialist Flyers Corps at its conception in 1937, and when war was declared two years later and the German Army occupied Holland, he was appointed officer commanding the occupied country—a post he held until the end of the war, when he was imprisoned by the Allies. On his release, Christiansen retired to West Germany and died at Innien in December 1972 at the age of 93.

Leutnant der Reserve Heinrich Gontermann, (1896-1917)
39 victories

Heinrich Gontermann, the son of a cavalry officer, was born on 25 February 1896 in Siegen, southern Westphalia. In August 1914 he joined the 6th Uhlan Cavalry Regiment in Hanau and after initial training was sent to the Front. The following months were hard, and he was slightly wounded in September and promoted to feldwebel. In the spring of 1915, because of his leadership qualities, he was given a field commission to leutnant and awarded the Iron Cross 2nd Class.

He applied for transfer to the Imperial German Air Service and was accepted for pilot training. On graduation early in 1916, he was sent to Kampfstaffel Tergnier as a reconnaissance pilot, flying the Roland C.II. In the spring he was posted to FA 25, where he flew both as a pilot and as an observer on AGO C.Is. After nearly a year of flying reconnaissance missions, Gontermann successfully applied for *Jastaschule* and transfer to a fighter unit, and after graduating on 11 November, was posted to *Jasta* 5. Within three days he had opened his score by shooting down an F.E.2b over Morval.

In March 1917, Gontermann scored another victory and was awarded the Iron Cross 1st Class on the 5th of the month. The following day he shot down an F.E.2b of 57 Squadron RFC, and by the end of the month had increased his score to six. One month later he had raised it to seventeen and was made squadron leader of *Jasta* 15.

On 4 May, Gontermann downed a SPAD south-east of Caronne, and two days later was awarded the Knight's Cross with Swords of the Royal House Order of Hohenzollern. Another victory followed on the 10th, when he shot down another SPAD and a Caudron R.4. The following day he dispatched another SPAD and received the Bavarian Order of Max Joseph. He was awarded his final decoration, the *Pour le Mérite*, on 14 May, with his score standing at twenty-one.

From June until the end of September, Gontermann added seventeen more victories, eleven of which were observation balloons, four being downed on the evening of 19 August within three minutes. His final victory came on 2 October, when he shot down a SPAD whilst on patrol over Laon.

On 30 October 1917, Gontermann was air testing the latest Fokker Triplane that had just been delivered to the *Jasta*. Minutes into the air test above the airfield, the upper wing of the Fokker suffered structural failure and the aircraft spun out of control into the ground. Gontermann was pulled from the wreckage still alive, but died from his injuries some hours later. He was just 21 years old.

Oberleutnant Hermann Wilhelm Göring, (1893-1946)
22 victories

After Manfred von Richthofen, Hermann Göring was probably the most famous—or infamous—German pilot to come out of the First World War. However, it was not for his actions during the Great War that his infamy spread but for his part in the Second World War.

Göring was born on 12 January 1893 in Rosenheim, Upper Bavaria—the son of Heinrich Göring, a very high-ranking Army officer who had also been the first Governor of German South West Africa. Graduating from Lichterfelde in 1912 with brilliant results, Hermann Göring was commissioned into the Prinz Wilhelm Regiment No. 112 and posted to its headquarters at Mülhausen. It was here that he contracted rheumatic fever.

While in hospital, he was visited by his friend Bruno Loerzer, who had served with him in his regiment but had transferred to the German Army Air Service and become a pilot. Göring applied to his commanding officer requesting a place at Freiburg flying school, but after waiting over two weeks and receiving no reply, he obtained the necessary papers and signed them himself, including a transfer paper to the flying school. During this two-week period he had been flying with Loerzer at every opportunity, getting in all the training he could. However, his transfer was refused and he was ordered to return to his unit—something that Göring had no intention of doing.

This situation posed a very serious problem for Göring. He was open to a charge of desertion and forging papers, so immediately telegraphed his godfather, Ritter von Epstein, who moved in extremely high circles. Crown Prince Friedrich Wilhelm suddenly intervened, asking that Göring be posted to the German Fifth Army field air detachment. The charges were reduced to one of lateness and he was given a medical certificate to confirm that he was not fit for duty on the front line.

In the autumn of 1914, Göring completed his training with FEA 3 as an observer before joining Loerzer at FFA 25. They soon acquired a reputation for carrying out the most dangerous of missions and, in March 1915, they received the Iron Cross 2nd Class.

In May, Göring and Loerzer were tasked to carry out a reconnaissance of the French fortresses in the Verdun area and photograph them in detail. Many others had tried but failed, and for three days both airmen flew over the Verdun area and came back with photographs so detailed that Gen. Erich von Falkenhayn asked to see them personally. So delighted with the results were the High Command, that Crown Prince Wilhelm exercised his royal prerogative and invested both Göring and Loerzer with the Iron Cross 1st Class in the field.

The following month, Göring was sent to Freiburg for pilot training, graduating in October. He was then posted to FA 25 and opened his score on 16 November by shooting down a Maurice Farman patrol over Tahure. In 1916, he was posted from one unit to another, first to Kek Stenay flying Fokker E.IIIs and then, in March, to Kek Metz. On 30 July he shot down a Caudron whilst escorting bombers over Mamey before returning to FA 25 on 9 July, and then back again to Kek Metz on 7 September. From there he went to *Jasta* 7, and on 20 October to *Jasta* 5.

It was whilst on patrol on 2 November he was attacked by British fighters and wounded in the hip. He passed out but came to as his aircraft plunged toward the ground. Managing to regain control of his aircraft, he steered it towards what looked like a cemetery just over the German lines, but as good fortune would have it, it turned out to be an emergency hospital and within a very short time of crash-landing he was on the operating table being repaired.

After recuperating, Göring was posted at the beginning of February 1917 to *Jasta* 26, which was now commanded by Loerzer. By the end of the month his victory score had risen to six and he was again attracting the attention of the High Command. He increased his score again on 10 May, when he shot down a DH.4 of 55 Squadron RFC, and one week later was given command of *Jasta* 27. By the end of October, Göring's score had risen to fifteen and he was awarded the Military Karl-Friedrich Merit Order, the Knight's Cross with Swords of the Royal House Order of Hohenzollern and the Knight's Cross 2nd Class with Swords of the Baden Order of the Zähringer Lion. Göring had sixteen kills to his name by the end of the year.

Throughout 1918 his victory score increased steadily. By the end of June it had risen to twenty-two and Göring had been decorated with the *Pour le Mérite*. On 9 July he was given command of JG I—the Richthofen Squadron—and promotion to oberleutnant, at which point he decided that his fighting days were over.

At the end of the war, Göring was ordered to instruct his pilots to fly their aircraft to an Allied field. He knew that the Allies wanted the latest Fokkers, so he ordered his pilots to do so but to set fire to the aircraft the moment they were on the ground. He later went to Denmark in a flight advisory capacity after fighting in the post-war revolution, but returned to Germany in the early 1920s.

Göring joined the Nazi Party and became Adolf Hitler's right-hand man, progressing through the party as its strength grew and taking over command of the newly formed Luftwaffe. He held a number of other posts throughout the Second World War, but the Luftwaffe was his forte. During the conflict he received the Knight's Cross of the Iron Cross and the Grand Cross of the Iron Cross—the only person to receive it—and was promoted to the rank of feldmarschall and later to Reichsmarschall, the heir apparent to Hitler. Captured by the Americans at the end of the war, he stood trial for war crimes. On being convicted, he was sentenced to death by hanging, despite his pleas to be executed by firing squad. In the end he cheated the Allies by committing suicide on 15 October 1946, using poison he had concealed on his person since his capture.

Oberleutnant Max Immelmann, (1890-1916)
15 victories

The son of a wealthy factory owner in Dresden, Max Immelmann was born on 21 September 1890. He joined a Railway Regiment in Berlin-Schöneberg with the rank of fähnrich and, after obtaining a commission, entered the War Academy but on the outbreak of war was returned to his regiment. He successfully applied for a transfer to the German Air Service and was sent for basic flying training at Johannisthal, Berlin, in November 1914. On completion of his training he was posted to Adlershof for advanced training before qualifying as a pilot.

In February 1915, Immelmann was posted to FFA 62 (later to become Kek Douai), flying LVG two-seaters on observation and escort patrols. With him on these patrols was another recently qualified pilot, Oswald Boelcke, and within a few months they had established a reputation as top scouting pilots.

In May, Immelmann was moved from the LVGs to the unit's single-seat fighter, the Fokker Eindecker, and his first victory came on 1 August—a B.E.2c of 2 Squadron RFC. By the end of September, with a score of three confirmed and two possibles, he was awarded the Iron Cross 2nd Class. October and November not only brought another four victories but also promotion to oberleutnant. Further awards followed—the Iron Cross 1st Class and the Knight's Cross with Swords of the Royal House Order of Hohenzollern. On 12 January 1916, Immelmann, or the 'Eagle of Lille' as he became known, was also awarded the *Pour le Mérite*.

His victory score had increased to thirteen by the end of March, when he also received the Saxon Commander's Cross to the Military Order of St Henry 2nd Class, the Knight's Cross to the Military Order of St Henry, the Saxon Albert Order 2nd Class with Swords, the Saxon Friedrich August Medal in Silver and the Bavarian Military Merit Order 4th Class with Swords.

On 18 June 1916, he was in a dogfight with F.E.2bs of 25 Squadron flying his Fokker 246/16. Twisting and turning around in the packed skies, he came under fire from an F.E.2b flown by Capt. G. R. McCubbin with his gunner Cpl J. H. Waller. It is unclear whether Waller's shots hit the Fokker's propeller or whether, as had happened before, a defective synchroniser gear had caused him to shoot off his own propeller, with the result that the torque on the engine ripped it from its mountings, plunging Max Immelmann to his death.

Leutnant Josef Carl Peter Jacobs, (1894-1978)
41 victories

The son of a middle-class businessman, Josef Jacobs was born in Kreuzkapelle, Rhineland, on 15 May 1894. He learned to fly at the age of 18, and on the outbreak of war enlisted in the German Army Air Service and was posted to FEA 9 to be trained as a military pilot. On graduating, he was posted to FA 11 as a reconnaissance pilot and for over a year was engaged in missions over the lines. Early in 1916, he was posted to Fokker Staffel West, flying Fokker E.IIIs.

Jacobs unofficially opened his score on 1 February, when he claimed a Caudron—but it was unconfirmed—and the end of March brought a claim for a balloon, for which he was awarded the Iron Cross 2nd Class. On 25 October, he was posted to *Jasta* 22 at the request of its commander Oberleutnant Erich Hönemanns, a long-time friend, and within weeks of arrival was posted temporarily to *Jastaschule* I as an instructor, where he spent part of the winter.

Returning to *Jasta* 22 at the end of January 1917, he was awarded the Iron Cross 1st Class, having increased his score by shooting down a Caudron R.4 over Terny-Sorny on the 23rd of the month. By the end of August, his score had risen to five and he was appointed commander of *Jasta* 7. With the appointment came the award of the Knight's Cross with Swords of the Royal House Order of Hohenzollern.

By the end of 1917, Jacob's victory score had risen to twelve and his *Jasta* was re-equipped with Fokker Triplanes. Jacobs had his aircraft painted all black, and it was soon to become instantly recognisable by Allied airmen. The beginning of 1918 was quiet for *Jasta* 7, but the lull did not last long and, in April, Jacobs claimed his next victim—an R.E.8 of 7 Squadron RFC over Ostend. By the end of July, after surviving a mid-air collision with another Fokker Triplane, his score had risen to twenty-four and he was awarded the *Pour le Mérite*.

Jacobs became Germany's greatest exponent of the Fokker Triplane, and by the end of 1918 had shot down forty-one Allied aircraft. He survived both World Wars and died in Munich in July 1978.

Oberleutnant Ernst Udet, (1896-1941)
62 victories

Ernst Udet was born in Frankfurt-am-Main and grew up in Munich. He was fascinated with aviation from early youth and enjoyed visitng a nearby aeroplane factory and an army airship detachment. In 1909, he helped found the Munich Aero-Club. After crashing a glider he and a friend constructed, he finally flew in 1913 with a test pilot in the nearby Otto Works, which he often visited.

Udet tried to enlist in the Army on 2 August 1914, but he was only 160 cm (5 ft 3 in) tall and did not qualify.Through a friend, Gustav Otto, owner of the aircraft factory he had visited in his youth, he received private flying tuition and received his civilian pilot's licence at the end of April 1915 and was immediately accepted by the German Army Air

Service. In the summer of 1915 Ernst Udet came to the notice of Obertleutnant Justinius of *Flieger-Abteilung* (Aviation Section) 206 and sent for him to join his unit at Darmstadt.

He began flying Justinius' Aviatik B two-seat observation plane. Based at Heiligkreuz, they spotted for the artillery, relatively oblivious to enemy aircraft, as none were armed. On 14 September, they were more ten miles beyond German lines, flying at 3,500 m, when the Aviatik began to spin down. Using all his strength, Udet stopped the spinning, but the aircraft still listed as it glided down. He shut off the engine, as it caused the plane to spin. Obertleutnant Justinius climbed out on the wing as a counterbalance. Udet opened up the throttle briefly, but still could not hold the plane level. Justinius joined Udet in the pilot's cockpit; with their combined strength and intermittent use of the engine, they managed to struggle along.

They hoped to get to Neutral Switzerland. At five miles from the frontier, they were down to 1,000 m. They passed the border town of St Dizier with 600 m of altitude remaining and began to hope they might reach Germany. They continued to descend and touched down just over the barbed-wire, on the German side. A local blacksmith promptly fashioned a replacement for the shackle that had failed, when an aviation *Hauptmann*, drove up. He insisted on recovering the failed shackle for testing; another Aviatik had been lost the same day for the same reason.

On a later bombing mission their Aviatik was overloaded with bombs, extra fuel, two machine guns, and a new radio. Just after take-off, the plane crashed when Udet banked left. Both he and Justinius were hospitalized and adding insult to injury Udet was sentened to seven days' arrest for 'careless manoeuvring which endangered the life of his observer and caused the destruction of a valuable aircraft.' During his week-long confinement, Udet had to recite a little confessional speech. On the day of his release, another officer-observer grabbed him and then went to bomb Belfort. On this sortie, a live bomb got stuck in the plane's undercarriage, and only through 'careless manoeuvring' was Udet able to free it.

Udet was now assigned to single-seater, *Jagdflieger* (fighter-pilot) Combat Command at Habsheim. He was provided a brand-new Fokker to fly there, but it crashed on take-off due to a mechanical fault.

In his first encounter with a French Caudron, he froze and could not fire. The French gunner shot off Udet's goggles, cutting his face with glass splinters but nothing worse. Shamed by his freezing in action Udet took great efforts with gunnery practice. This practice paid off when on 18 March 1916 a telephone report came of enemy airplanes heading towards Mülhausen. Alone, Udet went up to 2,800 m in his Fokker to intercept. He found over twenty French bombers: a large Farman in the middle, flanked by other Farmans and Caudrons. This time, he kept his nerve, closed with the Farman, and opened up at forty metres, flaming it. This was his first victory. He continued diving through the formation as other French planes went after him, diving steeply to escape. When he pulled out he saw more fighters from Habsheim had joined the fray. He spotted a lone Caudron retiring and he pursued it, firing a burst at long range, over 150 metres. He approached to 80 m and fired again, this time kocking out one of the Caudron's engines. But as he closed in for the kill, his gun jammed, and Caudron limped away.

Udet remained at Habsheim until March 1917 and downed three more planes in that area, and Staffel 15 was then transferred to La Selve, opposite the sector patrolled by The Storks, the French squadron of Guynemer and Nungesser. On 24 April Udet achieved his first victory on this front, a Nieuport over Chavignon, his fifth overall. At the end of April, Obertleutnant Heinrich Gontermann took over as CO; he was already an accomplished ace, with 18 victories to his credit at that point (his final tally was 39). On an evening patrol on 5 May 1917 Gontermann got a Nieuport and Udet a SPAD. During two weeks in command of Staffel 15, Gontermann shot down eight more planes. He was then awarded the *Ordre pour le Mérite* and four weeks leave. He appointed Obertleutnant Ernst Udet acting CO in his absence. On 25 May while on a solo mission, Udet got into a duel with a SPAD with Guynemer's markings. After some spirited, skilful jockeying, neither one could get behind the other. Then Udet's gun jammed, and in an increasingly rare chivalrous gesture, Guynemer waved to him and flew off.

In mid-1917 Udet transferred to Jasta 37 in Flanders and by February, 1918 his score had reached 20. Ernste Udet then had the honour of being invited by Manfred von Richthofen to join *Jagdgeschwader 1*, comprising Jasta 4, 6, 10, and 11. Udet arrived at Richthofen's group at 10 a.m. on 27 March 1918. At noon he flew his first sortie with them in his new steed, a Fokker Dr.1 triplane, and shot down a British R.E.8 reconnaissance plane. In the same patrol, they pounced on a flight of Sopwith Camels, Richthofen knocking down one of them. Then they strafed a column of British infantry. Evidently impressed with Udet's head-on attack on the observation plane, Richthofen gave him command of Jasta 11.

By this time, the Allied air forces vastly outnumbered the Germans. Udet later wrote, 'The French fly only in large units, fifty, sometimes a hundred aircraft. They darken the skies like locusts. . . . When one of our aircraft rises, five go up on the other side. And when one of theirs comes down near us, we fall on him and strip him bare, because we have long run out of such fine instruments, shining with nickel and brass.' Fuel was also in short supply. On the ground, Allied tanks and American manpower finally broke through the stalemated trench warfare. But for Ernst Udet and the crack pilots of the Richthofen group, hunting was good. In June, he shot down 12 planes, raising his total score to 36. In July, another 4, for a total of 40. And in August, Udet brought down 20 airplanes, for 60 altogether. He usually flew a Fokker D.VII, with his girlfriend's name, 'Lo,' painted on the fuselage, and on the tail, the words *'Du doch nicht!!'*—'You and who else?'

The end came quickly. Göring took over as CO of the Richthofen group; Oberleutnant Udet claimed two more victories, totalling sixty-two overall. When the Armistice came, the war was over and fighter pilots were no longer in great demand.

Ernst Udet struggled to make a living in the early 1920s. He built aeroplanes, he raced, and travelled to the USAs and Argentina for air shows.

During the Nazi regime Göring promoted Udet to the rank of *Generalmajor* and he was made head of the Luftwaffe's Technical Office. In April 1941 he led a German delegation inspecting Soviet aviation industry in accordance with the Molotov–Ribbentrop Pact. Udet informed Göring that the Soviet air force and aviation industry were very strong and technically advanced. Göring decided not to report this to Hitler. Udet realised that the upcoming war on Russia might destroy Germany, and, torn between truth and loyalty, suffered a psychological breakdown and even tried to tell all the truth to Hitler, but Göring had Udet under control by giving him drugs at drinking parties and hunting trips. Udet's drinking and psychological condition became a problem, but Göring used Udet's dependency to manipulate him. On 17 November 1941 he committed suicide, shooting himself in the head while on the phone with his girlfriend. Evidence indicates that his unhappy relationship with Göring, Erhard Milch, and the Nazi Party in general was the cause of his mental breakdown.

Imperial German Air Service Victory Totals

Rittmeister Manfred von Richthofen—*80 victories*
Oberleutnant Ernst Udet—*62 victories*
Oberleutnant Erich Löwenhardt—*54 victories*
Leutnant Werner Voss—*48 victories*
Leutnant Fritz Rumey—*45 victories*
Hauptmann Rudolf Berthold—*44 victories*
Leutnant Paul Bäumer—*43 victories*
Leutnant Josef Carl Peter Jacobs—*41 victories*
Hauptmann Bruno Loerzer—*41 victories*
Hauptmann Oswald Boelcke—*40 victories*
Leutnant Franz Büchner—*40 victories*
Oberleutnant Lothar von Richthofen—*40 victories*
Leutnant Karl Menckhoff—*39 victories*
Leutnant Heinrich Gontermann—*39 victories*
Oberleutnant Hermann Wilhelm Göring—*22 victories*

If published lists are to be believed, there were 391 German Aces during the First World War.

Early Aircraft used by Germany and the famous Fokker Eindecker

The Taube was designed in 1909 by Igo Etrich of Austria-Hungary, and first flew in 1910. It was licensed for serial production by Lohner-Werke in Austria and by Edmund Rumpler in Germany, and called the Etrich-Rumpler-Taube. Poor rudder and lateral control made the Taube difficult and slow to turn.

A flimsy Taube downed. The Taube proved to be an easy target for the faster and more mobile Allied fighters, and just six months into the war, the Taube had been removed from front line service to be used to train new pilots. Many future German aces would learn to fly in a Rumpler Taube.

German soldiers carrying wings from and unidentified biplane.

The Albatros B.II was an unarmed German two-seat reconnaissance biplane. It was designed by Ernst Heinkel based on his 1913 Albatros B.I, the B.II was the aircraft that brought the aircraft manufacturer Albatros Flugzeugwerke to the world's attention.

From top to bottom:

First flying in 1914, large numbers of the B.II were built and, though it was relegated from front-line service in 1915 following the introduction of the armed C-type two-seaters, the B.II remained in service as a trainer until 1918.

In 1914 the Albatros B.II set an altitude record of 14,800 ft (4,500 m). The seating arrangement was not ideal; the pilot occupied the rear cockpit, the observer sat in front over the wings which greatly reduced his downward view while the protruding engine block almost completely obscured the view over the nose.

The Aviatik C.I was a reconnaissance aircraft which came into service in April 1915. It was the successor to the Aviatik B.I and B.II. The observer sat in front of the pilot, with two machine-guns, mounted on rails on each side of the observer's cockpit. About 500 Aviatik C were built of which the majority were the C.I, only about 49 C.II and 80 C.III appear to have been completed. The Aviatik C.II and the C.III had more powerful engines. This observation Aviatik C-I 1429-15 is of *Artillerie Flieger Abteilung 206*

The Junkers J 1, nicknamed the *Blechesel* ('Tin Donkey'), was the world's first practical all-metal aircraft. Built early in the war when designers relied largely on fabric-covered wooden structures, braced with struts and exposed rigging lines, the Junkers J 1 was a revolutionary development in aircraft design and in many ways ahead of its time. Only the prototype was built, but it failed to meet any service standards and the concept faded for a long time.

Ground crew relax in front of a Fokker Eindecker—one of the early German aircraft types with frontal through propeller arc firing capability due to Fokker's mechanism. The success of this type gave rise to the expression 'the Fokker scourge'.

A Fokker E.II/35 from *Feldflieger Abteilung 14* preparing to land on the Eastern Front.

Oswald Boelcke in relaxed pose along with ground crew in front of his Fokker Eindecker.

It is not known who this pilot is with his puppy perched on the wing and 'Huckchen' lettered on the front of the cowling. It is from a mass-produced postcard. There no aces of the name Huckchen and the pilot appears to be wearing a *Kaiserliche Marine* cap.

Fokker Eindeckers outside the Fokker works. The Fokker E.I was the first purpose-designed fighter aircraft to enter service with the *Luftstreitkräfte* (known before October 1916 as *Die Fliegertruppen des deutschen Kaiserreiches*— Imperial German Flying Corps). Its arrival at the front in mid-1915 marked the start of a period known as the 'Fokker Scourge' during which the E.I and its Eindecker successors achieved a measure of air superiority over the Western Front due to the adoption in August 1915 with a front-firing gun.

The E.I was essentially an armed version of the Fokker M.5K single-seat reconnaissance aircraft, which was in turn very closely based on the design of the 1913 French Morane-Saulnier Type H.

Max Immelmann in the cockpit of an Eindecker E.I, probably serial number E .I 13/15, in which he scored his first five victories. Powder burns at the top of the cowling indicate gun firing activity.

The Eindecker in many ways was an unremarkable derivative of the Morane-Sauliner, but what transformed it into a formidable fighting machine was when it was fitted with the newly-developed synchronizer gear, the Fokker *Stangensteuerung*, firing a single 7.92 mm Parabellum LMG 14 or Spandau LMG 08 machine gun through the spinning propeller.

Left: Otto Parschau, (1890-1916). *Right:* Anton Fokker with Kurt Wintgens, (1894-1916).
Two German pilots, Leutnants Otto Parschau and Kurt Wintgens, worked closely with Anthony Fokker in early 1915 during evaluation of the M.5K/MG. Wintgens is known to have downed a two-seat Morane-Saulnier Type L parasol monoplane on 1 July 1915 while flying his M.5K/MG, but as the victory occurred in the airspace behind Allied lines, over the Fôret de Parroy woods near Lunéville, this could not be confirmed at the time. A similar victory over another Morane 'Parasol' two-seater, again unconfirmed, was scored by Wintgens three days later.

Kurt Wintgens and one of his air victories. On the 15 July, Wintgens scored his first confirmed victory over a third Morane Parasol, the earliest known confirmed aerial victory for anyone flying a Fokker E-series monoplane in combat.

Fokker E.IV. This was the last variant of the Fokker Eindecker and only 49 E.IVs were built out of the total Eindecker production run of 420 aircraft. It was an unsuccessful model with persistent engine problems and poor manoeuvrability. With only 420 Fokker Eindeckers built, it appears that the aircraft has created a legend out of all proportion to its actual importance.

A German AEG C.IV of *Flieger Abteilung 300* on the airfield at Huj, 10 miles north-east of Gaza, Palestine. The AEG [*Allgemeine Elektrizitäts-Gesellschaft*] C.IV was a two-seat biplane reconnaissance aircraft that entered service in 1916. The C.IV was based on the AEG C.II, but featured a larger wingspan and an additional forward-firing Spandau-type 7.92 mm (.312 in) machine gun. In addition to reconnaissance duties, the C.IV was used as a bomber escort and was easily the most successful of AEG's reconnaissance aircraft, with some 658 being built. It remained in service right up to the end of the war. (*Library of Congress*)

The LFG [*Luft-Fahrzeug-Gesellschaft*] Roland C.II, usually known as the *Walfisch* (Whale), was an advanced reconnaissance aircraft first introduced in 1916. The C.II had much lower drag than comparable aircraft of its time. It featured a monocoque fuselage built with an outer skin of two layers of thin plywood strips at an angle to each other. This had both lower drag and better strength per weight than typical of the time, but it was relatively slow and expensive to build.

An LFG Roland C.II being fuelled. British ace Albert Ball, whose first victim was a C.II, said in the latter half of 1916 that it was 'the best German machine now'. Some 400 were built.

DFW C.V (serial number 5845/16), photographed by a colleague. This excellent close-up shot provides us with a better feel for the aviator's life aloft. The DFW C.V was one of the most common German aircraft of 1916 with 3,250 of them built. About 2,000 were manufactured by DFW and about 1,250 licence-manufactured by Aviatik (as the DFW C.V(Av) or Aviatik C.VI). This is one of the latter as an Aviatik badge is visible on the strut.

The DFW C.V was used as a multi-role combat aircraft, for reconnaissance and bombing . It could outmanoeuvre many allied fighters of 1916 but lost its edge later in the war. It remained in service until 1918 and 600 were still in use at the end of hostilities.

'Good People Don't Shoot'. It is not clear why this was painted; it might cause a British pilot a second of Biblical reflection but a Frenchman might not understand it! The Rumpler C.IV was a reconnaissance aircraft, a development of the C.III with different tail surfaces and using a Mercedes D.IVa engine in place of C.III's Benz Bz.IV. Flying at 20,997 feet it was above the range of most fighters. 650 C.IVs were built.

A Rumpler C.-IV reconnaissance aircraft a with flexible Parabellum gun, 1917. Note the signal pistol and cartridge mounted on the fuselage beside the rear cockpit. (*National Museum of the USAF*)

The Rumpler C.VII could reach 23,950 feet. It was developed from the C.IV and optimised for high-altitude missions that would allow it to operate at heights that would render it immune to interception by enemy fighters. The most significant difference between the C.IV and C.VII was the choice of the Maybach Mb IVa engine to replace the Mercedes D.IV. Although the Maybach engine was around 8 per cent less powerful at sea level than the Mercedes, it could continue to provide most of its power output while at altitude, where power from the Mercedes engine decreased more rapidly as height increased. The crew were provided with oxygen generators and electrically-heated flight suits.

The Rumpler 6B1 was the first iteration of the 6B series and 39 of these were produced, with all but one of the number having been delivered by the end of May 1917. Born out of a requirement of the *Kaiserliche Marine* for a seaplane fighter, the Rumpler 6B was, like its contemporaries the Albatros W.4 and Hansa-Brandenburg W.9, an adaptation of an existing landplane design. In Rumpler's case the new floatplane fighter was based on the company's two-seat C.I reconnaissance aircraft.

Albatros D.III fighters of *Jagdstaffel 50*, 1917. The D.III was flown by many aces, including Manfred von Richthofen, Ernst Udet, and Kurt Wolff. It was the pre-eminent fighter during the period of German aerial dominance which known as 'Bloody April' 1917. This followed the British ground advance on Arras. German defensive policy inflicted very high losses on the RFC but failed to stop British air reconnaissance, artillery spotting, and tactical bombing operations, which contributed to successes on the ground. In many ways, although the Germans caused very heavy British aerial casualties, they may be considered as having lost the battle.

Wreckage of a German Albatross D. III fighter biplane. The D.III entered squadron service in December 1916, and was immediately acclaimed by German aircrews for its manoeuvrability and rate of climb. Soon after entering service faults were discovered, the most serious of which was a failure of the lower right wing spar. On 24 January 1917 Manfred von Richthofen suffered a crack in the lower wing of his new D.III. All D.IIIs were withdrawn in February for the faults to be rectified. Approximately 1,866 Albatros D.IIIs were built. (*Library of Congress*)

An excellent photograph of an Albatros D.III 2249 with superior-looking ace Heinrich Gontermann, (1896-1917). During 'Bloody April', Gontermann had 12 victories. On the 8th, he achieved his first success as a balloon buster. On 26 April 1917, he brought his victory total to 17 victories. Gontermann was also promoted to *Staffelführer* of *Jagdstaffel 15* four days later, replacing Max Reinhold, who was killed in action on 26 April 1917.

The Albatros D.V and D.Va were successful additions to the Albatros stable and 900 D.V and 1,662 D.Va were built. The D.Va had a slightly improved rate of climb and range, but both models were capable of 116 mph at sea level. The D.Va continued in operational service until the end of the War.

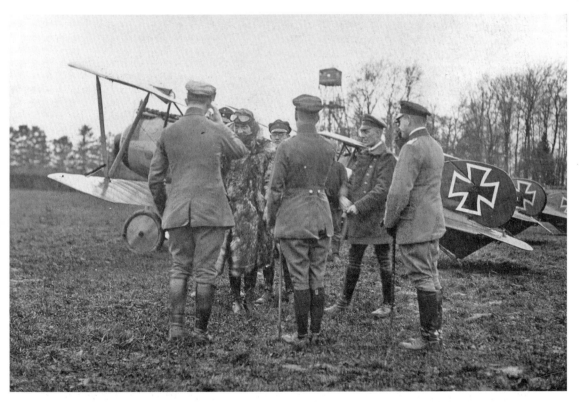

The instantly recognisable eyes show that this is Manfred von Richthofen having stepped out of his Albatros D.V 4479, at Boistrancourt, 17 March 1918.

The Hannover CL.II was developed as an escort fighter in response to the requirement to protect reconnaissance aircraft over Allied territory. Smaller than the usual C-class reconnaissance aircraft, it was easy for enemy pilots to mistake it for a single-seat fighter; a mistake that would bring them into the line of fire of the tail gun when closing from astern. The CL.II was also produced under licence by LFG, under the designation CL.IIa. 439 CL.IIs were built followed by 167 CL.IIIs, both types remained in service until the end of the War. Later in the War it was increasingly employed as a ground attack aircraft

Richard Scholl and his co-pilot Lieutenant Anderer, beside their Hannover CL.II biplane in 1918. (*Carola Eugster*)

Test pilot Wilhelm Eickhoff in a Roland D.VIa at Hannover Langenhagen, November 1917. The Roland D.VI was designed by the *Luft-Fahrzeug-Gesellschaft* (LFG), whose aircraft were made under the trade name 'Roland' after 1914 to avoid confusion with *Luftverkehrsgesellschaft* (LVG). 350 were built and it entered service in May 1918. It was one of the faster later aircraft at 124 mph, but its service ceiling at 16,400 feet was below later comparable aircraft.

The LVG C. VI was designed by Willy Sabersky-Müssigbrodt and developed by *Luftverkehrsgesellschaft* (LVG) in 1917, coming into service in 1918, approximately 1,100 of them were built. Most LVG C.VIs were used by for close reconnaissance and observation. It had a relatively poor speed at 103 mph but a good service ceiling of 21,300 feet. (*The U.S. National Archives and Records Administration*)

Four famous close-up views of Manfred Albrecht Freiherr von Richthofen, 'the Red Baron', (1892-1918).
Richthofen served as a cavalry reconnaissance officer on both the Eastern and Western Fronts, seeing action in Russia, France, and Belgium. In 1915 he transferred to the Air Service, becoming one of the first members of *Jasta 2* in 1916. He quickly distinguished himself as a fighter pilot, and during 1917 became leader of *Jasta 11* and then the larger unit *Jagdgeschwader 1* (better known as the 'Flying Circus'). (*Bundesarchiv*)

Two views of the 'Red Baron's half smile. His eyes are interesting and it is easy to identify him in photographs.

During a short spell flying two-seaters on the Eastern Front, Richthofen met Oswald Boelcke in August 1916. Boelcke was visiting the east in search of candidates for his newly formed fighter unit, and selected Richthofen to join one of the first German fighter squadrons, *Jagdstaffel 2*. (*Bundesarchiv*)

Manfred von Richthofen petting his dog Moritz.

Richthofen won his first aerial combat with *Jasta 2* over Cambrai, France on 17 September 1916. Boelcke was killed during a mid-air collision with a friendly aircraft on 28 October 1916; Richthofen witnessed the event.

Oswald Boelcke, (1891-1916). Boelcke was of the most influential patrol leaders and tacticians of the early years of air combat, the 'Father of Air Fighting Tactics'. He was the first to formalise rules of air fighting, which he presented as the *Dicta Boelcke*. While he promulgated rules for the individual pilot, his main concern was the use of formation fighting rather than single effort. The German air force was being reorganized from the *Fliegertruppe* into the *Luftstreitkräfte* in mid-1916; this reorganization was inspired by Boelcke. At this time, Boelcke codified his *Dicta*. He also shared his views on creation of a fighter arm, and the organization of fighter squadrons.

Oswald Boelcke and Max Immelmann as part of a group photograph. After Immelmann was killed on 18 June 1916 Kaiser Wilhelm II ordered Boelcke grounded for a month to avoid losing him in combat soon after Immelmann. He had become such an important hero to the German public, as well as such an authority on aerial warfare, that he could not be risked. He was sent on a tour of the Balkans. He transited Austria to visit Turkey. On the return trip he visited Bulgaria and the Russian Front. Along the way, he interviewed pilots. Boelcke was visiting Wilhelm in Kovel when he received a telegram from Hermann von der Lieth-Thomsen appointing him to raise, organise and command Royal Prussian *Jagdstaffel 'Jasta' 2*.

A photograph taken by Hermann Göring of Oswald Boelcke in the company of members of *Artillerie-Flieger-Abteilung 203*. Boelcke had been invited over from Sivry by their commanding officer Hauptmann Vogt [possibly third from the right, front row] to provide them with fighter protection during a reconnaissance mission that, according to Boelcke's correspondence home, occurred at some point between 12 and 18 June 1916. (*Library of Congress*)

Hauptmann Oswald Boelcke, *Staffelführer* of *Jasta 2* in front of his Albatros D.II, 1916. Boelcke set out on Saturday 28 October 1916 for his sixth sortie of the day with his two best pilots, Manfred von Richthofen and Erwin Böhme, and three others. In the ensuing melée of the dogfight there was a collision and Böhme's landing gear brushed Boelcke's upper wing. As the fabric peeled off the upper wing of his aircraft, Boelcke struggled for control. He and his aircraft fell out of sight into a cloud. When it emerged, the top wing was gone. Boelcke made a relatively soft crash-landing but he was not strapped in and did not survive the crash.

Oswald Boelcke, victor of 40 aerial engagements, was dead at the age of 25. Three days later, on Tuesday 31 October 1916, Manfred von Richthofen led the procession at Cambrai Cathedral.

Boelcke had been christened 'the Gentleman Pilot' by the British press. On 5 January 1916, Boelcke shot down a British B.E.2c biplane of No. 2 Squadron crewed by Lieutenant William Somervill and Lieutenant Geoffrey Formilli. He maintained contact with the two men when they were hospitalised and went to great lengths to deliver a letter Formilli wrote, informing people he was still alive.

Leutnant Immelmann

Two standard photography studio postcard views of Oberleutnant Max Immelmann, (1890-1916). These appear to have taken on the same day.

When Immelmann was called up he was immediately posted to the recently formed *Fliegertruppe* and was sent for pilot training at Johannisthal Airfield in November 1914. He was initially stationed in northern France. On 3 June 1915, he was shot down by a French pilot but managed to land safely behind German lines. Immelmann was decorated with the Iron Cross, Second Class for preserving his aircraft.

Leutnant Immelmann
an seinem Fokker-Flugzeug

Two early versions of the Fokker Eindeckers were delivered to Immelmann's unit, one Fokker M.5K/MG production prototype numbered E.3/15 for Oswald Boelcke's use, with Immelmann later in July receiving E.13/15 as a production Fokker E.I for his own use before the end of July. It was with the lMG 08-machine-gun-armed E.13/15 aircraft that he gained his first confirmed air victory of the war on 1 August 1915. In this photograph Immelmann poses in front of his Endecker.

Leutnant Immelmann
an den Trümmern eines von ihm abgeschossenen engl. Eindeckers.

Max Immelmann standing in front of one his victories, a British monoplane. Immelmann became one of the first German fighter pilots, quickly building an impressive score of air victories. During September, three more victories followed, and then in October he became solely responsible for the air defence of the city of Lille and became known as *Der Adler von Lille*. He gained two further victories during September, to become the first German ace. Immelmann and Boelcke competed with each other to have the highest number of victories. On 15 December 1915, Immelmann shot down his seventh British plane and moved into an unchallenged lead in the competition to be Germany's leading ace. He was the first pilot to be awarded the *Pour le Mérite*, Germany's highest military honour, receiving it on the day of his eighth win, 12 January 1916.

Max Immelmann had a lonely devotion to his pet dog, Tyras, who often slept within or on his bed. He didn't smoke or drink and wrote daily to his mother.

On Tuesday 25 April 1915 Immelmann received a sharp lesson regarding the recent improvement in the models of British aircraft coming into service. Describing the attack by two Airco DH.2s he said: 'The two worked splendidly together . . . put 11 shots into my machine. The petrol tank, the struts on the fuselage, the undercarriage and the propeller were hit. . . It was not a nice business.' On Wednesday 31 May, Immelmann, Max von Mulzer, and another pilot attacked a formation of seven British aircraft. Immelmann was flying a two-gun Fokker E.IV, and when he opened fire, the synchronising gear malfunctioned. A stream of bullets cut off the tip of a propeller blade. The shaking of unbalanced blade nearly shook the aircraft's engine from its mounting before he could stop the engine and glide to a landing. He was lucky to be over German-held territory.

At 21:45 on Sunday 18 June 1916, Immelmann in his Fokker E.III encountered No. 25 Squadron FE.2bs. He claimed one, his 17th victory claim. The crew of the second aircraft he closed on was piloted by Second Lieutenant G. R. McCubbin with Corporal J. H. Waller as gunner/observer, who was credited by the British with shooting Immelmann down. The Germans claimed he had fallen to friendly fire. The truth will never be fully known. At 6,000 feet the tail was seen to break away from the rest of Immelmann's Fokker, the wings detached or folded, and what remained of the fuselage fell straight down, carrying the 25-year old Oberleutnant to his death. His body was recovered by the German 6 Armee from the twisted wreckage,

Oberleutnant Ernst Udet, (1896-1941). Udet was the second-highest scoring German flying ace and was one of the youngest and highest scoring aces to survive the war. His 62 confirmed victories were second only to Manfred von Richthofen, his commander in the Flying Circus. Udet rose to become a squadron commander under Richthofen, and later under Hermann Göring.

An early photograph of Udet in a Fokker Eindecker in *Jasta 15*. Early in 1916 Udet served in *Kampfeinsitzer Kommando Habsheim* which became *Jagdstaffel 15* on 28 September 1916. Eventually, every pilot in *Jasta 15* was killed except Udet and his commander, Heinrich Gontermann. Gontermann became gloomy, saying to Udet, 'The bullets fall from the hand of God . . . Sooner or later they will hit us.'

An early photograph of Udet. On Gontermann's return to the unit Udet applied for a transfer to *Jasta 37*, and Heinrich Gontermann was killed three months later at the age of 21 when the upper wing of his new Fokker Dr. 1 tore off as he was flying it for the first time. Gontermann lingered for 24 hours without awakening, and Udet later remarked, 'It was a good death.'

Oberleutnant Ernst Udet in Fokker D.VII F 4253 of *Jasta 4*. In later years Udet was chosen by his former commander, Hermann Göring for the post of Director-General of Equipment for the Luftwaffe. However, the stress of the position and his distaste for administrative duties led to an increasing dependence on alcohol. A problematical life was ended on 17 November 1941; he committed suicide by shooting himself in the head.

Above: Ernst Udet's suicide was concealed from the public and he was given a state funeral and hundreds of thousands turned out. At his funeral he was lauded as a hero who had died in flight while testing a new weapon. The mourners were led by Hermann Göring and the guard of honour by Adolf Galland, the Second World War fighter ace. On his way to attend Udet's funeral, the another Second World War ace Werner Mölders died in a plane crash in Breslau. Udet was buried next to Manfred von Richthofen in the Invalidenfriedhof Cemetery in Berlin. Mölders was buried next to Udet. (*Bundesarchiv*)

Right: Leutnant Heinrich Gontermann, (1896-1917). Gontermann's personal reputation was that of an aloof man with few friends. He was granted four weeks leave upon receipt of the Blue Max, but on his return to the *Jasta* on 19 June 1917, he found that acting *Staffelführer* Ernst Udet had requested a transfer. Under Udet's leadership the Jasta had suffered three demoralising losses.

Leutnant Gontermann.

Heinrich Gontermann in front of an Albatros D.V of *Jasta 15*. By 2 October 1917, Gontermann had become a celebrated ace with 39 victories. He was credited with defeating 21 enemy aircraft and 18 balloons, plus an unconfirmed balloon shot down.

Left: The Fokker Dr.I 115/17 was the first production Dr.I to reach the frontlines and had been delivered *to Jasta 15* on 11 October 1917.

Below: Heinrich Gontermann in front of the Fokker Dr.I 115/17 that killed him a few days later. On Tuesday 30 October 1917 Gontermann took off in the Fokker Dr. I and tried aerobatics at approximately 700 metres altitude. He pulled out of the second loop and dived into a left turn. The upper wing collapsed and broke completely off. He plunged into the ground and was pulled from the wreck alive, but died from his injuries several hours later. His final total was 39 victories.

Right: Oberleutnant Erich Löwenhardt, (1897-1918). Löwenhardt was the 3rd highest German flying ace with 54 victories, behind only Manfred von Richthofen and Ernst Udet. Löwenhardt became locked into an 'ace race' with Ernst Udet and Lothar von Richthofen for the honour of being the top scoring ace in their fighter wing.

Below: The rivalry between Löwenhardt and the younger Richthofen was a friendly one, as they often flew as wingmen. In this postcard Löwenhardt stands beside a captured SPAD aircraft, in scruffy uniform, but still wearing his Blue Max.

Loewenhardt

On Saturday10 August 1918 Löwenhardt launched his yellow Fokker D.VII on a mid-day sortie. He encountered No. 56 Squadron RAF and shot down a Royal Aircraft Factory S.E.5a over Chaulnes, at 12:15 hours for his 54th victory. In the following melée, he collided with Leutnant Alfred Wenz from *Jasta 11*. Both pilots' aircraft were equipped with parachutes and both pilots bailed out, Löwenhardt's failed to open and the fall killed him. He was 21 years old at the time of his death.

Leutnant Werner Voss, (1897-1917). Voss followed Löwenhardt in the tally total with 48 victories. By 6 April 1917, Voss had scored 24 victories and awarded Germany's highest award, the *Pour le Mérite*. The medal's mandatory month of leave removed Voss from the battlefield during Bloody April; in his absence, Richthofen scored 13 victories. Nevertheless, Richthofen regarded Voss as his only possible rival as top scoring ace of the war.

Above left: Werner Voss with Anton Fokker. Soon after Voss returned from leave, he was detailed from his squadron to evaluate new fighter aircraft and was enthused by the Fokker Triplane. After transferring through three temporary squadron commands in two months, Voss was given command of *Jagdstaffel 10* on 30 July 1917 at Richthofen's request. By now, his victory total was 34. His last stand came on 23 September 1917, just hours after his 48th victory. After he fell in solo opposition to eight British aces, he was described by his pre-eminent foe, James McCudden, as 'the bravest German airman'. He was one of the younger aces.

Above right: Leutnant Fritz Rumey, (1891- 1918). After Voss, Fritz Rumey was the next highest scoring ace with 45 victories. With 29 victories to his credit, Leutnant Rumey received the coveted *Pour le Mérite* in July 1918. This made him one of only five pilots to have received both this award and the Golden Military Merit Cross. He went scoreless in August but in September, shot down 16 aircraft, a figure only surpassed by Franz Büchner.

The cause of Leutnant Fritz Rumey's death is unclear. The day is known, Friday 27 September 1917. One theory was that he was killed after a mid-air collision with the S.E.5a of Captain G. E. B. Lawson of No. 32 Squadron, who survived. Another suggestion is that Lieutenant Frank Hale of 32 Squadron actually shot Rumey down, while Rumey's squadron comrades believed that his full throttle diving pursuit of an RAF S.E.5a caused the fabric to peel off the upper wing of his aircraft. Whichever account is true, when he jumped from his damaged machine, his parachute failed entirely, sending the 27-year old ace plummeting to his death.

Above left: Hauptmann Oskar Gustav Rudolf Berthold, (1891-1920). With one less than Rumey, the next in line is Rudolf Berthold with 44 victories. Berthold had a reputation as a ruthless, fearless and—above all—very patriotic fighter. His perseverance, bravery, and willingness to return to combat while still wounded made him one of the most famous pilots of the War. After the War, Rudolf Berthold organized a *Freikorps* and fought the Bolsheviks in Latvia. He was killed in political street fighting in Hamburg on 15 March 1920.

Above right: Leutnant Paul Wilhelm Bäumer, (1896- 1927). Bäumer was nicknamed 'The Iron Eagle' and with a personal emblem of an Edelweiss on his aircraft. He received the *Pour le Mérite* shortly before the Armistice and was finally credited with 43 victories, ranking ninth among German aces.

Left: After the war Bäumer eventually became a dentist, and reportedly one of his patients, Erich Maria Remarque, used Bäumer's name for the protagonist of his anti-war novel *All Quiet on the Western Front*. Bäumer later founded his own aircraft company in Hamburg. He died in an air crash at Copenhagen on 15 July 1927, while test flying a Rohrbach Ro IX fighter.

Left: Leutnant Josef Carl Peter Jacobs, (1894-1978). After leave in April 1916, Jacobs was posted to Fokkerstaffel-West to fly a Fokker E.III Eindecker and he finally achieved his first official victory, over an enemy aircraft on 12 May when he shot down a two-seater Caudron crewed only by its pilot. From early 1918 onwards, Jacobs started flying the Fokker Dr.I triplane with *Jasta 7*, and had his aircraft finished in a distinctive black scheme. The Dr.I was his favoured mount until October 1918 and he used its manoeuvrable attributes to his advantage, becoming the triplane's highest scoring ace, with over 30 confirmed victories. Jacobs' victory tally slowly rose, until at 24 victories, on 19 July 1918, he was awarded the *Pour le Mérite*. Jacobs remained with *Jasta 7* until the armistice.

Right: Hauptmann Bruno Lörzer, (1891-1960). Hermann Göring flew as Lörzer's observer from 28 October 1914 until late June 1915. Transferring to fighters, Lörzer flew with two *Jagdstaffeln* in 1916 before joining *Jagdstaffel 26* in January 1917. By then he had scored two victories over French aircraft. His tally reached 20 victories at the end of October and he received the *Pour le Mérite* in February 1918.

Also in February 1918 Lörzer he took command of the newly formed *Jagdgeschwader III*, the third of Germany's famed 'flying circuses.' Lörzer proved a successful wing commander. Equipped with the new BMW-engined Fokker D.VII, *JG III* cut a wide swathe through Allied formations in the summer of 1918, and his own score mounted steadily. He achieved his last ten victories in September when he reached his final score of 44 victories. Shortly before the armistice, he was promoted to Hauptmann (captain).

May 1918 members of *Jasta 26*; *From left to right:* Buder, Klassen, Riemer, Zogmann, Weiss, Fritz Lörzer, Bruno Lörzer, Mar; at far right Fritz Beckhardt. (*Bundesarchiv*)

Bruno Lörzer was a close friend of Hermann Göring and there are countless photographs of the two young men together. Lörzer benefited from his long friendship with Göring, becoming Inspector of Fighters with rank of major general in 1938. During the early war years he was commander of *II Fliegerkorps* (Air Corps), being awarded the *Ritterkreuz des Eisernen Kreuzes* in May 1940.

Lörzer's II Air Corps participated in the invasion of Russia in the summer of 1941, as a section of Kesselring's 2nd Air Fleet—in support of Fieldmarshall von Bock. His unit was transferred to Messina, Sicily in October 1941, and he remained there until the middle of 1943, when his section returned to the Italian mainland. Göring promoted Lörzer to *Generaloberst* in February 1943 and in June 1944 was chief of the Nazi Leadership Branch of the Luftwaffe. He retired in April 1945.

Leutnant Franz Büchner, (1898-1920). In March 1917 Büchner became a fighter pilot, joining *Jagdstaffel 9* where he scored his first and only victory with them, on 17 August. He brought his tally to 40 victories by 22 October 1918. Three days later he was awarded the *Pour le Mérite* on 25 October 1918, one of the last awards before the Kaiser's abdication. After the War 22-year-old Büchner flew against communist revolutionaries but was killed during a reconnaissance flight near his hometown of Leipzig on 18 March 1920.

Oberleutnant Lothar von Richthofen, (1894-1922). Lothar was a younger brother of Manfred von Richthofen. His first posting as a pilot was to his brother's *Jasta 11* on 6 March 1917. His first victory claim followed on 28 March for an F.E.2b of No. 25 Squadron, RFC. Richthofen raised his total to 24 by 13 May, when, after shooting down a B.E.2, he was wounded in the hip by anti-aircraft fire and crash-landed; his injuries kept him out of combat for five months. On 14 May 1917 he was awarded the *Pour le Mérite*, and he resumed command of *Jasta 11* in September 1917. Of his total of 40 confirmed victories, Lothar scored 33 in just three months: 15 in April 1917, 8 in May 1917, and 10 in August 1918.

Leutnant Karl Menckhoff, (1883-1949). Menckhoff scored his first victory on 5 April 1917, downing a Nieuport 17 of No. 29 Squadron, RFC, flown by Lieutenant Norman Birks. On 23 September 1917, he is said to have come to the aid of Werner Voss during the latter's battle against an overwhelming force from the RFC. Lieutenant Arthur Rhys Davids reportedly turned from engaging Voss and damaged Menckhoff's Albatros so badly that he had to crash land it. Rhys Davids then shot down Voss. Menckhoff made no mention of this engagement in his later memoirs, and this account has been questioned.

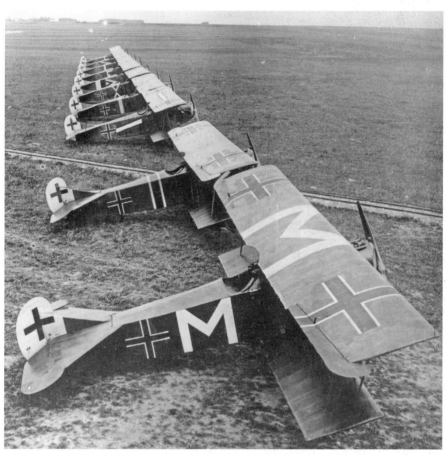

Karl Menckhoff's Fokker D.VII of *Jasta 72* at Bergnicourt 1918 with a large 'M' on the top. On 23 April 1918, Menckhoff was awarded Germany's highest decoration for valour, the *Pour le Mérite*, his victory total having reached 25. On 25 July 1918 Menckhoff was shot down by Lieutenant Walter Avery of the 95th Aero Squadron, United States Air Service. Following interrogation, Menckhoff was held as a prisoner of war, along with many other German pilots, at Camp Montoire, near Orléans.

Oberleutnant Hermann Wilhelm Göring, (1893-1946). In the first year of the War, Göring served with his infantry regiment in the area of Mülhausen, a garrison town only a mile from the French frontier. His friend Bruno Lörzer convinced him to request to transfer to the *Fliegertruppe* which the *Luftstreitkräfte* in October 1916, but his request was turned down. Later that year, Göring flew as Lörzer's observer in *Feldflieger Abteilung 25*. Göring had effectively informally transferred himself. He was discovered and sentenced to three weeks' confinement to barracks, but the sentence was never carried out. By the time it was supposed to be imposed, Göring's association with Lörzer had been made official. They were assigned as a team to FFA 25 in the Crown Prince's Fifth Army. They flew reconnaissance and bombing missions, for which the Crown Prince invested both Göring and Lörzer with the Iron Cross, first class.

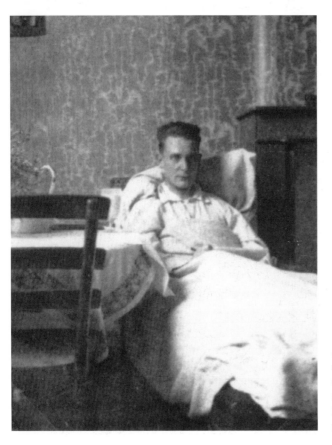

After completing the pilot's training course, Göring was assigned to *Jagdstaffel 5*. Seriously wounded in the hip in aerial combat, he took nearly a year to recover. He then was transferred to *Jagdstaffel 26*, commanded by Lörzer, in February 1917.

Right: A youthful and slim-looking Hermann Göring in the *Jasta's* map room. (*Library of Congress*)

Below: Hermann Göring diligently at his studies. (*Library of Congress*)

Hermann Göring (with cigarette in mouth) and Bruno Lörzer in their apartment. Apparently the two friends shared the same quarters. (*Library of Congress*)

This photograph is from Hermann Göring's personal album. His caption reads, 'Fighter Squadron 26 at Habsheim airfield', 1917. It shows early members of *Jagdstaffel 26* posed the photograph in late February 1917. *Seated left to right:* Offizierstellvertreter [Acting Officer] Fritz Lörzer, younger brother of Bruno Lörzer; and Leutnant Karl Wewer. *Standing, left to right:* Acting Officer Rudolf Weckbrodt, Sgt Langer, PFC Hansen, 1st Lieutenant Bruno Lörzer, two unknown, Leutnant Hermann Göring, Sgt Richard Linke, Reserve Leutnant Walter Blume, Reserve Leutnant Hans Auer, and Reserve Leutnant Theodor Rumpel.

Göring steadily served victories whilst serving with *Jastas* 5, 26 & 27 until May 1918 when he was assigned to the command of *Jasta* 27. In addition to his Iron Crosses (1st and 2nd Class), he received the Zaehring Lion with swords, the Friedrich Order, the House Order of Hohenzollern with swords third class, and finally, in May 1918, the coveted *Pour le Mérite*.

Göring finished the war with 22 victories. A thorough post-Second World War examination of Allied loss records showed that only two of his claimed victories were doubtful. Three were possible and 17 were certain, or highly likely. On 7 July 1918, following the death of Wilhelm Reinhard, successor to Manfred von Richthofen, Göring was made commander of the famed 'Flying Circus', *Jagdgeschwader 1*. His arrogance made him unpopular with the men of his squadron.

Two photographs from Hermann Göring's personal album; he obviously orchestrated them being taken. The first a photograph of the photographer! The second, the shot actually taken by the photographer. (*Library of Congress*)

Above: Göring wearing a flying helmet and goggles. In the last days of the war, Göring was repeatedly ordered to withdraw his squadron, first to Tellancourt airdrome, then to Darmstadt. (*Library of Congress*)

Right: Rittmeister Karl Bolle, (1893-1955). Bolle's final score of 36 victories included a preponderance of wins over enemy fighters; he downed 25. The other 11 victories were two-seater reconnaissance, ground attack, and bomber aircraft. More importantly, he led *Jasta 2* through the intense battles of 1918 to the second highest victory total in the German Air Force, with a total of 336 victories to the *Jasta.*

Leutnant Julius Buckler, (1894-1960). Buckler was credited with 36 victories. He shot down 29 aircraft and 7 balloons; two other victories went unconfirmed. He was one of only four German fighter aces to win Germany's highest decorations for valour for both enlisted man and officer.

Leutnant Max Ritter von Müller, (1887-1918). Müller was credited with 36 victories. With the death of Heinrich Gontermann in late October 1917, Müller was second only to Manfred von Richthofen as the highest scoring ace still at the front., On 9 January 1918, while on a patrol over Moorslede, Müller's flight came across an R.E.8 of No. 21 Squadron and two S.E.5a fighters of No. 60 Squadron. Bullets struck his fuel tank, and his Albatros D.Va began to go into a spiral several thousand feet up. With fire quickly burning through the interior panel of the cockpit, Müller, who was not wearing a parachute, jumped to his death.

Leutnant Gustav Dörr, (1887-1928). Dörr was credited with 35 victories. Dörr was the most successful ace to fly the Fokker D.VII, accumulating 30 victories with it. He had been wounded four times, twice as an infantryman, twice as a pilot. He had refused an assignment to the rear echelon to remain in the front line. He failed to receive the *Pour le Mérite* as Kaiser abdicated before the ceremony could take place.

Leutnant Otto Könnecke, (1892-1956). Könnecke was also credited with 35 victories. Könnecke had been awarded a Golden Military Merit Cross while still a *Vizefeldwebel*; this was the highest decoration for valour an enlisted man could receive. On 15 June, he was commissioned as Leutnant. On 20 July 1918, he was awarded the Knight's Cross with Swords of the Royal House Order of Hohenzollern. On 26 September 1918, the day before his comrade Fritz Rumey was killed in action, Könnecke was awarded Germany's highest decoration, the *Pour le Merite*. He was one of the few former NCOs to receive the Blue Max, and one of only five pilots awarded both the Golden Military Merit Cross and the Blue Max.

Eduard Ritter von Schleich, (1888-1947). When his best friend on the *Jasta*, Leutnant Erich Limpert was killed in a dogfight, Schleich ordered his plane to be painted all black. This black plane soon led to Schleich being dubbed 'The Black Knight'. He was awarded the *Pour le Mérite* in December, and after a spell commanding *Jastaschule 1*, on 15 March 1918 he took command of *Jagdgruppe Nr. 8*, a collection of *Jastas 23, 34* and *35*, in the last month of the war he commanded *Jasta 21*. By the war's end his score was 35, matching that of Dörr and Könnecke. He became a *Luftwaffe* general in Nazi Germany and his final command was *Luftwaffe* Ground Forces Commander in Norway. Held by British forces after the Second World War, he died in custody on 15 November 1947.

Josef 'Seppl' Veltjens, (1894-1943). Veltjens received the *Pour le Mérite* on 16 August 1918. His victory total was 31 when he went on leave, leaving Oscar Freiherr von Boenigk in charge. Upon his return, he resumed command of the prestigious *Jagdgeschwader 2* on 28 September, only to be bumped down once again to command *Jasta 15* from 12 October to Armistice Day. During this time, he raised his victory total to 35. Veltjens in later life became a personal emissary from Hermann Göring to Benito Mussolini.

Above left: Oberleutnant Kurt Wolff, (1895-1917). Karl-Heinrich Bodenschatz, who became a general who was the liaison officer between Hermann Göring and Adolf Hitler was also adjutant to Manfred von Richthofen during the First World War. He said of Wolff: *At first glance, you could only say 'delicate little flower'. A slender, thin little figure, a very young face, whose entire manner is one of extreme shyness. He looks as if you could tip him backwards with one harsh word. But below this friendly schoolboy's face dangles the order Pour le Mérite. And so far, these modest looking eyes have taken 30 enemy airplanes from the sky over the sights of his machine guns, set them afire, and made them smash to pieces on the ground.*

Above right: Vizefeldwebel Sebastian Festner, (1894-1917). Under the command of Manfred von Richthofen, Festner quickly claimed two victories in February 1917 (A B.E.2 on 5 February and a F.E.8 of No. 40 Squadron on 16 February) before claiming another ten during 'Bloody April'. Flying Albatros D.III 2251/17, Festner was killed in action on 25 April 1917, near Oppy. He crashed behind the British lines, between Gavrelle and Bailleul. With the area under German artillery fire, there was no attempt to recover either plane or body. Festner was therefore declared missing in action with no known grave.

Right: Karl Emil Schäfer, (1891-1917). With one single victory, Schäfer somewhat cockily telegraphed Manfred von Richthofen, who was assembling a 'top' squadron at *Jasta 11*, 'Can you use me?' Richthofen replied, 'You have already been requested.' Schäfer was then posted to *Jasta 11* on 21 February 1917. In intensive operations during 'Bloody April' he became a flying ace, being credited with 21 victories and awarded the *Pour le Mérite*. Schäfer was shot down and killed in action on 5 June 1917 in combat with No. 20 Squadron, by ace crew Lieutenant Harold Satchell and Lieutenant Thomas Lewis. Satchell and Lewis' fire did not strike Schäfer, but disabled his plane, which broke apart in mid-air.

It is not easy to identify these 18 officers and some (or most) of the following attributions may be incorrect. If any reader can make corrections or additions please email *office@fonthillmedia.com*.

Standing, left to right: 1) Friedrich Wilhelm Lubbert; 2) Erich Von Hartmann; 3) Hans Hinsch; 4) Ernst Luth; 5) Wilhelm Reinhard; 6) Friedrich August Von Schoenenebeck; 7) ????; 8) Wolfgang Plüschow; 9) Manfred von Richthofen. *Seated, left to right:* 1) ????; 2) Hanns Joachim Wolff; 3) Erich Löwenhardt; 4) ????; 5) ????; 6) Kurt Wolff; 7) Oskar Barth?; 8) Lothar von Richthofen; 9) Konstantin Krefft.

Manfred von Richthofen shaking hands with General Ernst Wilhelm von Hoeppner, (1860-1922), *Kommandierender General der Luftstreitkräfte*. During early 1917, it became apparent to the German High Command that they would always be outnumbered in air operations over the Western Front. The average *Jasta* could only muster some six or eight aircraft in total for a patrol, and would often face one Allied formation after another. In order to maintain some impact and local command of the air the *Jastas* began, at first unofficially, to fly in larger, composite groups. By mid-1917 the first official grouping of *Jastas* saw *Jagdgeschwader 1* (JG 1) formed. Its role was simple; to achieve localised air superiority wherever it was sent and to deny Allied air operations over a specific location. Hoeppner selected Richthofen to command this new unit.

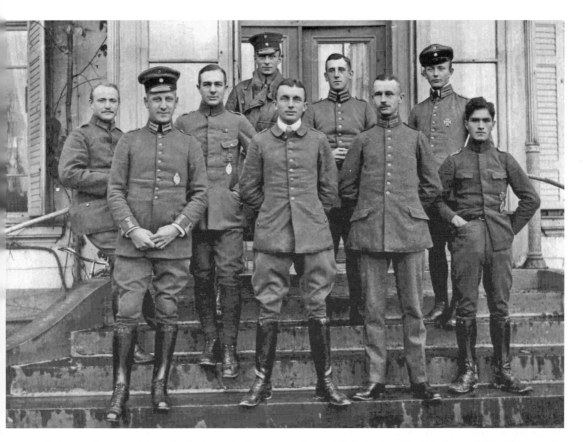

A clear and presumably early photograph of some members of *Jasta 11*. No Blue Max's are visible. If any reader can identify any of these officers please email *office@fonthillmedia.com*.

A smiling Manfred von Richthofen with fellow officers of *Jasta 11*. The unit was highly mobile, and JG 1 and its supporting logistical infrastructure travelled to wherever local air superiority was needed, often at short notice. JG 1 comprised of four squadrons, (*Jagdstaffels*, commonly shortened to *Jastas*), and these were *Jasta 4, 6, 10* and *11*. JG 1 became known as 'The Flying Circus'. Whether this is because of the bright colours of its aircraft, or because it frequently transferred from one area to another—moving like a travelling circus in trains is unclear, but the name soon stuck. Officers and ground crew frequently set up in tents on improvised airfields.

Kurt Wolff and Konstantin Krefft in conversation
with the Red Baron. Richthofen frequently
adopts that pose of looking at the camera, he was
conscious of being constantly photographed.

Manfred von Richthofen (in cockpit) with fellow officers of *Jasta 11*. *From left to right, standing*: Karl Allmenröder;
Kurt Wülshoff; Sebastian Festner; Karl-Emil Schäfer; Kurt Wolff; Wilhelm Reinhardt and Erich Löwenhardt.
Kneeling, left to right: Karl Esser (or Effer) and Konstantin Krefft. *Seated at front*: Lothar von Richthofen.

Initially based at Marke (*Jasta 11*), Cuene (*Jasta 4*), Bissegem (*Jasta 6*) and Heule (*Jasta 10*), Richthofen had *carte blanche* to select his unit commanders and recruit individual pilots into JG 1, and alternately to transfer out any pilots he did not feel were up to standard.

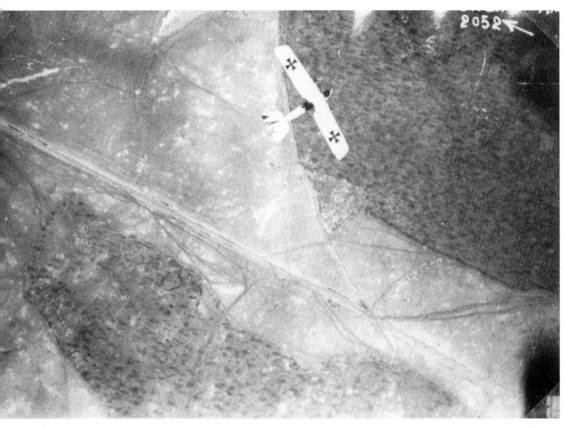

Two aerial photographs taken by Hermann Göring of *Jasta 11* and taken from his personal photograph album. (*Library of Congress*)

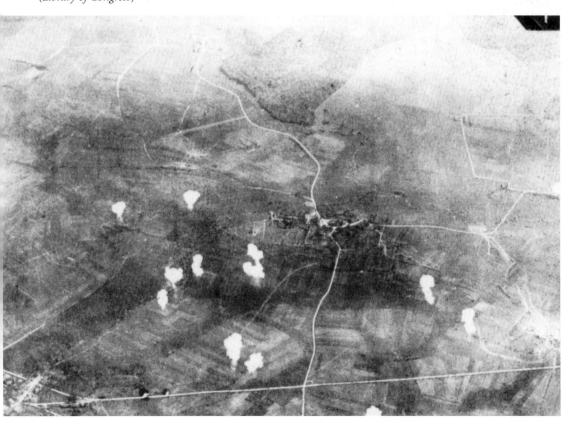

Manfred von Richthofen in flying helmet by his Albatros D.V 4693/17. This was taken summer 1917, probably just a few days before he was wounded and forced down. This occurred on 6 July 1917, leading elements of JG 1 in combat with F.E.2d's of 20 Squadron RFC. During the dogfight Richthofen was wounded in the head and momentarily blinded, but he managed to make an emergency landing behind German lines. He was treated in the field hospital 76 in St Nicolas, Courtrai and then went back to Château de Marcke-sur-Lys to recuperate.

Richthofen was billeted with other officers of *Jasta 11* at Château de Marcke-sur-Lys near Courtrai. Oberleutnant Kurt von Doering, Commanding Officer of *Jasta 4*, took over temporary command and *Jastas 4* and *11* shot down 9 Allied aircraft the next day. Richthofen resumed command on 25 July.

Château de Marcke-sur-Lys is south of Courtrai and the *Jasta* remained there from 2 July to 22 November 1917.

Manfred von Richthofen with Konstantin Krefft to his right jokes with other officers on the steps of Château de Marcke-sur-Lys, by their side is the broken propeller from a British aircraft.

On 11 July 1917 Kurt Wolff was shot in both his left hand and left shoulder by gunfire from a Sopwith Triplane flown by future ace Flight Sub-Lieutenant H. V. Rowley of No. 1 Naval Squadron RNAS. Wolff crash landed his aircraft on the Courtrai railway line. Here, with left arm in a sling, he joins a line-up on the steps of Château de Marcke-sur-Lys, presumably late July 1917. This is from Göring's personal photograph album and it is not quite clear if that is him front row second from the right. (*Library of Congress*)

A summer evening gathering in the park of Château de Marcke-sur-Lys. It does not look as if any of the young officers of *Jasta 11* are with this gathering of older personnel.

Richthofen met that Kaiser on 20 August 1917 near Courtrai when the Kaiser was inspecting the troops of the 4th Army.

On 3 September 1917 Richthofen downed Lieutenant Algernon Frederick Bird, (who survived) and his Sopwith Pup B1795 south of Bousbecque. Here he looks pleased with his conquest. On 6 September 1917 he left for a period of leave returning on 23 October.

From left to right: Sebastian Festner; Karl-Emil Schäfer; Manfred von Richthofen; Lothar von Richthofen and Kurt Wolff. Apart from Lothar, none survived the War.

Richthofen returned to JG 1 on 23 October 1917, and around this time a number of fatal crashes involving the Fokker Dr.I saw JG 1 Technical Officer Leutnant Konstantin Krefft ground the unit's triplanes until modifications were carried out in early December. The unit meantime soldiered on with the Albatros D.V.

A photograph taken outside Château de Marcke-sur-Lys with five *Pour le Mérite* holders. *From left to right:* Kurt Wüsthoff, Willy Reinhard, Manfred von Richthofen, Erich Löwenhardt and Lothar von Richthofen. Their combined victory total was 221. Kurt Wüsthoff received his award on Thursday 22 November 1917. JG 1 left Château de Marcke-sur-Lys that same day for Cambrai, so this would pinpoint the date of the photograph to the very day.

Back row from left to right: Carl Allmenröder; Lothar von Richthofen; Wolfgang Plüschow and Erich von Hartmann. *Front row, from left to right*: Georg Simon; Kurt Wolff; Manfred von Richthofen; Major von Richthofen, (father of Manfred and Lothar); Konstantin Krefft and Hans Hintsch.

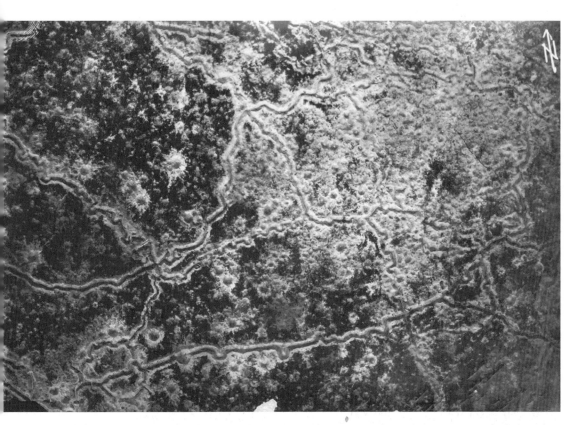

The Western Front from an aerial photograph. JG 1 was rushed from Ypres to Cambrai by 23 November 1917, following the launch of the British offensive, and did much to stabilise the air war over the battlefield when the weather permitted.

A dead German pilot in the wreckage of his aircraft. (*National World War I Museum, Kansas City, Missouri*)

By the end of 1917 the success of *Jagdgeschwader 1* meant several other similar formations were then formed in February 1918, with *Jagdgeschwader 2* operating against both the French and the British and *Jagdgeschwader 3* commander by Oberleutnant Bruno Lörzer on the Ypres front. At this time Richthofen recruited Hans Kirchstein and Fritz Friedrichs from two-seaters units, and Ernst Udet from *Jasta 37*.

Adolf, Ritter von Tutschek, (1891-1918). Von Tutschek was chosen to command *Jagdgeschwader 2*. He was killed in action on 15 March 1918 and the next day he was replaced by Rudolf Berthold.

Supposedly the remains of Richtofen's Fokker. Manfred von Richthofen received a fatal wound just after 11:00 am on 21 April 1918, while flying over Morlancourt Ridge, near the Somme River. There is a suggestion that on the day of Richthofen's death, the prevailing wind was about 25 mph easterly, rather than the usual 25 mph westerly. This meant that Richthofen, heading generally westward at an airspeed of about 100 mph, was travelling over the ground at up to 125 mph rather than the more typical ground speed of 75 mph. This was considerably faster than normal and he could easily have strayed over enemy lines without realising it, especially since he was struggling with one jammed gun and another that was firing only short bursts before needing to be re-cocked.

Australian soldiers with the wreckage of the tailplane. At the time of Richthofen's death, the front was in a highly fluid state and in the face of Allied air superiority, the German air service was having difficulty acquiring vital reconnaissance information. Richthofen was a highly experienced and skilled fighter pilot—fully aware of the risk from ground fire. Richthofen's judgment may also have been affected by his head wound from the previous summer. It seems most likely that Australian ground fire was the cause of death. Some sources suggest that Sergeant Cedric Popkin was the person most likely to have killed Richthofen. Popkin was an machine gunner with the Australian 24th Machine Gun Company, and was using a Vickers gun. He fired at Richthofen's aircraft on two occasions: first as the Baron was heading straight at his position, and then at long range from the right.

Gunner Ernest W. Twycross was the first man to reach the aircraft and Richthofen tried to say something in German to him. Richthofen then sighed and died. One witness, Gunner George Ridgway, stated that when he and other Australian soldiers reached the aircraft, Richthofen was still alive but died moments later. Another eye witness, Sergeant Ted Smout of the Australian Medical Corps, reported that Richthofen's last word was 'kaputt'.

Richthofen was buried in the cemetery at the village of Bertangles, near Amiens, on 22 April 1918. Six of No. 3 squadron's officers served as pallbearers, and a guard of honour from the squadron's other ranks fired a salute.

 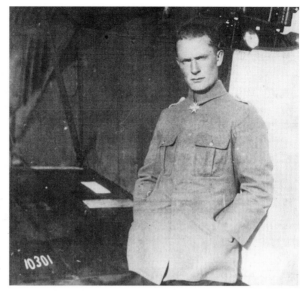

Above left: After von Richthofen's death, Hauptmann Wilhelm Reinhard, (1891-98) became JG 1 Commanding Officer. On 10 May JG 1 claimed its 300th victory while on 20 May the unit received the honorary title of JG 1 'Richthofen'. The unit then moved to the 7th Army front to support the forthcoming Aisne offensive, commencing on 27 May. JG 1 moved to Guise, and then Puiseux Ferme, operating primarily against the French and the newly arrived American Air Forces. On Wednesday July 1918, Wilhelm Reinhard attended aircraft trials near Adlershof. After Hermann Göring finished test flying a Dornier-Zeppelin D.I prototype that was supposed to have been grounded pending structural upgrades, Reinhard took it up for a test flight and was killed when the top wing broke free while pulling out of a dive. Following Reinhard's death, Göring assumed command of JG 1 on 8 July 1918. (*Library of Congress*)

Above right: A sullen-looking Hermann Göring who now left *Jasta 26* of *Jagdgeschwader 3* to take command of *Jagdgeschwader 1*. This unit moved again on 19 July to Soissons, claiming its 500th victory on 25 July. Yet another move followed on 10 August, to the 2nd Army front west of Saint Quentin. JG 1's then top scorer, Leutnant Erich Löwenhardt, was killed in an air collision on the same day. (*Library of Congress*)

A rear view of Göring's own mounted Spandau machine gun on the cowling of his fighter, a photo from earlier in the War. From August until the end of the war shortages of fuel and spares, increasing Allied numerical air superiority and continual retreats in the face of Allied ground advances meant JG 1 struggled to emulate earlier successes. From June 1917 until November 1918, JG 1 claimed 644 Allied aircraft destroyed, while losing 52 pilots killed in action and 67 wounded. In the last days of the war, Göring was repeatedly ordered to withdraw his squadron, first to Tellancourt, then to Darmstadt. At one point, he was ordered to surrender the aircraft to the Allies; he refused. Many of his pilots intentionally crash-landed their planes to keep them from falling into Allied hands. (*Library of Congress*)

Above: Hermann Göring and other officers fooling about on oil drums. Most of the young officers were late teens and early twenties. Letting off steam and fooling about were antidotes to the pressures of combat. (*Library of Congress*)

Left: Hermann Göring relaxing with cigar while someone clowns around behind him. (*Library of Congress*)

Göring (far left, seated) and Lörzer (third from left), of *Jasta 26* both in summer whites, enjoying an evening meal in summer time. Note the presence of Göring's cane— he needed it due to his rheumatism. (*Library of Congress*)

From Göring's personal photograph album: 'After the lineup of *Jagdstaffel 26* at Colmar', 1917. This appears to have been a very sedate tea party. (*Library of Congress*)

A drunken Christmas part with NCOs enjoying Champagne and wine—presumably purloined.

A slightly less drunken party with German white wine.

A haze of tobacco smoke.

Senior officers drinking beer. Some are already on the floor.

Revelries with *Jasta 5*, 1916. Oberleutnant Hans Berr and Oberleutnant Ernst Freiherr von Althaus with their Blue Max medals visible.

Putting on theatrical shows was a pastime enjoyed by all sides during the War.

Ballons were filled with hydrogen and filling them could be a lengthy operation. German soldiers attend to a stack of gas canisters attached to a manifold, inflating a captive balloon on the Western Front. (*National Archives/Official German Photograph*)

An Army observation signaller with a signal pistol. A static line parachute is attached to the side of the balloon's basket. Observation crews were the first to use parachutes, long before they were adopted by fixed wing aircrews. These were a primitive type, where the main part was in a bag suspended from the balloon, with the pilot only wearing a simple body harness around his waist, with lines from the harness attached to the main parachute in the bag. When the balloonist jumped, the main part of the parachute was pulled from the bag, with the shroud lines first, followed by the main canopy. This type of parachute was first adopted by the Germans and then later by the British and French for their observation balloon crews. (*U.S. National Archives*)

A German Type Ae 800 observation balloon ascending. The Germans used a copy of a French Caquot, the designation was 'Type Ae 800' for *Achthundert* (eight hundred) 800, which was a reference to the cubic metre capacity. (*Brett Butterworth*)

A German balloon being shot down. (*National World War I Museum, Kansas City, Missouri*)

Observation balloons near Coblenz. Positioning artillery observers on balloons, generally a few miles behind the front lines and at altitude, allowed them to see targets at greater range than they could on the ground. This allowed the artillery to take advantage of its increased range. (*Keystone View Company*)

A semi-inflated observation balloon. This may have been hit by machine gun fire and gradually deflated without bursting into flames. Ordinary bullets would usually simply pass through the balloon.

The Parseval-Sigsfeld *Drachen*. This was probably the most common German balloon from an original design by August von Parseval, (1861-1942), a German airship designer. In the garrison town of Augsburg he came into contact with August Riedinger and also came to know his later partner Rudolf Hans Bartsch von Sigsfeld, (1861-1902) with whom he developed *Drachenballons*: (Dragon balloons) used by the military for observation.

A captive balloon with its lorry, equipped with a motor winch, June 1918, after the battles at Soissons. (*National Archives/Official German Photograph*)

Fregattenkapitän Peter Strasser, (1876–1918) was Chief Commander of Germany's Zeppelin force during the First World War. He is pictured here, *c.* 1916, on the right, at Count Ferdinand Zeppelin's left side. To the left of the photograph is Hugo Eckener, the head of the Zeppelin company. Strasser died on 6 August 1918, on board *LZ 112* (*L 70*) when it was intercepted and destroyed over North Sea by British de Havilland DH-4 flown by Major Egbert Cadbury with Captain Robert Leckie as gunner.

Count Ferdinand Zeppelin, (1838-1917) had pioneered the development of Zeppelins and by 1914 the Germans had a modest fleet available. *LZ 36* (*L9*) made 74 successful reconnaissance missions in the North Sea and took part in four raids on England dropping a total of 5,683 kg of bombs. It also made several attacks on British submarines, at least one of which was successful. It burnt out in its hangar at Fuhlsbüttel in the north of Hamburg on 16 September 1916 after the Navy Zeppelin *LZ 31* (*L 6*) it was alongside caught fire during inflation.

LZ 37 was brought down by Sub-Lieutenant Reginald Warneford, 1 Sqdn RNAS, flying a Morane-Saulnier Type L, during its first raid on Calais on 7 June 1915. LZ 37 crashed at Sint-Amandsberg, near Ghent. Warneford was awarded a VC for his actions. This sketch was drawn by Reg Warneford himself.

LZ 96 (L 49) was forced to land near Bourbonne-les-Bains on 20 October 1917 and was captured almost undamaged by French forces. The design of LZ 96 influenced the design of the first American rigid airship, the USS Shenandoah (ZR-1) and the British R 38.

Opposite above: LZ 38 was one of a new 'P' Class of Naval Zeppelins and it carried out the first bombing raid on London on 31 May 1915 killing seven and injuring 35 people. This was followed by raids on Ipswich, Ramsgate, Southend (twice) and London, dropping a total of 8,360 kg of bombs. On 7 June 1915 this Navy Zeppelin, along with LZ 37 was returning to Evére to the east of Brussels and they ran into a counter-raid by RNAS aircraft flying from Furnes, Belgium. LZ 38 was destroyed on the ground. As a consequence of the RNAS raid both the German Army and Navy withdrew from their bases in Belgium.

Searchlights over London.

Zeppelin caught in the searchlights during a bombing raid in 1916.

Wreckage of airships and warehouses in Ahlhorn after the explosion and possible sabotage on 5 January 1918. Ahlhorn hangars exploded destroying five airships, killing 15 and injuring 134 people.

LZ 112 (L 70) was a tragedy for the German authorities as on its last flight on 5–6 August 1918 it has on board *Fregattenkapitän* Peter Strasser, Commander of the Navy Airship Department. It was intercepted and destroyed over North Sea by British de Havilland DH-4 flown by Major Egbert Cadbury with Captain Robert Leckie as gunner.

The control station on a Naval Zeppelin.

THE AUSTRO-HUNGARIAN EMPIRE
Naval Air Service—Luftahrtruppen

T HE AUSTRO-HUNGARIAN AERONAUTICAL INSTITUTE was created in 1892 and ranks as one of the oldest flying establishments in the world. The Imperial Austro-Hungarian Navy Air Service emerged in 1909, when several naval officers were selected to learn to fly and sent to France and Britain for instruction. On their return a flying base was set up near Pola, where a floatplane aircraft was constructed and flown in July 1912.

The Austrians foresaw the flying machine as a weapon of war, and an Army engineer—Emil Uzelac—was requested to form an air arm to the Austro-Hungarian armed forces. Oberst Uzelac was a non-flying officer but quickly gained pilot skills within a period of four months.

Early in 1913, the Navy decided to buy nine foreign flying boats—two Curtiss aircraft and four Donnet Lévêques, plus three others for spares and training. In 1913, a *Fliegerkompanie* (Flying Company) was established with six aircraft, and by the outbreak of war the strength of the Austro-Hungarian Air Arm had increased to thirty-six aircraft, made up of Etrich Taube A.I and A.II types and Lohner Pfeil (Arrow) biplanes, plus an airship and about ten balloons.

The Navy had twenty-two aircraft at its air bases at Teodo and Pola (there was a temporary base at Tivat, and another was built at Kumbor), its first combat coming on 12 August 1914—a bombing run against the enemy at Lovćen. This was followed by combat missions on 17 October against shipping, on 23 October—a mass raid on Antivari—and on 9 November—a first-time night raid on Antivari. By the end of the year the Naval Air Service had twenty-nine aircraft at Kumbor, and forty-seven by May 1915.

Austria-Hungary had declared war on Russia on 5 August 1914, on Japan on 25 August, and on Belgium on 28 August. As they were allies with Germany, the Austro-Hungarians asked the Germans for aircraft, and a few obsolete Rumpler and Aviatik aircraft were supplied, but it became clear that Austria-Hungary would have to build its own aircraft—some, like the Phonix Albatros, under licence.

No real aerial conflict occurred during the initial stages of the conflict, as the Russians and their Serbian allies had no substantial air warfare capability, but on 24 May 1915, Italy joined the Allies and declared war on Austria-Hungary. At first the Italians, like the Russians, posed no real threat, and the Austro-Hungarians—flying a variety of Fokker

E.Is, Lohner Bs, Albatros B.Is (Phonix-built), Lloyd C.IIs and Aviatik Bs—conducted a somewhat phoney war with desultory bombing, recce and observation sorties.

The Naval Air Service began a concerted build-up of its establishment, with fifty-five new Lohner flying boats on strength, followed by another sixty-six Lohners, and six Phonix fighters later in 1916. Earlier in the year, the situation had begun to take on a new dimension as the Italians—equipped with French Nieuport 10s and 11s and Caproni bombers—began to be more dashing and aggressive, the crews of the three-engine Caproni bombers causing severe damage and disruption. The Italian ace Francesco Baracca came to the fore in a Nieuport 11 when he shot down his first Austro-Hungarian aircraft on 7 April 1916.

As the air war hotted up, the Germans sold fifty Fokker B.IIs to the Austro-Hungarians. Two home companies—Phonix Aeroplane Works and UFAG (Hungarian Aeroplane Factory)—built under licence the outstanding Brandenburg D.I (KD) 'Star Strutter', and OEFFFAG (Austrian Aeroplane Factory) built the German D.II. The Naval Air Service took delivery of seventy-nine Hansa Brandenburg A-types and eighty-two K-type two-seat biplanes during 1917.

The opposing Italians flew the French Hanriot HD.1, the Nieuport 17 and the formidable SPAD S.7. Italian SAML, SIA 7B and Pomilio types were brought into action to replace obsolete pusher-type aircraft. With German-crewed aircraft combining with the Austro-Hungarian Air Arm in October 1917, their ground troops broke through the Italian front at Caporetto. The German *Jasta* 39 decimated the Caproni bombers and the Italians lost their front-line airfields.

However, French and British squadrons came to the Italians' aid just in time, stemming the onslaught and regaining air superiority. All lost ground was retaken. German forces were withdrawn in March 1918, leaving the Austro-Hungarians to fight on alone with no more than thirteen squadrons. The Italians began to increase the pressure on their enemy with probing long-range raids on Vienna and aggressive fighter patrols. They also used to great effect their Macchi fighter flying boats (some copied from the Lohner flying boat.)

Austria-Hungary's Naval Air Service had lost some ninety flying boats and about seventy-four seaplanes, mostly in combat, by the time of the Armistice in November 1918. When the new Hungarian state was established after the conflict, it was forbidden to build an air force.

AUSTRO-HUNGARIAN ACES

AUSTRIA-HUNGARY ONLY CLASSED AIRMEN as aces if they scored more than ten confirmed victories. Some records show the following scores—others differ.

Hauptmann Godwin von Brumowski, (1889-1937)
40 victories

Of Polish descent, von Brumowski was born on 26 July 1889 at Wadowice, Galicia. He became a career soldier with Field Artillery Regiment No. 6 in 1914–15 on the Eastern

Front. In 1915, he transferred to the air service as an observer, learning to fly by instruction from his sergeant pilots. He became commanding officer of Flik (*Fliegerkompanie*) 12 after he had self-qualified as a pilot, and a year later was posted as commanding officer to Flik 41, equipped with Brandenburg D.Is. He had a white skull on a black background painted on the fighter squadron's aircraft as an identifying badge.

In the summer of 1917, when the outstanding OEFFFAG Albatros D.III came on Flik 41 strength, von Brumowski had the new scouts painted red, again with a white skull on the fuselages. At this stage his victory score stood at six, and on 17 July he made it seven when he shot down a Voisin. On 11 August he shot down a Caudron and a Nieuport, and by the end of the month his score had risen to nineteen.

Another Flik 41 ace—Frank Linke-Crawford—was flying as von Brumowski's wingman, and the combination began to wreak havoc on the opposing Italians. An Italian balloon was downed on 4 October, followed two days later by the shooting down of two seaplanes, and then two Nieuports on the 23rd. By the end of the year von Brumowski had taken his score to twenty-seven.

During the last year of the war von Brumowski increased his number of kills to forty—becoming Austria-Hungary's top ace. He survived the war but died in an air crash in Holland in 1937.

Offizierstellvertreter Julius Arigi, (1895-1981)
32 victories

Julius Arigi was born on 3 October 1895 of Czech descent at Tetschen and graduated as an NCO pilot on 23 November 1914. At this stage of the war, rank and class (especially in Germany) prevailed: officers were in charge; observers and NCOs flew the aircraft.

Arigi saw action inasmuch as his aircraft came under AA fire, but did not participate in aerial combat until 4 September 1916, when he and his observer shot down an Italian Farman aircraft of No. 34 Squadriglia over Fier, Albania. A transfer to single-seaters and duty with Flik 60 commanded by Frank Linke-Crawford came in the spring of 1917, after which Arigi began to shoot down enemy aircraft at a steady rate.

Awarded four gold, eight silver and three bronze medals, Arigi became the most decorated NCO in the air arm. Inexplicably, he remained a warrant officer throughout the war in spite of his thirty-two victories. After the First World War, Arigi flew as a test pilot, and after Hitler annexed Austria in 1938, joined the Luftwaffe as an instructor. He survived the Second World War and died on 1 August 1981.

Oberleutnant Benno Fiala Ritter von Fernbrugg, (1890-1964)
28 victories

Benno Fiala was born in Vienna on 16 June 1890. When war was declared, he applied for flying duty but this was refused and he was gazetted as an engineer officer with Flik 1. Fiala wanted to fly and again applied for flying training, and this time was given training as an observer and sent to the Russian Front. He was then posted to Flik 10 on the Italian Front, flying as observer in Brandenburg C.Is.

On 4 May 1916, Fiala scored an impressive and unusual victory when he shot down the Italian airship M 4 over Gorizia on the Isonzo Front. Flying with Hauptmann Adolf Heyrowsky as pilot, he poured incendiary bullets into the drifting airship (which was believed to have run out of fuel) and M 4 flamed into the ground. By this time, Fiala had scored five victories.

He then qualified as a pilot, continuing to fly Brandenburg C.Is, before moving to D.Is early in 1917, flying out of Aidussina airstrip and scoring several more victories. These led to the award of the Order of Leopold, the Gold Medal of Merit, the Order of the Crown and the German Iron Cross 1st Class, and to him being given command of Flik 51J.

A notable victory occurred on 30 March 1918, when flying an Albatros D Scout, Fiala shot down Camel B5648 of 66 Squadron RFC, flown by Lt Alan Jerrard. In a superb display of flying and marksmanship, he poured 163 rounds into the Camel during an intense dogfight, causing it to crash at Gorgo al Monticano. (Lt Jerrard was believed to have shot down six Austrian aircraft in the dogfight, and was invested with the VC on 5 April 1919.) The gentlemanly Fiala landed his Albatros nearby, went to the scene of the crash and chivalrously took charge of Lt Jerrard.

Fiala ended the war with twenty-eight victories. He served in the Second World War in the rank of hauptmann and died in Vienna on 29 October 1964.

Oberleutnant Frank Linke-Crawford, (1893-1918)
27 victories

Of Polish descent, Frank Linke-Crawford was born at Cracow on 18 August 1893. Between 1914 and 1916 he was in action with a dragoon cavalry regiment on the Russian Front, and applied for, and was granted, transfer to the air service in April 1916, being posted to Flik 12 after completing his flying training. Three months later he transferred to von Brumowski's Flik 41 flying Brandenburg D.Is. Linke-Crawford acquired the nickname 'The Red Head' from his habit of wearing a glaring red flying helmet.

Flik 41 acquiring formidable Albatros D.III aircraft in the summer of 1917, and Linke-Crawford's machine had a 'displayed' (outspread) eagle emblazoned on the fuselage as an escutcheon. This shield became well known to the Italian Air Arm, as Linke-Crawford shot down several Italian SP.2 aircraft.

In November, he was given command of Flik 60 at the age of only 24 years, and continued to increase his victory score to twenty-seven during the remaining few months of his life. On 30 July 1918, Frank Linke-Crawford died in aerial combat over Montello when his aircraft went down in flames and he was burned beyond recognition. As was the custom, he was buried locally but his remains were exhumed after the war and re-interred at Salzburg.

Leutnant Josef Kiss, (1896-1918)
19 victories

Josef Kiss was born in Pressburg (now Bratislava) on 26 January 1896, and when war broke out he enlisted in the Army and volunteered for the air arm. Accepted for training as a pilot, he graduated as a sergeant pilot in April 1916 and began his operational flying career on the Isonzo Front, flying alongside the top ace Godwin von Brumowski.

A courageous and skilful pilot who disregarded danger and was always eager for battle, Kiss was wounded twice in air action. In 1917, his victories increased sharply when he was posted to the Trentino area. He had his Albatros D.III painted with a black nose and wheels. Later he had the Albatros (OEFFFAG series 153, 200 hp) painted black all over, with the letter 'K' (for Kiss) on both sides of the fuselage. He was decorated with a total of three gold and four silver medals for bravery in the air.

On 24 May 1918, the 22-year-old feldwebel took off for his final flight in the black Albatros. He was killed in action over Valsugana and posthumously commissioned to leutnant to mark his courage and bravery. He had nineteen victories to his credit.

Linienschiffsleutnant (Naval Lieutenant Commander) Gottfried von Banfield, (1890-1986)
9 victories

Gottfried von Banfield was born at Pola on 6 February 1890 into a naval family. After education at St Pölten Military School and Fiume Naval Academy, he joined the embryo Imperial and Royal Navy of Austria-Hungary in 1912 and learned to fly fighter flying boats. When war broke out, Banfield was stationed on the Istrian coast at Pola naval base, which had a strength of twenty-two aircraft.

On 12 August 1914, the Navy went into action for the first time at Mount Lovćen in Montenegro. With Italy a short 25 miles across the Adriatic, it was easy for the Austrians to raid military targets by night and day. Banfield's first four victories were against balloons on the Isonzo Front.

The Italian and French Air Arms were raiding Trieste, and Banfield went up to intercept the intruders, managing to shoot down a Caproni bomber and three FBA flying boats by September 1916, earning him the nickname 'The Eagle of Trieste'. The following month, flying Hansa-Brandenburg CC (Camillo Castiglioni) fighter flying boat—the A.13 prototype—he shot down an Italian Farman and was also put in command of the naval air station at Trieste.

In January 1917, Banfield clashed with the Italian ace Francesco Baracca over the River Isonzo. Banfield was in his Brandenburg KDW fighter flying boat, A.24, and Baracca in his Nieuport 11 fighter. However, this unusual duel fought in appalling weather did not bring victory to either pilot and the fight was broken off. He became Freiherr von Banfield when, in March 1918, he was admitted to the Order of Maria Theresa as a military knight.

Gottfried von Banfield emigrated to England in 1920, but moved to Trieste six years later and became an Italian citizen. He died in Trieste at the age of 96 on 23 September 1986.

Austro-Hungarian Victory Totals

Hauptmann Godwin von Brumowski—*35 victories*
Offizierstellvertreter Julius Arigi—*32 victories*
Oberleutnant Benno Fiala—*28 victories*
Oberleutnant Frank Linke-Crawford—*27 victories*
Leutnant Josef Kiss—*19 victories*
Leutnant Franz Gräser—*17 victories*
Feldwebel Eugen Bönsch—*15 victories*
Feldwebel Stefan Fejes—*15 victories*
Offizierstellvertreter Kurt Gruber—*14 victories*
Oberleutnant Ernst Strohschneider—*14 victories*
Hauptmann Raoul Stojsavljevic—*12 victories*
Hauptmann Adolf Heyrowsky—*10 victories*
Hauptmann Josef Maier—*10 victories*
Oberleutnant Friedrich Navratil—*10 victories*
Leutnant Franz Rudorfer—*10 victories*
Linienschiffsleutnant Gottfried von Banfield—*9 victories*

Another fourteen airmen were believed to have shot down between five and ten enemy aircraft.

Oberleutnant Godwin von Brumowski, (1889- 1936). Brumowski was the most successful fighter ace of the Austro-Hungarian *Luftahrtruppen* during the War. He was credited with 35 victories. In July 1915 he was posted to *Fliegerkompagnie 1* (*Flik 1*) at Czernowitz, commanded by Hauptmann Otto Jindra. On 12 April 1916 Jindra and von Brumowski crewed one of the seven Austro-Hungarian planes that participated in bombing a military review attended by Czar Nicholas II. In the process, they shot down two of the seven Russian Morane-Saulnier Parasol two-seaters that attempted to drive them off.

The Hansa-Brandenburg D.I, also known as the KD (*Kampf Doppeldecker*) was a German fighter aircraft built for Austria-Hungary. It was designed by Ernst Heinkel to meet the requirements of the Austro-Hungarian Air Force (*Kaiserliche und Königliche Luftfahrtruppen or K.u.K. Luftfahrtruppen*). It was a single seat, single engined biplane, of wooden construction, with plywood fuselage skinning and fabric wing skins. Despite some poor handling problems, the aircraft was ordered by Austro-Hungary as the D.I. A total of 122 D.Is were built, with 50 built by Hansa-Brandenburg in Germany—powered by 110 kW (150 hp) Austro-Daimler engines—while a further 72 were built under licence by Phönix in Vienna, powered by 138 kW (185 hp) Austro-Daimler engines.

Brumowski quickly demonstrated a natural ability at the controls and was soon flying a variety of types, both observation aircraft and single-seat fighters, quickly finding himself in command of a *Fliegerkompanie* (*Flik*) where he was able now to develop his leadership qualities. By 1917, he had become an ace for the first time and was rewarded with the command of *Flik 41J*, the first Austro-Hungarian fighter squadron. Before assuming this command he sought permission to be posted temporarily to Germany's *Jasta 24* so that he could observe and absorb their tactics. Brumowski implemented the new ideas on the Italian Isonzo front where, now equipped with the Hansa-Brandenburg D.1 Starstrutter, he could press the fight home. His aircraft proved to be comparable in performance with most contemporary German fighters, apart from armament, and massively superior to most Italian aircraft.

Brumowski's Albatros D.III with his distinctive skull emblem which he adopted in October 1917. In August 1917 von Brumowski scored a remarkable streak of victories, being credited with 12 confirmed and 6 unconfirmed kills between the 10 and 28 August. Two of these victories, on 19 and 20 August, were the result of a partial transition to a newer fighter plane, a German Albatros D.III with twin synchronized guns. On the 20th he scored once with the Albatros and twice with the Hansa-Brandenburg D.I. By the end of August the transition was complete; he would use the Albatros to score the rest of his victories.

On 9 October 1917 he shot down and burned an observation balloon for his 22nd victory; it was the first of five balloons he would down. His Albatros that day was painted all red, in emulation of von Richthofen, with the addition of mustard coloured skulls on either side of the fuselage. This paint scheme would become characteristic of his aircraft until war's end.

Brumoski and Linke-Crawford by the side of Brumowski's Albatros D.III (Oef) 153.52 after a forced landing at Passarella. On 1 February 1918 von Brumowski became involved in a fight with eight Sopwith Camels of 28 Squadron. Some of the 26 bullets striking his Albatros ignited the fuel tank built into the upper wing. He managed to land at his home field, without serious injury, becoming a rare survivor of an in-craft fire.

The fire ate the fabric off the upper wing and the inboard portions of the lower one, leaving only the scorched bare spars and struts of the wing roots.

Three days later, while flying another Albatros he fought eight English fighters and took multiple machine gun hits. With his wings breaking up he managed to land but the Albatros turned over and was totally destroyed. Brumowski fought on until 23 June 1918, when he was ordered on extended leave. His last successful fight was on 19 June; he scored his 35th victory and suffered 37 hits in his plane. He had flown 439 combat sorties, but his combat career was ended.

Right: Julius Arigi, (1895-1981). In March 1914, Arigi transferred to the *Luftfahrtruppen* to train as a pilot, and passed final tests on 26 November 1914, to become *Zügsführer* (sergeant). Initially during the War, Arigi was assigned to *Fliegerkompanie 6*, based in southern Dalmatia, flying Lloyd Type LS 2 and Lohner biplane aircraft in operations against Serbian and Montenegrin forces. On 20 December 1914, Arigi and his observer, Leutnant Levak, crashlanded a Lohner 140 in the Adriatic Sea; fortunately for them, in the shallow water.

Middle: A Lloyd C.1 of the Hungarian Lloyd Aeroplane and Motor Company, Ltd., of Aszod, Budapest.

In October 1915, Arigi became a prisoner of war when he was forced down due to engine failure during a reconnaissance flight behind enemy lines in Montenegro. He escaped captivity in January 1916 on his sixth attempt by stealing a staff car belonging to Prince Nicholas of Montenegro. He re-joined his unit which later moved to Albania.

Below: Lloyd C.III, 1916, 78 mph, 50 built.

Lohner B.VII & Lohner C.I, 1915. 70–85 mph, 113 built.

Julius Arigi in his Lohner B.VII 17.19. Towards the end of 1916, Arigi was transferred to the Isonzo front in Italy where he mostly flew escort missions in a Hansa-Brandenburg D.I single-seat fighter. By May, 1917, his victory total was up to 12. He was unhappy with the tail assembly of this aircraft because he felt it lacked directional stability. He redesigned the horn-balanced rudder with a low aspect fin and a plain rudder. His redesign was later copied from his plane and became standard on the D1. He was awarded 500 kronen for his innovation.

In April, 1918, Arigi was transferred back to *Flik 6* on the Albanian front. In his short stay there, he scored 3 more kills while flying an Avatik D1. In summer, 1918, he was again transferred, to *Flik 1J* at Igalo in Dalmatia. There he was equipped with two new Avatik D1 fighters, which he used to score his final four victories. His combat career extended over four years; his last victory was scored on 23 August 1918. He spent the last days of the war as a factory test pilot.

Above: Design of the Austrian Aviatik, or Berg D I commenced very early in 1917, slightly ahead of Austria's other indigenous fighter, the Phönix D I. During the early stage of its flying career, the Berg D I suffered catastrophic structural wing failure, but once generally 'beefed-up', the machine proved to be both fast, agile and have a good climb, cited as reaching 13,000 feet in 11 minutes 15 seconds. Initially powered by a 185hp Austro-Daimler, these Bergs had top level speed of 113 mph at sea level.

Right: Oberleutnant Benno Fiala Ritter von Fernbrugg, (1890-1964). Although trained as an observer, Fiala's duties in this beginning of the war consisted mainly of arming planes with machine guns, and experimenting with aerial cameras. He also rigged a 30 kg radio transmitter in an unarmed plane. It was used in May 1915 at the Battle of Gorlice-Tarnow on the Russian Front; by sending corrections to a receiver on the ground, it successfully adjusted mortar fire.

Below: In January 1916. Fiala was transferred to *Fliegerkompany 19* on the Italian Front, there he flew a Hansa-Brandenburg C.I two seated reconnaissance plane, scoring his first confirmed triumph on 29 April 1916. The Hansa-Brandenburg C.I had a long service life and 1,300 produced, although in many variants. Initially slow enough to be caught by the DH.2 or Macchi M.3, later variants improved reaching 88–96 mph.

On 4 May 1916, Fiala was piloting a Hansa-Brandenburg C.I when he teamed with a second C.I to shoot down the Italian airship M-4. The semi-rigid dirigible had been returning from a bombing raid when Fiala shot it down above Gorizia. Fiala was wounded by anti-aircraft fire in the beginning of 1917. It was during this recuperation that he decided to apply for pilot's training. After he recovered, he moved into *Fliegerkorps 41J*, then into a Hansa-Brandenburg D.I fighter in *Fliegerkorps 12D*.

Flight Lieutenant Alan Jerrard, VC, pictured after crashing and capture. He became a PoW for the remaining three months of the War. Fiala racked up number 28 on 20 August 1918. He continued to fly until October, but then was posted to nonflying staff duties until war's end. The engineer turned fighter pilot had flown on two fronts which had more hazardous flying conditions and less opportunity for air combat than the Western Front in France.

Oberleutnant Frank Linke-Crawford, (1893-1918). Linke-Crawford scored his first confirmed aerial victory on 21 August 1917, using a Hansa-Brandenburg D.I to down a Nieuport. In the next five days, he scored three more confirmed wins using this plane, with one claim going unconfirmed. Linke-Crawford's switch to flying an Albatros D.III armed him with twin Spandau machine guns synchronized to fire through his propeller. Flying the Albatros D.III, he shot down a seaplane on 23 September 1917 bringing his tally to that of an ace. Continuing to use the Albatros, he ran up a score of 13 by 13 December.

In late December 1917, Linke-Crawford was appointed commander of *Fliegerkompanie 60*. This unit was stationed at Grigno in northern Italy until March, 1918. *Flik 60j's* seven pilots flew against an opposition of British, Italian, and French pilots. Linke-Crawford's plane in *Flik 60j* was a Phönix D.I. He used this slow but sturdy twin-gunned fighter to run up seven triumphs in the first three months of 1918. *Flik 60* transferred to Feltre, also in northern Italy.

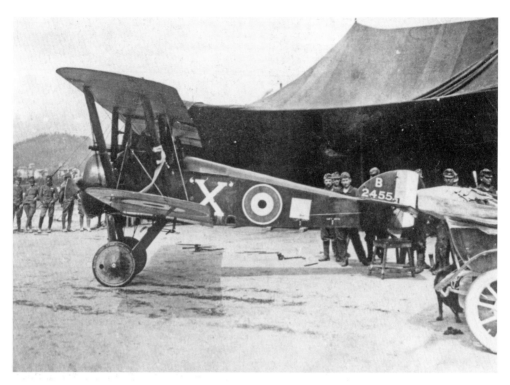

On 10 May 1918, Linke-Crawford switched to an Aviatik (Berg) D.I (115.32) At least five of his seven victories in this machine were over superior aircraft, such as the Sopwith Camel and Bristol F.2 Fighters. The following day, Monday 11 March 1918 he captured Sopwith Camel 1F.1 B2455 'X' of 28 Squadron piloted by Lieutenant E. G. Forder.

Linke-Crawford in front of his Aviatik (Berg) D.I (115.32). On Tuesday 30 July 1918, the day after his final victory, he was flying his Aviatik (Berg) D.I in a formation of four when he was attacked and shot down in flames by a pair of Italian Hanriot HD.1 fighters, with his plane disintegrating before impact.

Left: Lieutnant József Kiss de Elemér et Ittebe, (1896-1918). After pilot graduation he was assigned to the newly founded Flik 24. He scored his first victory on 20 June 1916 while flying a two-seater Hansa-Brandenburg C.I. By November 1917 he had amassed seven victories, including four forced down and captured.

Right: József Kiss was then transferred to *Flik 55J* flying the Albatros D.III. Kiss' personal aircraft was painted black with a large white 'K' on either side of the fuselage. Comrades included fellow aces Julius Arigi and Josef von Maier, who formed the rest of his flight, and the three of them became known as the *Kaiser Staffel* (Emperor's Squadron).

József Kiss was seriously wounded again in late January 1918, but returned to duty only two months after having some of his bowel surgically removed. His last victory was on 28 January 1918. He flew without any further triumphs until he was killed in action on 24 May 1918 by Lieutenant Gerald Birks of No. 66 Squadron. His final score of 19 included at least seven enemy aircraft forced down and captured and 9 victories shared with other pilots.

József Kiss was posthumously promoted to Leutnant; he was the only non-commissioned officer in the Austro-Hungarian military to be so promoted. His funeral was held three days after his death, at the Italian airfield at Pergine Valsugana. A sizable flyover of opposing Allied planes, including British, French, and Italians, dropped a funeral wreath with a note attached. It read: 'Our last salute to our courageous foe.' Kiss's girlfriend Enrica Bonecker never married, and she visited his grave daily for the next 52 years.

Ocffag C.II 52.03 before dismantling and transportation to the Russian front .

Sopwith Camel B7167 of 'C' Flight 66 Squadron shot down by *Flik 30*, 8 July 1918.

A front view of the same Sopwith Camel B7167 of 'C' Flight 66 Squadron.

Fregattenleutnant Stephan Wollemann on the wing of his Phönix D.1 fighter A-118. In company with three other Austro-Hungarian Navy Phönix D.IIIs from Pola Air Station (A-102 flown by Fliegermaat Josef Gindl, A-111 flown by Fregattenleutnant Emil Paramberger and A-117 flown by Fregattenleutnant Friedrich Lang) they had previously attacked a USN flight of four Italian-built Macchi M-5s (13015, flown by Ensign George H Ludlow, 7299, flown by Ensign Austin Parker, 7225, flown by Ensign Dudley Voorhees and 7229, flown by Landsman for Quartermaster Charles Hammann) and one M-8 (19008, flown by Ensign Walter White (Pilot) and Ensign Albert Taliaferro (Observer)). Ludlow's aircraft was brought down by Wollemann, and Hammann was awarded the Medal of Honor for rescuing him.

Friedrich Nauratil of *Flik 3J* by his Albatros B.1 (PN) 3rd series 22.28.

The pilot and observer in an H.B.C1.

THE LESSER MILITARY AIR SERVICES OF THE FIRST WORLD WAR

Brazil
Brazilian Army Air Service

Brazil created an Army Balloon Corps in 1908, which became the Brazilian Army Air Service in 1918.

Bulgaria

The Bulgarian Army Aviation Corps was formed in 1912 and acquired twelve Blériot and Bristol aircraft. As Bulgaria did not have any military pilots, it had to rely on foreign pilots to fly its machines during the Balkan Wars of 1912–13. The Corps was disbanded when the Balkan Wars ended, but reappeared in 1915 during the First World War when Bulgaria aligned itself with Germany and Austria-Hungary. Again, the Bulgarians had no military aircraft or pilots—these were loaned to Bulgaria by the Central Powers. When the war ended in 1918, Bulgaria was forced by the victorious Allies to scrap its small air arm.

Bulgaria used captured as well as purchased aircraft. On 12 February 1917 RFC pilot 2Lt A. C. Stopher landed Armstrong-Whitworth FK3 Nr. 6219 by mistake on Bulgarian territory. In this photograph smiling Bulgarian airmen pose in their trophy at Belitsa Airfield in the province of Blagoevgrad.

Finland

Finland is included in this book purely as a reference point, as Finnish forces did not use aircraft during the First World War. The Finns seized their independence after the Russian Revolution of 1917 and commandeered the naval bases left by the occupying Russian Navy.

The Finnish Army acquired several Russian aircraft, including a Devjatka flying boat and several German-made Friedrichshafen floatplanes. When the Imperial German Navy revolted in October 1918, Finland's Army seized all German naval aircraft from every German base on the Baltic.

Greece
Stratiotiki Aeroporia (Army Air Service)
Naftike Aeroporiki Ypiresia (Naval Air Service)

In 1911, the Greek Government sent officers to France to receive flying training, the first officer to gain a flying licence being Lt Dimitrios Kamberos in May 1912. During the Balkan Wars, an aircraft squadron was formed under Lt Kamberos at Larissa, equipped with two Farman aircraft. Another aircraft squadron, also using two Farmans and commanded by Lt Bares, flew out of Epirus. Both these units gave valuable assistance to ground forces, and this encouraged the Greek Navy to acquire two Astra seaplanes and base them at Mudros. In 1913, a Sopwith two-seater seaplane was bought as a trainer for a projected Royal Hellenic Naval Air Service.

Impressed with the Sopwiths, Greece ordered six more from Britain, but the outbreak of war intervened and the order was cancelled by Britain. However, four Farman F.22 seaplanes were bought and commanded by Lt Aristeidis Moraitinis, the Hellenic Navy's first naval pilot.

All Greek air units had been brought under one authority and joint command and control, but in May 1917 they were separated into Army and Navy Air Services. The Army Air Service, under French control, had twenty-two Dorand AR.1s, fourteen Nieuport 24s, sixteen SPAD S.7s, eight SPAD S.13s and twelve Bréguets. By November, the Greeks had their first squadron (531 Fighter Squadron) in action in Macedonia, equipped with French aircraft. In 1918, 532 Bomber Squadron formed and flew alongside 531 Squadron, and on 1 June, a third unit (533 Squadron) was formed as a bomber and reconnaissance squadron. A further squadron, No. 534, did not see action.

The Royal Hellenic Naval Air Service, under the control of the RNAS at Mudros, was divided into four flights. Some pilots were sent to RFC flying training units in the Middle East. All British equipment was used—Sopwith Camels and Pups, Sopwith Baby seaplanes, Short 184 seaplanes and several DH.4 and DH.9 bombers. A Henri Farman floatplane was also on loan from the RNAS.

Japan
Imperial Japanese Army Air Service

Interest in aviation in Japan began in 1877, with the use of observation balloons. Designed and constructed by two naval engineers, Shinpachi Baba and Buhei, the balloons had been developed after a rebellion had broken out in the Kyushu area where Government forces had been besieged. The idea of using balloons had come about after Japanese military authorities had studied how they had been used by the French during the Franco-Prussian War of 1870–71 when Paris was under siege. However, before the new Japanese balloons could be used, the Kyushu rebellion was quashed and military interest evaporated.

But use of balloons in Japan did not disappear entirely. A number of Japanese civilians maintained an interest in their development, and it was this interest that was put to good use by the Japanese Army some years later. During the Russo-Japanese War of 1904, the Army ordered one of the civilian balloon enthusiasts, Isabura Yamada, to construct two small observation balloons. These two balloons, plus another bought from an Englishman, Charles Spencer, were used to good effect for artillery ranging and observation during the invasion of Port Arthur, and the Japanese military became convinced of the need for lighter-than-air craft.

In 1909, the Japanese Army and Navy established a joint organisation—Rinji Gunyo Kikyu Kenkyu Kai (the Provisional Committee for Military Balloon Research)—commanded by Lt Gen. Gaishi Nagaoka, and two army officers—Capts Yoshitoshi Tokugawa and Kumazo Hino—were sent to France and Germany respectively to learn to fly, in April 1910. They returned to Japan on completion of their flying training, each bringing an aircraft with them: Tokugawa brought a Henri Farman, and Hino a Hans Grade monoplane.

These aircraft were demonstrated by the two pilots to the Japanese military in the first such demonstration of heavier-than-air craft in Japan, heralding the beginning of Japanese aviation. The flying demonstrations being successful, an airfield was set up at Tokorozawa just outside Tokyo. Several more officers were sent for flying training as future instructors, and aircraft were bought as trainers for use by the new instructors.

Bitter inter-service rivalry between the Army and Navy caused the latter to form its own aviation service—Kaigun Kokujutsu Kenkyu Kai (the Naval Committee for Aeronautical Research) early in 1912. The Committee promptly sent three lieutenants to France and another three to America for flying training, those sent to America being authorised to buy two suitable aircraft for flying training. A Curtiss seaplane and a Farman floatplane were bought and shipped to Yokosuka for training purposes. Lt Yozo Kaneko returned to Japan with two Maurice Farman aircraft and Lt Sankichi Kohno with two Curtiss seaplanes, and on 2 November the first flights of these new aircraft took place from the Japanese naval base at Yokosuka.

On 23 August 1914, when Japan declared war on Germany, its Army Air Service consisted of four Maurice Farmans and one Nieuport NG.2, with an aircrew strength of eight pilots. The Naval Air Service comprised four Maurice Farman seaplanes with an aircrew strength of seven pilots. Japanese naval aircraft went on the offensive against the German enclave at Tsingtao during September and October 1914, recce flights were made and a mine-laying ship sunk.

A handful of Japanese Army pilots were sent to France during the First World War, but it is thought that they did not see combat. Interestingly, a Japanese-born RFC pilot, FS

O'Hara (!), flew on the Western Front and was wounded six times, but it is not recorded if he shot down any enemy aircraft.

Portugal
Serviço de Aeronáutica Militar

A military aviation unit—the *Serviço de Aeronáutica Militar*—was originally proposed by the Portuguese Government in 1912, but this came to nothing as money was short. However, a public subscription was made and managed to raise enough to buy three aircraft from France. When it was proposed to establish a military flying school at Nova da Rainha in May 1914, money was still short and nothing came of it either.

Portugal entered the war on 23 November 1914—aligned with its oldest ally, Britain—but did not declare war as such until 1916. However, after Germany invaded Portugal's colony of Mozambique from German East Africa, the Portuguese clashed with German forces on 24 August 1914. Germany declared war on Portugal on 9 March 1916, and Austria-Hungary followed suit six days later.

As Portugal had no flying training infrastructure, volunteers were requested from the Army and Navy to train as pilots in Britain, France and America. Twelve officer volunteers were selected and sent abroad, the intention being that they in turn would act as flying instructors at a newly formed flying training school—the aircraft strength being one old rickety French Deperdussin!

On 17 July 1916, the first training course began with the one aircraft, but two Farman MF.11s were acquired in August, followed by five Farman F.41s, two Caudron G.3s and a Morane-Saulnier—all bought from France. In mid-July 1917, Portugal had its first squadron—the Mozambique Expeditionary Squadron—on operational status with three Farman F.40s.

The Portuguese Expeditionary Corps Air Service was deployed with the Allies in France, but owing to an aircraft shortage, some dozen Portuguese pilots flew with the French Air Arm. (The Corps was returned to Portugal before the Armistice.) Another similar unit was formed—the Angola Expeditionary Squadron—which was equipped with Caudron G.4s, but the war ended before it went into action.

The Portuguese Navy also had a small air service—*Escola de Aviação Naval*—based near Lisbon and equipped with three FBA flying boats. These were used from late 1917 for coastal and sea patrols.

Portugal ended the First World War heavily in debt—some £1.5 million in gold having been lost to the war effort. (£23 million had been borrowed from Britain in 1916). More than 7,000 Portuguese servicemen lost their lives, and 95,000 tons of shipping were lost.

Romania
Romanian Army Flying Corps

The Romanian Army Flying Corps was established in 1910, and by the following year had four Blériots and four Henri Farmans. Two Morane-Saulnier Type Fs and three Bristols were acquired in 1912. When the First World War broke out, Romania was on the Allied side and acquired a few Nieuport 12 and 17 fighters. However, these few aircraft were soon wiped out by German and Austro-Hungarian air power. After the war ended, the Corps was renamed the Romanian Air Division.

Serbia
Serbian Military Air Service

Serbia became independent from Turkey by the Treaty of Berlin in 1878, after almost 500 years of Ottoman rule. During the Balkan Wars of 1912–13—when Serbia conquered Novibazar and Macedonia from Turkey—only Montenegro and Russia sided with Serbia.

Created in 1913, the Serbian Military Air Service bought French aircraft. Having no flying schools or aircraft, the novice pilots were sent to France to learn to fly the aircraft.

Serbia declared war on Germany on 6 August 1914 and repulsed its enemies for over a year before suffering defeat by the Central Powers in October 1915. Its decimated forces—40,000 of whom were killed—retreated into Albania and across the Adriatic to Italy and Corfu.

When Yugoslavia was created in 1918, the Serbian Military Air Service became the Aviation Department of the Yugoslav Army.

Turkey
Turkish Army Aviation Section

The Ottoman Empire became interested in military aviation during the Balkan Wars. In March 1912, Turkey bought two French aircraft and formed an embryo Army Aviation Section at Yesilkoy. However, as Turkey had no aircraft industry, it was obliged to buy its machines from Germany, Britain and France—including R.E.P., DFW Mars, Nieuport, Bristol and Deperdussin.

Serbian Air mechanics on Farman MF.11 at Corfu, March 1916.

In 1918 the Serbian Air Service was reformed with French officers and squadrons were staffed with French and Serbian personnel. On 17 January 1918, the command was given for two Serbian squadrons to be formed and staffed with Serbian personnel. In April 1918 Prva Srpska Eskadrila (First Serbian Squadron) became operational with 12 Dorand AR type I A2 and 3 Nieuport XXIV C1 from French-Serbian composite Squadron AR 521.

During the Balkan Wars, Turkey hired foreign pilots to fly its aircraft. One such pilot was Mario Scherff, who took off from Constantinople's San Stefano airfield on 7 April 1913 in a DFW Mars biplane with an observer. They were heading, or rather staggering, at a mere 300 feet, towards the Bulgarian positions near the Sea of Marmara. As the DFW Mars approached it came under intensive ground fire from the Bulgarians and the observer released the Mars' bomb load on the village of Kawakscha, right on the Bulgarian positions. Scherff managed to take the aircraft higher as the observer took photographs of the enemy positions and recorded their artillery and supply routes. With fuel running low and the weather becoming foul, Scherff turned for home through a thunderstorm and made it back safely to San Stefano.

Another foreign pilot who flew for the Turks was Oberleutnant Reinhold Jahnow, holder of German pilot's licence No. 80. Jahnow flew many recce missions during the Balkan Wars, but was killed in an air crash at Malmedy, Belgium, on 12 August 1914.

Russia went to war with Turkey on 31 October 1914, leading Turkey to ally itself with the Central Powers of Germany and Austria-Hungary, Britain declaring war on Turkey on 5 November. Most of the Turkish Army Aviation Section's aircraft were German and flown by German pilots, Turks flying as observers only. Several German floatplanes were supplied to the Turks, and it was reported on 21 August 1916 that one of the floatplanes had clashed with two Russian torpedo boats in the Black Sea.

The Army Aviation Section became the Turkish Flying Corps in 1914, and the Turkish Army Air Service in 1917.

APPENDIX

THE ROYAL AIRCRAFT FACTORY

T HE ROYAL AIRCRAFT FACTORY began life early in the Victorian era (1878) and moved to Farnborough in 1904–06 as the Army Balloon Factory. This was part of the Army School of Ballooning, under the command of Colonel James Templer. In 1912 the Balloon Factory was renamed the Royal Aircraft Factory and among its designers was Geoffrey de Havilland who later founded his own company; John Kenworthy who became chief engineer and designer at the Austin Motor Company in 1918 and who went on to found the Redwing Aircraft Co. in 1930, and Henry Folland—later chief designer at Gloster Aircraft Company, and founder of his own company Folland Aircraft. Other engineers included Major F. M. Green, G. S. Wilkinson, James E. 'Jimmy' Ellor, Professor A. H. Gibson, and A. A. Griffith. Both Ellor and Griffith would later go on to work for Rolls-Royce Limited. In 1918 the Royal Aircraft Factory was once more renamed, becoming the Royal Aircraft Establishment (RAE) to avoid confusion with the Royal Air Force, which was formed on 1 April 1918, and because it had relinquished its manufacturing role to concentrate on research.

Between 1911 and 1918 the Royal Aircraft Factory produced a number of aircraft designs. Most of these were essentially research aircraft, but a few actually went into mass production, especially during the war period. Some orders were met by the factory itself, but the bulk of production was by private British companies, some of which had not previously built aircraft.

Up to about 1913 the designation letters referred to the general layout of the aircraft, derived from a French manufacturer or designer famous for that type:

S.E. = Santos Experimental (Canard or tail-first layout)
B.E. = Blériot Experimental (Tractor or propeller-first layout)
F.E. = Farman Experimental (Pusher or propeller behind the pilot layout)

From 1913–14 onwards this was changed to a designation based on the role for which the aircraft was designed:

A.E. = Armed or Armoured Experimental
C.E. = Coastal Experimental
F.E. = Fighting experimental

N.E. = Night Experimental

R.E. = Reconnaissance experimental (two-seat machines)

S.E. = Scout experimental fast single-seat aircraft.

The B.S.1 of 1913 was a one-off anomaly, combining both systems: Blériot (tractor) Scout (fighter). R.T. & T.E. were also used for strictly one off prototypes.

Because Royal Aircraft Factory type designations are inconsistent or confusing the following explanations are given.

The 'F.E.2' designation refers to three quite distinct types, with only the same broad layout in common, the F.E.2 (1911), the F.E.2 (1913), and finally the famous wartime two-seat fighter and general purpose design, the F.E.2 (1914). This last aircraft was the one that went into production, and had three main variants, the F.E.2a, F.E.2b, and the F.E.2d. There was also the F.E.2c; in which the crew positions were reversed to improve the pilot's view, especially for landing at night.

The B.E.1 was basically the prototype for the early B.E.2 but the B.E.2c was almost a completely new aeroplane, with very little common with the earlier B.E.2 types. On the other hand the B.E.3 and B.E.4 were effectively prototypes for the B.E.8. The B.E.8a was a B.E.8 fitted with the wings and tailplane of the B.E.2c.

The S.E.4a had nothing in common at all with the S.E.4, while the S.E.5a was simply a modified S.E.5 with a strengthened wing structure.

Several early RAF designs were officially 'reconstructions' of existing aircraft, because the Factory did not initially have official authority to build aircraft to their own design. In most cases the type in question used no parts whatever from the wreck, in some cases not even the engine. Included in this list are the Cody and Dunne designs built and/or tested at Farnborough, although these were not strictly Royal Aircraft Factory types.

Royal Aircraft Factory types with dates

British Army Dirigible No. 1—1907	B.S.1—1913	B.E.9—1915
Dunne D.1—1907	R.E.1—1913	F.E.8—1915
British Army Aeroplane No. 1—1908	R.E.2—1913	S.E.4a—1915
Dunne D.5—1910	B.E.8—1913	F.E.4—1916
S.E.1—1911	R.E.3—1913	R.E.8—1916
F.E.1—1911	H.R.E.2—1913	R.E.9—1916
F.E.2—1911	F.E.2—1914	S.E.5—1916
B.E.1—1911	S.E.2—1914	S.E.5a—1917
B.E.2—1912	R.E.5—1914	F.E.9—1917
B.E.3—1912	S.E.4—1914	N.E.1—1917
B.E.4—1912	F.E.6—1914	A.E.3—1918
F.E.3—1913	R.E.7—1915	C.E.1—1918
B.E.7—1913	B.E.12—1915	Ram—1918